BRIAN
BORU

ABOUT THE AUTHOR

Máire Ní Mhaonaigh is a University Senior Lecturer in the
Department of Anglo-Saxon, Norse and Celtic at the University
of Cambridge and a Fellow of St John's College. She lives in
Cambridge.

BRIAN BORU

IRELAND'S GREATEST KING?

MÁIRE NÍ MHAONAIGH

TEMPUS

Front and back cover illustration: An imaginative portrayal of the battle of Clontarf (WH Holbrooke). Courtesy of the National Library of Ireland.

First published 2007

Tempus Publishing
Cirencester Road, Chalford
Stroud, Gloucestershire, GL6 8PE
www.tempus-publishing.com

Tempus Publishing is an imprint of NPI Media Group

British Library Cataloguing in Publication Data.
A catalogue record for this book is available from the British Library.

ISBN 978 0 7524 2921 2

Typesetting and origination by NPI Media Group
Printed and bound in Great Britain

Contents

Acknowledgments

It is a real pleasure to acknowledge with gratitude the invaluable assistance of family, friends and colleagues in the writing of this book. Jonathan Reeve of Tempus Publishing first approached me about the project and applied judicious use of baton and carrot to facilitate its completion. His colleague, Pascal Barry, saw it expertly through the press. Elizabeth Boyle compiled much of the Index, while Keith Boyle assisted with the Tables. Pádraig Ó Riain, Dagmar Ó Riain-Raedel and Rosalind Love supplied references and much encouragement, while Torsten Meißner commented on many aspects of the work and provided essential and ever-ready assistance. To Jonathan Grove I owe a wonderful 'hooked o'.

The staff of various institutions were helpful in supplying illustrations, in particular Con Brogan of the Department of the Environment, Heritage and Local Government, Dublin, Finbarr Connolly of the National Museum of Ireland, Joanna Finnegan of the National Library of Ireland and Rikke Johansen of the Viking Ship Museum, Roskilde. The Honourable Gráinne O'Brien-Weir kindly provided me with a copy of a portrait of her most famous ancestor. My colleague, Fiona Edmonds, generously allowed me to use some of her photographs and meticulously prepared two of the three maps. The third I owe to Seán Duffy who readily gave permission to use his previously published map, 'The Age of Brian Boru', and to Malcolm

Swanston and his colleagues at Red Lion Mapping who prepared it for re-use. Generous grants from St John's College, Cambridge, and the Dorothea Coke Fund made the publication of this material possible.

Fiona Edmonds has put me further in her debt by reading the complete typescript, as have Anita Bunyan, Denis Casey, Howard Clarke and Colmán Etchingham; their incisive comments and invaluable suggestions have benefited the work immeasurably. Denis Casey cheerfully and painstakingly also proof read the entire work, saving me from numerous errors in the process. In addition, the Clontarf chapter was read by Meidhbhín Ní Úrdail upon whose own insightful work on the later account of the battle I have profitably drawn, as well as by my colleagues, Jonathan Grove and Judy Quinn. Their contributions too have added much to the work, as have the discriminating remarks of another colleague, Simon Keynes, who was kind enough to read the final chapter of the book. This and various other sections were also read by Margaret Kelleher whose unerring eye and excellent judgement has infinitely improved the work.

To Margaret Kelleher I also owe loyal friendship and constant support, and to Meidhbhín Ní Úrdail and Jürgen Uhlich; their hospitality in Dublin is always warmly offered (and received). My Clare sister, Bríd Dillon, along with Kenneth Miller, provided shelter in Brian Boru's home territory; for their enthusiastic engagement with the project I remain touched and ever grateful. The involvement of all of them with two small semi-Dalcassians is also much appreciated. That pair of brothers nourishes me, while their Scandinavian-named father provides vital and continual sustenance, both academically and personally. It is to that trio of men this book is dedicated, and to the memory of my father who first awoke in me an interest in history on what I now know were fieldtrips of the most precious kind.

Abbreviations

Full bibliographical entries for these works can be found in the Bibliography.

AB	The Annals of Boyle, ed. and trans. Freeman (= 'Annals in Cotton MS.')
AClon.	The Annals of Clonmacnoise, ed. Murphy
AFM	The Annals of the Kingdom of Ireland by the Four Masters, ed. and trans. O'Donovan
AI	The Annals of Inisfallen, ed. and trans. Mac Airt
ALC	The Annals of Loch Cé, ed. and trans. Hennessy
ASC	The Anglo-Saxon Chronicle, trans. Whitelock
ATig.	The Annals of Tigernach, ed. and trans. Stokes (references are from the facsimile reprint of 1993)
AU	The Annals of Ulster, eds and trans. Mac Airt and Mac Niocaill
AU[1]	The Annals of Ulster, eds and trans. Hennessy and Mac Carthy
Misc. Ir. Ann.	Miscellaneous Irish Annals, ed. and trans. Ó hInnse
CS	Chronicum Scotorum, ed. and trans. Hennessy
s.a.	*sub anno*, referring to the year in which an annalistic entry is recorded

Accessing Brian

Brian Boru needs no introduction to many, his place in the Irish imagination being assured. Renowned as a fearless fighter, it is as defender of his people against encroaching Vikings that he is primarily remembered, his death at Clontarf in 1014, in what is perceived to be the premier Irish-Norse battle, making certain that his fame would endure. Already an old man at the time of that conflict, the reign of almost forty years that preceded it is viewed as a triumph in which the Munster hero overcame not merely oppressive foreigners, but defeated neighbouring dynasties to make himself 'Emperor of the Irish' (*Imperator Scotorum*) and 'the Augustus of the whole of north-west Europe' (*August iartair tuaiscirt Eorpa uile*) besides.[1] Such was his superiority that none could surpass him; by common acclamation down through generations, Brian is indeed Ireland's greatest king.

Popular perception is one thing, historical happening another and distinguishing between them is always a difficult task. In Brian's case it is made more complex by the millennium or more separating the mythologized mogul from the medieval man. Contemporary sources are limited and those that survive do not provide the whole truth. Extant chronicles may appear to do this, but these, too, reflect particular interests on the part of their partisan authors at any given time. The Annals of Inisfallen, the only annalistic compilation to have come down to us that was written in Munster, Brian's homeland, during his reign, proffers an elaborate account of his activities. The details are suspect, however, since the contemporary annalist was certainly favourable to the southern ruler and may even have been in his pay. Other sets of annals of differing orientation provide complementary accounts, against which we can measure the Munster source.[2] Yet these, too, need to be sifted. What are known as the Clonmacnoise-group chronicles – the Annals of Tigernach and *Chronicum Scotorum* – exalt Brian's primary opponent, the ruler of the midland territory of Mide, Máel Sechnaill mac Domnaill, and to this end the deeds of the former are perhaps deliberately downplayed.[3] The Annals of Ulster may appear more neutral, yet its account of the Clontarf battle shows signs that the rewriting of history is already taking place. Not alone is Brian north-west Europe's Augustus, as noted above; he is 'over-king of the Irish of Ireland and of the Vikings and Britons' (*ardrí Gaidhel Erenn ocus Gall ocus Bretan*) in its record of the event. As befitted the greatest of rulers, he was buried in Armagh, Ireland's premier church, the community there waking him for twelve consecutive nights 'in honour of the dead king' (*propter honorem regis possiti*).[4]

Had he been in a position to read the notice, Brian would undoubtedly have approved, since the evidence suggests that image-cultivation was something of which he was profoundly aware. When his confessor, Máel Suthain, accorded him the grandiose title 'Emperor of the Irish' in his presence in 1005, the cleric was presumably taking the lead from his lord who was acutely conscious of the imperial resonances of the term.[5] In media-management Brian had good teachers, none other than his own immediate ancestors who, on their rise to power, reinvented themselves as the seed of Cas (Dál Cais), fabricating an association with a figure from whom Munster's sovereignty was indirectly derived.[6] Preserved in medieval genealogies, the story underlines the care needed when drawing on sources of even early date.

The pitfalls of source-analysis become more perilous the further we move forward from Brian's own time, not least since his descendants were to prove themselves masters in the art of message-manipulation, taking their lead from the great king himself. Moreover, Brian became central to the image, the great towering beacon in whose illustrious illumination his descendants continued to glow. Naming themselves after him, Uí Briain (the O'Briens) cultivated their eponymous ancestor, an intense period of such activity being datable to the reign of Brian's great-grandson, Muirchertach, whose power waned when he fell ill one hundred years after the battle of Clontarf. The first of his kin to be termed Ua Briain (O'Brien), Muirchertach's link with his great-grandfather was reinforced through the composition at his behest of a literary narrative concerning Brian's reign. The production of the text in question, *Cogadh Gáedhel re Gallaibh* (The Viking-Irish Conflict), in the early years of the twelfth century, perhaps even with Clontarf's centenary in mind, can, with hindsight, be seen as Brian's defining moment, since it is in its pages that his posterity lies. The king that adorns them outstrips Augustus and places even an Ottonian Emperor in the shade. A holy Christian ruler, he overthrows Viking heathens, enforcing all-Ireland rule in the process. As such, he provides literary legitimisation to his descendants, and to Muirchertach in particular, whose own ambitious policy is cast as the natural continuation of his great-grandfather's glorious rule.

It is as a work of propaganda that the *Cogadh* must be read and as a tract written about a hundred years after the events it purports to describe. Its author drew on existing annals, including local records not preserved elsewhere; thus authentic information forms part of its core. Laying bare those basic nuggets is an intricate business and many must perforce remain hidden from our view, occluded by the layers of legend that clothe the made-over Brian. In his revamped guise, the Dál Cais ruler is set forth, the popularity of the *Cogadh* assuring his acclaim. In the ensuing centuries, kinsmen are lauded as his descendants and are urged to emulate his deeds; even Connacht and Leinster rulers are feted as the best since Brian's time.[7] When in the seventeenth century Geoffrey Keating came to write his history of Ireland, it was the twelfth-century bombastic biography that informed his retelling of Viking-Irish affairs, his contemporary, An Dubhaltach Mac Fhirbhisigh, also having access to the work. The events of Clontarf were given a new lease of life at about the same time in the Modern Irish tale, *Cath Cluana Tarbh* (The battle of Clontarf), which is dependent on the earlier narrative. Its seventy or so manuscript versions indicate its enormous popularity, Brian's story proving to have a timeless appeal.[8]

This story also crossed geographical boundaries, Norse renderings of the conflict at Clontarf being written as Irish literary accounts of the encounter were taking shape. These, too, furnish information on the monarch; as imaginative compositions, however, dramatic distortion will also have occurred. *Brennu-Njáls saga* (The Story of Burnt Njáll) and related narratives may not reflect the interests of Brian's descendants, yet in the Irish ruler they present a good and moral leader, both a martyr and a saint, the seeds of whose depiction may be found in Brian's evolving state. English authors, too, revisited his story, providing their own rendition of the battle of Clontarf.[9] Indeed it was to furnish the material for an early historical novel attributed to Sarah

Butler and published posthumously just over seven hundred years after the actual encounter in 1716.[10]

If Brian's legend proved enduring, its longevity and the liberty taken with facts in its formation create difficulties when trying to access the historical Brian. Yet, the creation of his literary alter ego is a subject of interest in its own right. For this reason, both person and persona are treated in what follows, every effort being taken to distinguish between them. Two threads are simultaneously unravelled, the one pertaining to a tenth-/eleventh-century Dál Cais king of real ability who succeeded, over the course of a long reign, in becoming Ireland's most powerful ruler; the other which is considerably more convoluted, concerning his medieval mythologizing and the literary reception of the man. Both are significant stories superimposed on one another in the formidable figure of Brian. As a catalyst for creativity, he may indeed be Ireland's greatest king.

Before Brian: The Growth of Cas's Seed

Some time around the middle of the tenth century Brian Boru was born. The surviving sources record the event under the year 941 but may have done so retrospectively, in recognition of the fame he acquired relatively quickly in death.[1] His epithet 'Boru' (Bórama) was also acquired posthumously and refers to Béal Bórama, just north of Killaloe, the heart of his home territory. In a poem attributed to the eleventh-century poet, Cúán ua Lothcháin, he is termed 'Brian of Ireland from Bórama' (*Brian na Banba a Bórumi*).[2] The Ireland into which he was born was one in which Vikings had long since settled; indeed exactly a century before Brian made his way into the world, Norsemen spent the winter in Dublin.[3] From their earliest recorded onslaught on Rechru (Lambay Island or Rathlin Island) in 795[4] down to the 830s, raids on coastal monasteries form a dominant pattern.[5] In the 830s and 840s Vikings venture further inland intensifying their campaign, taking prisoners presumably for slave-trading and for ransom in the process. Part of this strategy involved the establishment of more permanent bases (*longphoirt*) in various places, including Dublin.

However, prolonged periods in Ireland provided opportunities for alliance as well as attack. One hundred years or so before Brian's birth, Commán,

abbot of Linn Duachaill (Annagassan, Co. Louth) was slain by a combined
group of Irish and Vikings in 842.[6] While fierce plundering continued for
some time, it gradually gave way to increased involvement by Scandinavians
in local political affairs. Cináed mac Conaing of Brega is the first known Irish
dynast to collaborate extensively with them, rebelling with their assistance
against his main rival, Máel Sechnaill mac Maíle Ruanaid, in 851.[7] Nor did
the Vikings themselves always present a unified front: newly arrived *dubgenti*
'black heathens' confronting the more established *finngenti* 'white heathens' at
Linn Duachaill the following year.[8] A state of uneasy equilibrium ensued, the
Scandinavian groupings constituting yet further elements in what was often a
volatile scene. They married the daughters of Irish kings and very many of them
converted to Christianity. Communication continued and some level of bilingualism may have prevailed. Amlaíb Conung (Norse Óláfr/Áleifr Konungr),
a mid-ninth-century king of Dublin, may have been the recipient of a
praise-poem in Irish that we may assume he understood and enjoyed.[9] If it
was not intended for him, Amlaíb Cuarán (Norse Óláfr/Áleifr Kváran), a
contemporary of Brian is being addressed.[10] Proclaimed in ink, the Norse
had penetrated to the heart of Irish affairs.

Early in the tenth century the Norse of Dublin suffered a severe setback,
being expelled from their *longphort* (settlement base) in 902 by a combined
force of men from Brega and Leinster.[11] Its leaders, the descendants of Ímar
(Norse Ívarr) who died in 873, did not return again until 917.[12] In the mean-
time, however, renewed raiding had begun, some of it perhaps perpetrated by
the Dublin Norse who may have based themselves temporarily on the River
Ribble, as James Graham-Campbell and Nick Higham have suggested.[13]
Viking activity intensified once more.[14] The Leinster allies of Niall Glúndub,
king of the northern dynasty of Uí Néill, were defeated by Sitric ua Ímair
(Norse Sigtryggr, grandson of Ívarr), in a major battle at Cenn Fuait in 917,
after which the Norse victor entered Dublin in triumph.[15] The northern king
faced Vikings again two years later but was killed at Dublin, alongside 'many
other noblemen' (*alii nobiles multi*).[16] Consolidating their power, the 920s and
930s saw the Norse of Dublin in particular increase their influence, though
they were to become increasingly preoccupied with their involvement in the
kingdom of York.[17] As well as battling the Irish, they also frequently allied
with them and they were often at war too with other Viking settlements, the
rivalry between Dublin and Limerick being especially strong.[18] The Munster-
based Norsemen were decisively defeated by their Dublin kinsmen, for
example, just four years before Brian was born.[19]

Brian's Contemporaries

In the year of Brian's birth the long-reigning Norse king of Dublin, Amlaíb Cuarán, entered the historical record for the first time, ruling over the Northumbrians, according to a northern English chronicle.[20] It was to be four years before he assumed control in Dublin, ousting his rival, Blacair,[21] who had perhaps been involved in the slaying of the prominent Irish kings, Muirchertach mac Néill of Uí Néill and the Leinsterman, Lorcán mac Fáeláin, in 943.[22] Blacair may have been weakened by a revenge attack in 944 by the successor of the Leinster ruler, alongside Congalach mac Maíle Mithig, over-king of Uí Néill, in the same year.[23] Indeed Congalach may have been actively supporting the rival Norseman, since both he and Amlaíb Cuarán raided the territory of Conaille together, as soon as the latter became king.[24] Moreover, they marched together against Ruaidrí ua Canannáin two years later in the battle of Slane.[25] The alliance with Congalach appears to have endured, although the Irish king was slain by a combined force of unspecified *gaill* (Vikings) and Leinstermen in 956.[26] In fact, it spanned a generation, since Amlaíb and Congalach's son, Domnall, were allies in battle in 970, as well as being linked through the marriage of Domnall with Amlaíb's daughter.[27] The Dublin king himself had also entered into a number of strategic marital alliances, including with Dúnlaith, sister of Domnall ua Néill, Congalach's successor as king of Tara, against whom he and Congalach's son, Domnall, had fought.[28] Amlaíb was also married to Gormlaith, daughter of Murchad, king of Leinster, with whom Brian Boru himself was later to unite.[29] It was their son, Sitric (Norse Sigtryggr Silkiskegg 'silkenbeard'), who was ruling Dublin when Brian Boru faced the Norsemen and their Leinster allies, led by Gormlaith's brother, Sitric's uncle, Máel Mórda, at the battle of Clontarf. What is more Sitric was married to his mother's stepdaughter, Brian's own offspring, Sláine, at the time.

Amlaíb Cuarán's marital affairs also linked him with Brian's main Irish rival, Máel Sechnaill mac Domnaill, who was in fact Amlaíb's step-son, being the son of Dúnlaith, sister of the king of Tara, Domnall ua Néill. The relationship was none too happy; in fact it was Máel Sechnaill who effectively ended the long career of the Dublin ruler, defeating him in 980 in the battle of Tara 'in which great slaughter was inflicted on the Vikings and Viking power [was ejected] out of Ireland' (*i rroladh derg-ar Gall ocus nert Gall a hErinn*).[30] The Clonmacnoise chronicles, which consistently favour Máel Sechnaill, claim that, together with Eochaid, king of the Ulaid, he besieged

Dublin aiming to free 'every Irishman who is in servitude and tribulation in Viking territory' (*gach aon do Gaoidelaibh fail a ccrich Gall a ndaoire, ocus a ndocraidhe*), in what the chronicles descibe as 'the Babylonian captivity of Ireland' (*brad Baibilóin na hErenn*).[31] While this is obviously exaggerated, it is likely that Amlaíb Cuarán did leave Dublin to go on pilgrimage to Iona at this point, as the texts assert. He had already been baptised[32] and his possible patronage of the Columban church of Skreen indicates that he may have had an earlier connection with Iona, the premier church of St Columba (Colum Cille).[33] It was there he died 'having received holiness and penance' (*iar sanct, iar n-aithrighe*),[34] a Viking king for the modern age.

In his ecclesiastical and secular activity Amlaíb resembled none more than his Irish contemporaries, with whom, like them, he fought and allied in turn. Moreover, his policy bore fruit; this 'first Irishman to rule in Dublin' in Alex Woolf's provocative phrase,[35] succeeded in strengthening and extending Dublin's power beyond the boundaries of the Norse settlement, playing a pivotal role in insular political affairs in the process.[36] As he cast his eye outwards, so too did his rivals look in his direction, since Dublin with its thriving economy and vast network of trading links was a very desirable prize.[37] It was to remain so and control over its valuable resources was undoubtedly a motivating force for Brian Boru when he sought to besiege it more than thirty years after Amlaíb's deposition.[38]

Brian's rival, Máel Sechnaill, whose Southern Uí Néill heartland had been considerably encroached upon by Amlaíb, had earlier sought to assert his power over Dublin, as we have seen. Relations between this Mide ruler and Amlaíb's son, Glún Iairn (Norse Jarnkné 'iron-knee'), who succeeded his father in the kingship, were more cordial. The two were in fact half-brothers, since Glún Iairn was the son of Máel Sechnaill's mother, Dúnlaith, by Amlaíb. In 983 they formed a formidable alliance against the Leinstermen and Vikings of Waterford 'and many fell, both by drowning and slaying' (*i torcratar ili, itir bádhudh ocus marbadh*).[39] As Clare Downham has chronicled, tensions increased again after Glún Iairn's death in 989, Máel Sechnaill being attacked by the Dublin Norse aided by various allies on two occasions in the following decade.[40] The Clonmacnoise chronicles suggest that he quickly recovered, seizing the symbolically significant 'ring of Tomar and sword of Carlus' (*fail Tomair ocus claidebh Carlusa*) from the Dublin Vikings.[41] In the end, however, the greatest threat to Máel Sechnaill's power was posed not by his Dublin neighbours, but by his exact Munster contemporary, Brian Boru.

North-South Divide

The north-south rivalry between the two rulers was nothing new. The eighth-century king of Munster, Cathal mac Finguine, had ventured northwards, devastating the territory of Brega in 721.[42] According to the Munster-biased chronicle, the Annals of Inisfallen, his success was such that he is called *rí Herend* 'king of Ireland' on his death in 742,[43] a term signifying Ireland's most powerful king.[44] In reality, however, it was his northern counterparts who had the upper hand in this period. Donnchad Midi mac Domnaill, king of Tara until his death in 797, was an ambitious ruler who succeeded in extending his power throughout much of Ireland, pursuing an aggressive policy towards Munster in the process. In 775, for example, 'Donnchad did great devastation in the territory of the Munstermen' (*fecit Donnchad uastationem magnam in finibus Muminensium*) and he may have been involved in a battle between Uí Néill and Munster in the following year as well.[45] The southern kingdom rallied somewhat during the ninth-century reign of Feidlimid mac Crimthainn, whose constant harrying against his northern rivals brought him a measure of success. He and his northern contemporary, Conchobar, son of Donnchad Midi, participated in a *rígdál* 'royal meeting' in 827,[46] suggesting that the Munster king had by then become a force with which one had to come to terms. His strength continued to grow and he and Conchobar's successor, Niall Caille, also came together at a *mordál* 'great meeting' just over a decade later in 838. According to the Annals of Inisfallen, Niall in fact submitted to Feidlimid 'so that Feidlimid became full king of Ireland on that day' (*corbo lánrí Hérend Fédlimmid in lá sein*).[47] Southern hyperbole notwithstanding, the Munster king had come far.

The year before Feidlimid's own death in 847, his northern contemporary was drowned, to be succeeded by a grandson of Donnchad Midi, Máel Sechnaill I.[48] The north-south pendulum swung back again in the other direction during the reign of this ruler of note. Munster became a particular target, Máel Sechnaill attacking the region frequently and with devastating effect.[49] When he took control of Osraige in 859, Máel Guala, king of Munster, could do nothing but assent.[50] Accorded the title *ri Herenn uile* 'king of all Ireland' in the Annals of Ulster, on his death in 862, Máel Sechnaill I had exerted control over many of the country's regions, having been in a position to marshal the forces of Munster, Leinster and Connacht on a march to Armagh two years previously.[51] His son, Flann Sinna, inherited his

ability, subjugating Munster three years after his accession to power in 879.[52]
After the assumption of the kingship of the southern territory by Cormac
mac Cuilennáin in 901, however, Flann had a formidable opponent. In 907
the Munster ruler was powerful enough to march northwards, securing the
hostages of Uí Néill as well as those of the Connachta, according to the
Annals of Inisfallen.[53] Flann wreaked the ultimate revenge the following
year; mobilising the forces of Leinster and Connacht against the Munster
king, Cormac was killed in the battle of Belach Mugna.[54] It appears to have
been a fatal blow for his dynasty, the Éoganachta, and it was to be eighty
years or so before Cashel sought to overpower Tara once more. When it
did, it was in the person of Brian Boru, whose harrying of the territories of
Mide and Uisnech in 988[55] signalled the resurgence of a northward-looking
southern power.

That power was of an entirely different hue, however, since Brian Boru
belonged not to the royal Éoganachta, but to their newly emergent rivals,
Dál Cais, as we shall see. His rival in Ireland's northern half, Máel Sechnaill
II, on the other hand, could look to a long established ancestry. Flann Sinna
was succeeded by a very able king, Niall Glúndub, who was killed fighting against Vikings in the battle of Dublin in 919. His successor was one
of Flann Sinna's many sons, Donnchad Donn, though in effect Niall's own
son, Muirchertach, was the real power in the region. Máel Sechnaill was the
descendant of both men, being the product of a marital alliance between
Donnchad's son, Domnall, and Muirchertach's daughter, Dúnlaith. Brian
Boru's rival was thus of vigorous royal stock. On the death of Donnchad
Donn, a grandson of Flann Sinna, Congalach mac Maíle Mithig, assumed
the kingship. He came into direct contact with Brian's kin-group, killing two of his brothers, Echtigern and Donn Cuan, on an expedition
in the south in 950.[56] His power at home was far from secure, however,
and he was challenged by Máel Sechnaill's maternal uncle, Domnall son
of Muirchertach; he subsequently became king of Tara, when Congalach
was killed by Vikings in 956.[57] Domnall failed to gain supremacy in the
north and was ousted from the kingship by Máel Sechnaill's paternal kin,
Clann Cholmáin.[58] Máel Sechnaill himself came to power in 978, just as
Brian Boru was establishing himself in Munster, having taken over the
reins of authority two years previously on the murder of his brother,
Mathgamain.

The rivalry between the two manifested itself a few years later, Máel
Sechnaill being perhaps responsible for the destruction of a symbolic sacred

tree in 982 in Brian's home territory of Mag Adair.[59] Fifteen years of military manoeuvring and political positioning ensued before the two men entered into an agreement in 997. Even if Ireland was not carved up between them at the time, as the Uí Brian-biased chronicle, the Annals of Inisfallen, triumphantly claims, the event clearly underlines the important position Brian had by then achieved on a national stage. For Máel Sechnaill worse was to come, Brian succeeding in taking his hostages five years later in 1002.[60] Moreover, the descendant of long-established Uí Néill stock was subordinate to the relative Munster newcomer just over a decade later when they faced Leinster and Viking forces at the battle of Clontarf.

Brian's Ancestors

Brian's own journey to Clontarf was long and arduous, spanning a period of thirty-eighty years from his acquisition of power after the murder of his brother in 976 to his own triumphant death in battle there in 1014. His own ancestors, however, gave him a considerable head start. Though not so firmly rooted as the forbears of his rival, Máel Sechnaill, they made themselves a force to be reckoned with in Munster, reinventing themselves as Dál Cais (the Seed of Cas). It is in their earlier incarnation as In Déis Tuaiscirt that Brian's group are first attested, a name that brings with it connotations of subservience, since déis means 'vassal'. Notwithstanding this, they were involved with the promulgation of two laws in the late seventh century, which is indicative of some measure of importance. *Cáin Fhuithirbe* (The Law of Fuithirbe), concerned with the relative rights of ecclesiastical and secular authorities and put together about 680, refers to an unnamed king of the territory in a catalogue of various Munster people associated with the *cáin* 'law'.[61] The guarantors of a slightly later law, *Cáin Adomnáin* (The Law of Adomnán) promulgated in 697, form a much more diverse grouping. Among the ninety-one church and lay figures listed who come from all over Ireland is Aindlid, king of In Déis Tuaiscirt.[62]

Sparse though the annalistic entries from this early period concerning Brian's ancestors are, they also give some sense of a burgeoning community. They attacked the neighbouring Clare territory of Corcu Mo Druad in 744,[63] perhaps with some success, if Torpaid, who died as king of that territory in 769, was one of their number.[64] The death in battle somewhere in Clare of a member of the powerful Éoganachta, Corpre mac Con Dínisc, some years before is also worthy of note, if it signifies that Munster's ruling classes were taking an interest in what was happening on the other side of the Shannon at the time.[65] The Éoganachta continued to dominate southern politics in the ninth century and no record of the activity of In Déis Tuaiscirt survives, apart from a defeat they suffered at the hands of Vikings in 836.[66] That they did not go into oblivion, however, is indicated by the emergence in the first half of the tenth century of a particular sub-group of the dynasty, Uí Thairdelbaig, who planted the seeds that would eventually blossom in their scion, Brian.

If a later account of the battle of Belach Mugna is to be believed, two members of Uí Thairdelbaig, Conadar and Aineslis, were killed in 908 fighting on the side of the Éoganacht king of Munster, Cormac mac Cuilennáin, against a combined force of Leinstermen and Uí Néill. The source in question, the Fragmentary Annals, provides a florid description of the encounter, however, and while it agrees in its broad essentials with the more laconic notices in other annalistic compilations, the elaborate details are suspect.[67] Notwithstanding this, the presence of a group of men from North Munster alongside the other specified southern groups would not be unexpected and, if the two names had been inserted retrospectively, they would probably have been labelled Dál Cais. It is likely, therefore, that Brian's ancestors did provide the king of Munster with a military contingent in the early tenth century and were sufficiently significant to have their names recorded for posterity.[68]

However, not Uí Thairdelbaig but their dynastic rivals, Uí Óengusso, it was who may have produced the first ruler termed *rí Dál Cais* 'king of the Dál Cais' in the chronicles, Rebachán mac Mothlai, who was so described on his death in 934.[69] Abbot of Tuaim Gréine (Toomgraney, Co. Clare) as well, he has been described as a compromise candidate, though this must remain speculative.[70] His successor in the kingship was Lorcán mac Lachtnai, Brian's grandfather, whose great-great-great grandfather was the eponymous Tairdelbach from whom Uí Thairdelbaig were descended.[71] During the reign of Lorcán's son, Cennétig, the power of Brian's kin-group dramatically increased, his father being described in the Annals of Inisfallen as *rígdamna Cassil* 'heir-apparent of Cashel', and hence worthy of the kingship of Munster, on his death in 951.[72] Even allowing for the bias of that southern chronicler, other evidence also suggests that Cennétig was an active, ambitious ruler.[73] He challenged his Éoganacht rival, Cellachán of Cashel, in a significant encounter 'in which many fell' (*ubi multi ceciderunt*) in 944.[74] Although he was defeated, he was clearly a force with which to be reckoned upon the Munster scene. He had also come to attention further afield, since the name of one of his daughters, Órlaith, is recorded in the eleventh- or twelfth-century catalogue of women known as the *Banshenchas* (Women-lore), as one of a trio of wives of the powerful Uí Néill king, Donnchad mac Flainn.[75] If this were so, the North Munster dynast had connections in high places. Whether they were ultimately useful is another matter: her northern husband is said to have killed Órlaith after she was accused of sexual intercourse with his son.[76] Moreover, Donnchad's successor, Congalach mac Maíle Mithig, killed two sons of Cennétig on an expedition in Munster in 950, a year before the death of their father, as already noted.[77] Another son, Lachtna, succeeded the latter but reigned for a mere two years, dying in 953.[78] Later sources suggest that he was in fact murdered by rival local segments, Uí Fhlainn who were of Uí Thairdelbaig, and Uí Chernaig of Uí Oengusso.[79] If so, the Dál Cais home base was still far from secure.

Mathgamain, Brother of Brian

The situation was very different some twenty-three years later when Brian inherited the mantle of authority from another son of Cennétig, Mathgamain, who became king on Lachtna's death. The first Dál Cais leader to be termed king of Munster in extant king-lists,[80] it was Brian's older brother who carefully nurtured the seeds of power sown by his father and ensured that a sturdy sapling had taken root by the time his more famous sibling took control.[81] Like his father before him, Mathgamain too was expansionist. In the first decade of his rule, he sought to assert authority in the strategically significant Shannon basin, plundering Clonmacnoise in 959.[82] Later expeditions in the region were less successful; a Thomond host was slaughtered on the Shannon in 963 and Mathgamain himself was defeated by Fergal ua Ruairc somewhere between Clonfert and Clonmacnoise shortly afterwards, the Bréifne ruler adding insult to injury by raiding Dál Cais lands on the same expedition.[83] Four years later Mathgamain had bounced back and captured a richer prize, Limerick itself, having defeated its Viking rulers at the battle of Sulchóit.[84] He was ably assisted in this encounter by his right-hand man, Brian, according to later accounts of this battle; contemporary annalistic notices, however, give no indication that this was in fact the case.[85]

Mathgamain then sought to extend his newly-acquired authority over Munster neighbours, plundering Uí Énna Áine in 968 and taking the hostages of his Éoganacht arch-rival, Máel Muad mac Brain, the following year.[86] Some time later he was raiding in West Munster in the territory of Ciarraige Luachra and he was also active against Viking opponents about the same time.[87] Significantly, working alongside Máel Muad mac Brain, he was one of three Munster rulers to enact a trio of ordinances (*cána*) pertaining to the Vikings of Limerick in the same year: 'the banishment of the [Norse] officials, the banishment of the foreigners from Limerick and the burning of the fortress' (*innarba na suaitrech ocus innarba na nGall a lLumniuch ocus in dún do loscud*). Furthermore, placing him first in the list of royal legislators, the annalist of Inisfallen evidently wanted to indicate his pre-eminence in this regard.[88] If secular laws were now his concern, he was also mindful of the important role of the Church, specifically Armagh. Thus, the following year, acting as the premier Munster ruler, he was instrumental in settling a dispute between the abbot of Emly and the abbot of Armagh who was on a visitation in the south. That the rights of the northern Church were upheld need not surprise us.[89] In the first place, Mathgamain would not have been sympathetic to the claims of Emly, an Éoganacht church. Moreover, it may be that he too, like his brother after him, had perceived the benefits of an alliance with the country's chief ecclesiastical centre and one for long associated with Ireland's most powerful dynasty, Uí Néill.[90]

That Brian's own dynasty, Dál Cais, were actually associated with Uí Néill at this period has been suggested by John Kelleher, who attributes their rise to prominence in the first half of the tenth century to the support of the northern group. There was nothing altruistic in Uí Néill sponsorship of the Munster party, Kelleher has argued, suggesting that Dál Cais was promoted as a direct challenge to Éoganacht authority, in an attempt to ensure that Munster remained divided and weak.[91] His argument is weakened, however, by his claim that the northern dynasty aided the prominent Éoganacht ruler, Cormac mac Cuilennáin, simultaneously.[92] A more likely scenario is one of ever-shifting allegiances as the northern power bastion sought to keep its eye firmly on the southern ball. The situation in Munster was undoubtedly complex, a number of interlinked factors contributing to the emergence of a revitalised group, Dál Cais, on the political scene. The inherently unstable nature of Munster overlordship, as indicated by the number of different groups entitled to supply its kings, may have had a role to play, enabling the North Munster dynasty to join the fray.[93] This may well have been made easier by a gradual decline in the power of the Éoganachta, although their king, Cellachán of Cashel succeeded in defeating Brian's grandfather, Cennétig, not long after Brian himself was born.[94] Notwithstanding this, Dál Cais invigoration continued, not least because of its prime geographical position, which a succession of strong rulers could skilfully exploit.[95]

These enterprising Dál Cais personnel, among whom Brian's father and older brother were to the fore, were key to the success of the dynasty. Their military exploits were accompanied by astuteness off the battlefield, as Mathgamain's involvement in law-making and ecclesiastical politics shows. Like all newly-made men, they were also concerned with perception and may have had recourse to a medieval media machine. In any event, con-comitant with their gains by might was the justification of them by right. To this end their genealogy was augmented and a name reflective of their enhanced status adopted, as Kelleher and Ó Corráin have discussed. Thus did the 'northern vassal-group' (In Déis Tuaiscirt) become the 'seed of Cas' (Dál Cais), descendants of Cormac Cas, brother of Éogan Már, from whom their royal rivals, the Éoganachta, claimed descent.[96] Cleverly connected with Munster's long-established ruling dynasty, their prerogative to the kingship was artificially authenticated; an audacious claim that the Dál Cais in fact shared with the Éoganachta an equal alternate right to rule in Cashel was manufactured in the process.[97]

If the link with Munster's royalty through Éogan's brother, Cormac Cas, was designed to accord relatively recent claims to authority in the south the all-important seal of antiquity, another document may have served to emphasise the long-enduring nature of the Dál Cais connection with Armagh through its premier saint, Patrick. An episode in that holy man's Tripartite Life (*Vita Tripartita*) is keen to stress that Cairthenn mac Blait, ancestor of Brian's Uí Thairdelbaig forbears, believed in Christ and was baptised by Patrick himself. Having fathered what are termed misshapen children up to that point, the chosen one then had a perfectly formed son, Echu Ballderg, whose 'red member' (*ball derg*) served as a reminder of the miracle that was his creation.[98] The precise date of the text is conten-tious and its language exhibits many tenth- and eleventh-century features in its present form.[99] However, historical references therein, including perhaps the passage under discussion, suggest a stratified text.[100] In a tenth-century context, the depiction of *sen Clainde Tairdelbaig* 'the ancestor of

Uí Thairdelbaig' as Patrick's chosen one could be taken to reflect a growing aspiration on the part of Cairthenn's descendants, and Mathgamain perhaps specifically, to forge an association with Armagh. As we shall see, Brian too was acutely aware of the significance of the northern church; but were the account to date from his period we might expect the appellation, Dál Cais, to be employed, which was by his time long established. The precise date of the story, therefore, remains unclear.

The term 'Dál Cais' is used in annalistic notices as early as 934, in which year Rebachán mac Mothlai is described as king of that group, as we have seen.[101] According to Kathleen Hughes, this entry is retrospective, as are, in her view, a number of others, including the death-notice of Brian's grandfather, Cennétig.[102] Why a later partisan of Uí Briain should choose to accord this honorific title to Rebachán who was of Uí Oengusso, rather than to an Uí Thairdelbaig claimant, is uncertain. The animosity between the two groups is underlined by the killing of Rebachán's son, Dub Gilla, in the same year that his father died, by a member of Uí Thairdelbaig, Congalach mac Lorcáin, brother of Cennétig, according to the Annals of the Four Masters.[103] It seems more likely that a later copyist substituted *rí Dál Cais* 'king of Dál Cais' for the 'king of Thomond' or the like that was in his exemplar for the entry of 934. Uí Briain manipulation of the Annals of Inisfallen can certainly be detected from the time Brian himself came to power.[104]

That Mathgamain also wielded control over centres of learning is not in doubt and the attention he paid to the written word is also a characteristic feature of a number of his successors, including Brian. It undoubtedly paid dividends and he is acknowledged as king of Cashel in a northern source, the Annals of Ulster, on his death in 976.[105] The manner of his passing also gives some indication of his standing, since he was murdered, having been treacherously seized by an Uí Fhidgeinti opponent, Donnubán mac Cathail, working in conjunction with Mathgamain's main Munster rival, the Éoganacht king, Máel Muad mac Brain.[106] That this is said to have happened in direct contravention of, and despite the interdiction of *sruthi Muman* 'the elders of Munster', highlights the success of the deliberate policy of the Dál Cais ruler in courting favour with the Church.

A twelfth-century account of the crime preserved in the biography of Mathgamain's more famous brother, Brian, *Cogadh Gáedhel re Gallaibh*, provides additional detail on ecclesiastical involvement in the fatal incident. The older sibling is said to have been under the protection of Colum mac

Ciarucáin, abbot of Cork, at the time of his slaying. Moreover, Mathgamain attempted in vain to protect himself with the gospel book of Bairre, Cork's founding saint.[107] The central role assigned to the southern monastery in the later narrative, however, casts light on Dál Cais-Church relations not in Mathgamain's time but in the period when the text was actually composed. Links between Cork and Brian's descendants at the time were strong:[108] at least two Dál Cais candidates succeeded to the southern abbacy in the late eleventh and early twelfth centuries, Mac Bethad Ua hÁilgenáin and Gilla Pátraic Ua hÉnna. In addition an anchorite of Uí Thairdelbaig, the dynastic group to which Brian's family belonged, as we have seen, died in Cork about the same time. The *Cogadh* highlights these connections by portraying one of the Cork clerics weeping bitterly at the sight of Mathgamain's blood splattered across the sacred gospel-book. Thus Dál Cais rather than the ineffectual Éoganachta are that monastery's true protectors, according to the text, particularly since Máel Muad's murderous deed demonstrated utter contempt for Cork, ignoring as it did Colum mac Ciarucáin's edict that the honourable Mathgamain be neither killed nor blinded (*ar ná marbhtha ocus ar ná dallta é*).[109] The Éoganacht ruler is seen to have received his just reward by being buried on the northern, obscure side of a hill where 'the sun will never shine on it, as the cleric and ecclesiastic foretold' (*ni thaitnend grian fair co brath, amhail ro tircan in clereach ocus in credal*).[110] By contrast, Mathgamain, and by association his descendants, will bask in southern sunshine of all kinds.

Mathgamain's glow is not allowed to shine over-brightly in the literary narrative, however, which is in essence an elaborate extolling of his brother Brian. Alongside his precocious sibling he is one of 'two brave, strong, valorous towers, two fierce, lacerating, vigorous heroes, two battle defences, two poles of combat, two sheltering bushes' (*da tuir croda comnerta comcalma, da laech lonna letarracha luchtmara, da comlaid catha, da cleith ugra, da dos didin*).[111] Even when second-in-command, the younger man is seen to direct proceedings, chiding his older sibling for yielding to the Viking threat, besmirching the memory of their glorious ancestors in the process. Conceding the truth of the allegations, Mathgamain assembled the Dál Cais and all agreed unanimously to adopt the policy of war advocated by Brian.[112] Victory at the battle of Sulchóit ensued, Mathgamain's assumption of the kingship of Munster being presented as a direct consequence of it.[113] That he owed his sovereignty to his brilliant brother, therefore, is being subtly implied. This sibling rivalry may also be deliberately resonant of another more difficult relationship between Brian's great-grandson, Muirchertach, and his half-brother, Diarmait, which was being played out as the *Cogadh* was being composed. Ostensibly at peace between the latter's submission to his sibling in 1093 and his assumption of power and banishment of Muirchertach when that king fell ill in 1114,[114] tensions would undoubtedly have remained. Echoes of these may well have been captured in the literary narrative, Muirchertach's equation with the younger heroic brother being made abundantly clear.[115]

The glorification of Brian at the hands of Muirchertach's image makers in the early twelfth century ensured that his older brother, Mathgamain, was effectively cast in the shade. Considerable though his achievements may have been, they were inevitably less significant than those of a revamped Brian whose adoption as auspicious ancestor obscured the substantial successes of other members of the kin. In reality, however, Brian was very much building on a foundation set in place by his older brother and father in particular. Furthermore, many of the policies practised by Brian had been tried and tested by Mathgamain to good effect. In the military sphere both brothers sought to maintain control of the Shannon waterway, having recourse to naval power in the process. Consolidation of the home base was followed by expansion elsewhere in Munster and, in Brian's case, beyond. Battle strategy was only one avenue pursued; legislative activity and ecclesiastical interaction were also actively engaged in by the two men. The latter ensured access to the tools of writing that both effectively employed. Although Mathgamain's authority never extended beyond Munster, he displaced its firmly entrenched royal rulers, the Éoganachta, as Brian was to challenge the supremacy of their northern equivalents, Uí Néill, a few years later. The sibling-successor was indeed 'a strong man in the place of a strong man' (*tren i n-inad trein*) and 'a vigorous one coming after a vigorous one' (*tend iar tend*), as *Cogadh Gáedhel re Gallaibh* proclaims;[116] it was Mathgamain's strength and vigour, however, that accorded Brian a considerable head start.

3

'Emperor of the Irish': The Road to Clontarf

Into a dynasty on the make Brian Boru was born,[1] the activities of his father, Cennétig, and brother, Mathgamain, ensuring that it remained on the move. As things transpired, Brian was certainly his father's son and proved himself to be more than his brother's equal. Under his leadership Dál Cais became players on a larger political stage and the Munster king carved out for himself a dominance of sorts throughout the island of Ireland. His descendants certainly perceived it thus, commemorating him in his augmented obituary in the Annals of Ulster as 'high-king of the Irish of Ireland and of the Vikings and the Britons; the Augustus of the whole of north-western Europe' (ardrí Gaidhel Erenn ocus Gall ocus Bretan, August iartair tuaiscirt Eorpa uile).[2] Less biased commentators also recognised his achievement: a list of the kings of Ireland preserved in the twelfth-century manuscript Rawlinson B502 admits Brian, alongside Báetán mac Cairill of the Ulaid, to an illustrious list of what are otherwise kings associated with the dynasty of Niall, ancestor of Uí Néill.[3] Even narratives designed to elevate the northern dynasty do not always write the southern pretender out of the story, the eleventh-century propaganda tract, Echtra mac nEchach Muigmedóin (The Adventure of the Sons of Eochaid Mugmedón) citing him as one of very few holders of the kingship of Ireland who were not of Uí Néill stock.[4] Furthermore, a poem addressed to Mór, wife of Brian's arch-rival, the Southern Uí Néill king, Máel Sechnaill mac Domnaill, may include a reference to the Munster king therein (*Brian ro gab Éiblinn co n-ór* 'Brian whose rule over Éibliu [Ireland] is golden'), specifically stating that he is a good friend to her.[5]

That Brian's special status owes much to his military exploits and political manoeuvring is undeniable, even before these were transformed in the telling by an eager and enthusiastic following. Furthermore, in their effective employment of the literary record, his descendants can be seen to be following a lead set by their sage ancestor who was ever mindful of the power of the written word. At the height of his political power symbolised effectively by a tour of the northern part of the country in 1005, acting as chief benefactor of Armagh, Ireland's primary church, he deposited twenty ounces of gold on the altar there.[6] Ostentatious gesture though this was, it is overshadowed by another event that happened on the same occasion, at which a ninth-century manuscript, the Book of Armagh, was produced for Brian. Writing 'in Brian's presence' (*in conspectu Briain*), Máel Suthain, confessor of the Munster king, accorded him the title *Imperator Scotorum* 'Emperor of the Irish' in the valuable book.[7] Aubrey Gwynn has suggested convincingly that this may well reflect the adoption a short time earlier of a similar honorific label, *Imperator Romanorum*, by the Ottonian royal house.[8] Brian, or his adviser, knew the value of an outward look.

Family Man

Brian's beginnings, however, are to be found much closer to home. He is recorded in genealogical material as a member of Dál Cais, who were later to become known as Uí Briain 'Brian's descendants' after their most famous ancestor, Brian himself. As son of Cennétig and grandson of Lorcán, he is brought back through a further eighteen generations to Cormac Cas son of Ailill Óluimm, from whom the Dál Cais 'seed of Cas' got their name, as part of their attempts to legitimise their claim to the kingship of Cashel, as we have seen.[9] Although he was not his father's eldest son, Brian's supremacy over his older brother, Mathgamain, is indicated by his position in the genealogies as the first of Cennétig's five sons who left descendants after them.[10] His mother was the daughter of a king of western Connacht, Urchad son of Murchad; her name is recorded in the *Banshenchas* (Women-lore), as Bé Binn.[11]

Brian himself is recorded as having six sons, three of whom had offspring themselves, Tadc, Donnchad and Domnall, and three of whom had none, Murchad, Conchobar and Flann. This second trio is described as sons of the daughter of Eiden son of Cléirech.[12] That Brian's first wife was a daughter of Eiden, king of the southern Connacht territory of Uí Fhiachrach Aidne that bordered on the North Munster territory of Dál Cais, is also recorded elsewhere.[13] Contrary to what the genealogies suggest, her son, Murchad, had at least one son himself, Tairdelbach, but as both father and son were slain in the battle of Clontarf in 1014, their line ended at this point; they were thus genealogically insignificant. Of Conchobar and Flann nothing further is known; Brian's other trio of sons, however, have left historical marks. Alongside his half-brother, Murchad, Domnall took joint command of part of his father's army on a foray into the northern territory of Cenél Conaill in 1011, though his apparently peaceful death is recorded later that year.[14] Neither his mother's name nor that of any wife of his has been recorded; that an unnamed son killed a king of Ara in Munster twenty years later is known.[15]

Donnchad and Tadc, the two brothers with whom Domnall is paired in the genealogies, are of greater significance. The former succeeded to the kingship of Munster on his father's death, dying himself in Rome in 1064 where he had gone on pilgrimage earlier that year.[16] He was the son of Gormlaith,[17] daughter of the king of Leinster, Murchad mac Find, whose relationship with Brian is deemed to have been both tempestuous and hostile in twelfth- and thirteenth-century literary narratives in Irish and Norse.[18] A witty stanza preserved in genealogical material associates her with a trio of powerful men: Amlaíb Cuarán, Norse king of Dublin; the Mide ruler, Máel Sechnaill, friend and foe in turn of the Munster king; as well as Brian himself.[19] Although the verse suggests that Gormlaith's marriage to the southern ruler took place after her unions with the other two men, the fact that Donnchad was active at the time of the battle of Clontarf in 1014 places his birth and thus his parents' alliance in the 980s or 990s. His death in 1064 at what would then be a considerable age corroborates this. Since it was in this period that Brian attempted to extend his sway in Leinster, his marriage to the daughter of a king of that region might have been part of this process and was perhaps specifically linked with his incursion there in 984. If so, this marital diplomacy did not have the desired effect since he was forced to attack Leinster again in 991 and acquire its hostages five years later. Furthermore, Brian faced a combined force of Vikings and Leinstermen in 999 in the battle of Glenn Máma. Gormlaith's brother, Máel Mórda, who opposed him in that encounter was none the less installed by Brian in the kingship of Leinster in 1003. His loyalty did not endure and he was among the prime instigators of the move against the Munster king just over a decade later at Clontarf.[20] Máel Mórda's principal ally on that occasion was his nephew, Sitric Silkenbeard, son of Gormlaith by Amlaíb Cuarán, to whom she was married before Brian.[21]

By contrast, the mother of Brian's remaining son, Tadc, did not acquire quite the same notoriety. She was Echrad, daughter of Carlus mac Ailella, of the little known dynasty of Uí Aeda Odba in the region of the Southern Uí Néill.[22] The geographical position of this group in the heartland of the territory of Brian's chief opponent for the kingship of Ireland, Máel Sechnaill mac Domnaill, indicates that this marriage may have been designed to acquire for the ambitious Munster ruler a friendly foothold on enemy ground, as John Ryan suggested.[23] If 'Odba' of their dynastic affiliation refers to a place in the south of the plain of Brega, as Ailbhe Mac Shamhráin has proposed, it gave Brian a strategic resting place within striking distance of Dublin.[24] Brian made a number of forays northwards in the 990s and suffered some defeats at Máel Sechnaill's hands. By 997, however, his power was such that he and the Uí Néill king came to terms.[25] It may be that this marital alliance can be dated to this period; in any event Brian's son by Echrad was also old enough to fight at Clontarf in 1014. Moreover, on his death in 1023, he had a son, Tairdelbach, who deposed his uncle, Tadc's brother, Donnchad, as king in 1063, ruling himself until his death of old age in 1086.[26] Tairdelbach's own son, Muirchertach, took up the reins of power on his father's death and building on the latter's success consolidated Uí Briain power until illness struck in 1114.[27] Furthermore, as a great-grandson of Brian, he deliberately cultivated his ancestor's exalted image and it was during his reign that what is in effect an heroic biography of his glorious great-grandfather, *Cogadh Gáedhel re Gallaibh*, was composed. It was Brian's northern wife Echrad, therefore, who was the progenitor of the Uí Briain ruling line.

Brian is also known to have had a fourth wife, Dub Choblaig, daughter of Cathal mac Conchobair, king of Connacht, who worked actively with the king of Mide, Máel Sechnaill, against the Munster ruler in 1001. Brian had gained the upper hand a year later, as indicated by his acquisition of the hostages of both kings.[28] Moreover, the Connacht men formed part of his expedition northwards in 1005.[29] If, as seems likely, military and marital associations were linked in this case also, Brian's marriage to the Connacht woman can be dated to around this time. Dub Choblaig predeceased Brian by five years, dying one year before her father in 1009;[30] no account of children she may have had with the Munster king survives.

The maternal line of his three named daughters, however, is not known. Sadb who died in 1048 was married to Cian, the son of her Uncle Mathgammain's slayer, Máel Muad mac Brain.[31] Her sister or half-sister who bore their grandmother's name, Bé Binn, married the king of the Northern Uí Néill, Flaithbertach ua Néill. This may conceivably have been in the context of that ruler's submission to Brian in 1010, as a result of which the Munster king brought northern hostages southwards to his stronghold at Cenn Corad (Kincora, Co. Clare).[32] A third daughter, called Sláine, also appears to have had a strategic marriage arranged for her; she was wife of Sitric, king of Dublin, at the time of the battle of Clontarf.[33] Their alliance may date back more than a decade to the Norse ruler's reinstatement as king of Dublin by Brian in 1000 very much on the Munster king's terms.[34] *Cogadh Gáedhel re Gallaibh*, written long after her time in the early twelfth century, suggests that her loyalties lay with her paternal kin and has her taunt her husband as they watch the fight at Clontarf from the relative safety of Dublin's battlements.[35] That it was Brian who was responsible for her liaison with Sitric who was the son of one of his own wives, Gormlaith, seems likely. In pursuit of political advancement both might and mediation were employed to serve his cause.

Military Career

Family connections also served Brian well in other ways. As the son of a claimant to the kingship of Cashel and the brother to one who had certainly attained it, Brian succeeded to a home base that was relatively secure. Indeed, it is in his dead brother's shadow that he first appears in annalistic entries, loyally avenging Mathgamain's death, the circumstances of which have been outlined above.[36] Reading the various chronicle sources in conjunction with one another provides the following account of an active career.[37] In 977 he slew Ímar (Norse Ívarr), king of the Limerick Norse, along with his two sons,[38] who may have been involved in the plot to over-throw Mathgamain. This was followed by another attack on the Norse and on other participants in his brother's slaying, Uí Fhidgeinti.[39] One year later he turned his attention to the prime instigator of Mathgamain's murder, Máel Muad mac Brain, who had been in contention with his older brother for the kingship of Munster, slaying him in the battle of Belach Lechta.[40]

His familial duty thus dispatched, Brian then looked to expansion and may have directed an expedition of the Munstermen to Osraige in 982 in which 'a good number of them were slain' (co rubad sochaide díb and).[41] In the same year, the sacred tree of Mag Adair in Brian's home territory was destroyed by Máel Sechnaill mac Domnaill according to some annalists.[42] The Munster mover had evidently come to the attention of the most powerful king in Ireland's northern half, perhaps indeed as a direct result of the successful Osraige attack, since that territory had been alienated to the northern half of Ireland (Leth Cuinn) by that time. Brian is specifically named as head of the ill-fated fleet that attacked Connacht and the territory of Uí Briúin the following year.[43] He made further progress in Osraige in the same year, capturing its king and taking hostages there, as well as in Leinster.[44] He returned to harry the same two territories a year later, with the support of Vikings, the Haraldssons (meic Arailt), with whom he had exchanged hostages at Waterford.[45] If the Vikings of Waterford them-selves were involved in the alliance it was presumably as a reaction against a battle-rout upon them by Máel Sechnaill the previous year.[46] The joint hosting by Brian and the Haraldssons on Dublin was also designed to hurt the Mide ruler through his half-brother, Glún Iairn, who was ruling Dublin at the time.[47]

Máel Sechnaill had reason to be worried; Brian's control of Osraige from this point onwards seems relatively secure. Not so his power over neigh-bouring regions and, when the Déssi attacked his allies in 985, the Munster king turned his attention to them, devastating their territory.[48] An attack on a combined force of Munstermen and Waterford Vikings by Connachtmen may also be dated to around this time.[49] In addition, Brian's home base was still not fully secure and he was forced to imprison his nephew, Áed, son of Mathgamain, in 986.[50] Nonetheless, his strength was such that he was in a position to impose his authority in southern Munster (Desmumu 'Desmond') and to acquire the hostages of the three chief churches of Munster one year later.[51] Furthermore, he plundered the midland territories of Mide and Uisnech in 988, as well as enjoying considerable naval success in Connacht.[52] Among those slain fighting on his side was Dúnlaing, king of Éoganacht Raithlind, traditionally opponents of the Dál Cais. Involvement in ecclesiastical politics continued; a mere two years later he ransomed an official of the monastery of Ros Ailithir who had been captured by the Norse.[53] The appointment of his brother, Marcán, as abbot of Emly in the same year was also undoubtedly made with his brother's approval.[54]

There were setbacks, however, in the military field: his counterpart in Ireland's northern half, Máel Sechnaill, defeated the men of Brian's own territory of north Munster (Tuadmumu 'Thomond') in battle in 990.[55] Moreover, notwithstanding Osraige's general loyalty, Tadc mac Donnchada, brother of and potential heir to that territory's king, Gilla Pátraic, was killed by the Munstermen on a hosting to Leinster the following year in which Brian too lost men.[56] A further hosting to Mide about this time is recorded in some annalistic compilations, on which Brian obtained 'neither cows nor men' (nir' gab bai na duine).[57] He appears to have been more success-ful on a naval expedition in 993, venturing as far as Bréifne.[58] Perhaps as a result, Máel Sechnaill marched southwards and defeated the Munster king on his home ground.[59] Not surprisingly, defence was a major theme in 995 during which he had a number of major structures in Munster fortified, including Cashel.[60] He returned to Leinster one year later and succeeded in acquiring the hostages of Uí Chennselaig, as well as those of western Liphe.[61] By this time, his power was evidently such that Máel Sechnaill entered into an agreement with him, the terms of which are set out as favourable to Brian in the Annals of Inisfallen.[62] Furthermore, the Munster annalist portrays Brian as the leader of a successful expedition to Connacht the following year, the hostages of which territory he then handed over to Máel Sechnaill.[63] By contrast, other annalists make Brian at most co-protagonist,[64] or claim Máel Sechnaill as leader of the Connacht hosting while attributing military success in Leinster to Brian.[65]

The year 999 saw Brian gain a major victory against the Norse in the bat-tle of Glenn Máma,[66] although Máel Sechnaill is presented as joint-leader in a number of chronicles.[67] As a consequence of this, the Munstermen marched to Dublin and banished Sitric mac Amlaíb, the Norse king, who later returned on submitting to Brian.[68] A hosting to Brega about the same time was less successful; a combined party of Vikings and Leinstermen met Brian's forces there and Máel Sechnaill inflicted heavy losses on them, caus-ing the Munster king to retreat 'without giving battle or making incursion' (cen chath cen indriudh).[69] A foray into southern Mide the following year also resulted in the slaughter of many of Brian's men,[70] and Máel Sechnaill, working in collaboration with the Connacht king, Cathal mac Conchobair, sought to halt Munster's advance by building a construction across the Shannon at Athlone.[71] His efforts proved futile, however, the Clonmacnoise chronicles dating the beginning of Brian's reign, presumably as most powerful king in Ireland, to this period.[72] Moreover, Brian succeeded in taking the hostages of both the northern and the Connacht rulers in 1002.[73]

Towards the Kingship of Ireland

Brian's eyes were now firmly directed northwards. Leading a combined force of Munster, Mide and Connacht men, reinforced by the Leinstermen and the Norse according to some annalistic compilations, Brian marched against the northern territories of the Ulaid and Cenél nÉogain but failed to take their hostages and was forced to call a truce.[74] Nonetheless, the Munster king was soon in a position to intervene in Leinster politics, bestowing power on Máel Mórda mac Murchada in the process.[75] He went north again the following year but Cenél nÉogain halted his advance.[76] This may have been in the wake of the substantial victory of that group against the Ulaid in the battle of Cráeb Tulcha.[77] In any event, with the northern groups at war, Brian was more successful a year later in 1005, reaching Armagh and returning home 'with the pledges of the men of Ireland' (co n-etire fer nErenn laiss).[78] It was on this occasion, some annalists claim, that he left twenty ounces of gold on the altar at Armagh, aligning himself clearly with the primatial church.[79]

He demonstrated his supremacy again in 1006 when, at the head of a force of Munster, Leinster and Mide men, together with Máel Sechnaill, the Connachta and the Norse, he undertook an elaborate circuit of the north of Ireland.[80] Moreover, he was back there the following year, removing by force the Ulaid hostages that Flaithbertach ua Néill, king of Cenél nÉogain, had recently acquired.[81] The Annals of Ulster name one of the hostages, Ua Críchidéin, an ecclesiastical official (comarba) of the monastery of Mag Bile,[82] underlining the significant ecclesiastical dimension to Brian's political manoeuvring, further highlighted by the death of his nephew, Céilechair son of Donn Cuan, as abbot of Terryglass in 1008.[83] Another expedition northwards was necessary in 1010, on which occasion he brought the hostages of Leth Cuinn back with him to his own fortress at Cenn Corad and received the submission of Flaithbertach ua Néill.[84] Notwithstanding this, he was forced to march against Cenél Conaill twice in 1011, perhaps with the support of ua Néill, acquiring the 'complete submission' of its king in the process (*co tuc a ogréir do Brian*).[85] Significantly, the king in question, Máel Ruanaid ua Maíl Doraid, also endured the humiliation of journeying to Cenn Corad to submit.

According to the Annals of Ulster, Brian was also in the north the following year, acting as secular patron of Armagh.[86] Simultaneously pursuing a defence strategy, however, he constructed numerous fortifications in Munster.[87] The year 1013 saw him similarly engaged in ecclesiastical and secular politics. On his orders, Máel Sechnaill attacked the Conaille Muirthemne who had previously profaned Patrick.[88] He was also engaged against the Norse, a three-month campaign failing to bring about peace.[89] His son, Murchad, had greater success in Leinster where 'he took great spoils and countless captives' (*co ruc gabala móra ocus brait diairmhidhe*).[90] Hostilities continued, however, with the Norse and the Leinstermen allied against Brian.[91] These culminated in Brian's march to Dublin and the celebrated battle of Clontarf.[92]

Subjective Sources

The influence of literary hyperbole on the extant accounts of that particular battle has been noted; yet other events of Brian's career have also been recounted with a subjective spin. Not surprisingly the Annals of Inisfallen, a Munster compilation, and one that became the Uí Briain in-house chronicle during the reign of Brian's brother, Mathgamain,[93] is fullest and most flattering in its portrayal of the all-conquering Brian. Without it, little would be known of his activities through the 980s and 990s in particular, since entries pertaining to him are unique to the Munster compilation in the years 982, 983, 984, 985, 986, 987, 988, 990, 991, 993, 995, 996, 997 and 1003. Much of the additional information is concerned with Munster, including a hint at internal opposition to Brian (986), as well as detail concerning his building activity (995) and involvement with southern churches (987, 990). Yet it is in this source alone that a record of particular attacks on Osraige and Leinster (982, 983, 984, 996, 1003) and of the associated alliance with Vikings at Waterford (984, 985) is preserved. Certain expeditions further afield (988 to Mide, Uisnech and Connacht; 993 to Bréifne; 996 to

Leinster and Western Liphe) are similarly solely recounted therein. That this supplementary material is for the most part laudatory in tone is to be expected, the notice of a defeat in 983 at the hands of the Connachta and Uí Briúin being exceptional.

Moreover, setbacks suffered by the Munstermen and recorded in other chronicles do not always appear. A successful excursion by Máel Sechnaill into Brian's home territory (990) is not recorded in the Annals of Inisfallen, nor is what may be a retaliatory and ultimately futile attack by the Munster king in Mide about two years later. In the same way, losses at the hands of the Mide king in 994, 1000 and 1001 are also ignored, as is a repulse by Cenél nEogain in 1004.[94] And even when various descriptions of a particular event have survived, comparison between them frequently reveals a chronicler's evident bias. Thus, according to the Munster annalist, Brian simply killed the Norse king, Ímar, and his two sons, in 977, whereas the Clonmacnoise chroniclers behind *Chronicum Scotorum* and the Annals of Tigernach claim that he desecrated Inis Cathaig (Scattery Island) in the process.[95] Similarly, the 997 truce between the two kings is a meeting of equals, according to a number of reports; in the Munster chronicle, however, Brian reigns supreme. A triumph two years later at the battle of Glenn Máma is also a solo one, according to the account preserved in the Annals of Inisfallen, although Brian shares the glory with Máel Sechnaill in a number of other sources. The Annals of Tigernach in fact accord the midland ruler pride of place, the acquisition of hostages of the Connachta also being presented as a joint action with that king.[96] This particular annalist can scarcely conceal his hostility to Brian on occasion, as when he accuses him of retreating 'like a runaway' (*a coir n-éludha*) and of attacking Máel Sechnaill 'treacherously' (*tre mebail*).[97] We may compare a similar sentiment expressed somewhat more discreetly by the northern annalist who accords one particular defeat of Brian, not recorded in the Annals of Inisfallen, to God's will.[98] God works in other ways in the Munster compilation: a defeat of Vikings in 1013 in which Brian presumably took part 'was a great miracle of God and of St Finbarr' (*ba firt mór do Dia ocus do Barre*).[99]

Written from different vantage points, therefore, the individual chronicles provide varying perspectives on Brian's career. Nonetheless, balancing the positive noises of the Munster annalist with the more muted tones of his Clonmacnoise and northern counterparts, the main events of Brian's reign come into view. The ultimate hero in the southern source, his activities form the main focus of the annalist in the period between Mathgamain's murder in 976 and Brian's own death in 1014. By contrast, his early career is all but unrecorded in the Annals of Ulster: a notice of his killing of Máel Muad mac Brain in 978 excepted, his actions are not recounted until his power is such that he can realistically rival Máel Sechnaill in the late 990s. Thenceforth, his actions are frequently recorded, whether functioning independently (998, 999, 1000, 1004, 1005, 1006, 1007, 1012, 1013), in tandem with Máel Sechnaill (998, 1002) or against the Mide king (1000, 1002, 1010). Furthermore, on one occasion Máel Sechnaill is said to have been acting at Brian's behest when he raided the territory of Conaille Muirthemne in 1013.[100] The Clonmacnoise sources, on the other hand, favour Máel Sechnaill above the Munster king, claiming both rulers as joint leaders of expeditions to Connacht and, more significantly, to Glenn Máma, as we have seen.[101]

Almost from the beginning, therefore, Munster annalists were keen to give their highly polished monarch an extra sheen. When exactly they first took to their cleaning cloths is impossible to ascertain but they were certainly hard at work in the mid-eleventh century when various sets of Munster and Clonmacnoise annals were assembled and conflated, most probably in the monastery of Killaloe, to produce what we now know as the very much Uí Briain-orientated Annals of Inisfallen.[102] That they did far more than simply copy their exemplars is indicated by a retrospective entry concerning Brian inserted under the year 721,[103] as well as by a comparison of their account of Brian's career with that contained in other, differently biased, annalistic compilations, as we have seen. Ultimately, however, the precise degree of concoction must remain unclear.

Cogadh Gáedhel re Gallaibh and the Chronicles Compared

While a chronicle text, the Annals of Inisfallen, presents Brian's career as all but untarnished, a literary narrative, *Cogadh Gáedhel re Gallaibh*, which draws heavily on annalistic material,[104] does indeed depict the Munster king as entirely blemish free. Portrayed alongside Mathgamain, from the outset, the two brothers are 'two spears of victory and readiness, of honour and valour, of ferocity and strength, of kindness and vitality' (*da rind aga ocus urlaimi, enig ocus egnuma, brotha ocus brigi, bagi ocus beodachta*).[105] Furthermore,

it is Brian who is deemed to be the more courageous of the siblings fighting
to protect his ancestors' inheritance, in contrast with an unduly cautious
Mathgamain who quickly sought peace. It is Brian's approach that the Dál
Cais are said to support.[106] Accordingly, the brothers set out as joint leaders of an expedition to Sulchóit where the Vikings are soundly defeated,
their fortress at Limerick being plundered in the process.[107] In reality, it
was Mathgamain alone who was the victor,[108] Brian's political activities
commencing in earnest after his brother's death, as we have seen.

   Essentially, however, the career depicted in outline in the chronicles
corresponds with that described in greater detail in the more discursive
narrative text, as the following outline of Brian's activities in the *Cogadh* will
show. The killing of Ímar and his two sons by Brian recorded in annalistic
entries is stated explicitly in the tale to be in revenge for their involvement
in Mathgamain's murder;[109] the attack on Uí Fhidgeinti, also participants
in the crime, is termed in the *Cogadh* the battle of Cathair Cuan.[110] The
encounter at Belach Lechta, in which Mathgamain's principal opponent,
Máel Muad mac Brain, was slain is present in the literary narrative, as well
as in other sources.[111] According to the *Cogadh*, this battle was followed by
an attack by Brian on the Déssi;[112] in reality it was seven years before he
turned his attention to this particular group.[113] Brian's alleged seizure of the
hostages of the chief churches of Munster[114] might also reflect a later event,
his capture of the hostages of Lismore, Cork and Emly in 987, as recorded in
the Annals of Inisfallen.

   That Osraige and Leinster next became the focus of Brian's attention,
according to the author of the *Cogadh*, is in keeping with chronicle accounts.
These events are specifically dated by the narrator to eight years after
Mathgamain's death, namely 984.[115] Furthermore, he states that consequently
'Brian became king of Leth Moga (Ireland's southern half)' (*ba ri Lethi Moga
Brian*).[116] Telescoping activities of different years recorded in annalistic entries,
the literary account then presents as a single expedition an attack on Mide,
Uisnech, Connacht and Bréifne mounted from Lough Ree.[117] As well as killing
rígdamna Connacht 'the heir-apparent of Connacht', as the Annals of Inisfallen
also note,[118] Brian is said to have slain a duo of other western nobles in the
process.[119] The agreement with Máel Sechnaill is then recorded in the *Cogadh*,
each ruler being assigned one of Ireland's halves.[120] It is dated to two years
before the battle of Glenn Máma, a detailed description of which ensues.[121]

   The account of the events of 1002 in the narrative is also considerably
embellished, Brian's power being depicted as far greater than that of his

counterpart in the northern half of Ireland as a result. Thus, what constitutes a brief record of the taking of Máel Sechnaill's hostages by the Munstermen in the chronicles[122] is described as a stand-off between the two rulers during which the Mide ruler, Máel Sechnaill, sought in vain to muster the support of neighbouring Cenél Conaill and Cenél nÉogain.[123] This is linked in the *Cogadh* with the notice of Brian's journey to Dún Delca in the same year to obtain the hostages of Máel Sechnaill's opponents. What is a joint venture by the two rulers, according to entries in various chronicles,[124] is presented as a show of supremacy by Brian in the narrative text.[125] In this context, his gift of gold to Armagh[126] and his northern circuit the following year,[127] which are also described in the *Cogadh*, serve to portray the southern king, having conquered the north, at the pinnacle of his power.[128] Such is his influence at this time, according to the imaginative author, that Brian can levy tribute and obtain hostages in neighbouring territories overseas as well.[129] Literary tropes then prevail: Brian's territory is said to have flourished during his reign, being in a state of such peace that a lone woman could bear a golden ring from north to south without being robbed.[130] Learning similarly prospered, intellectual contacts overseas being actively pursued.[131] Annalistic echoes remain, however; Brian is said to have strengthened 'the forts and fortifications ... and the notable royal strongholds of Munster' (*dúin ocus daingni ... ocus rigpuirt aireda na Muman*),[132] perhaps reflecting the construction work that he did in fact engage in at various points in his career.[133]

Notwithstanding these resonances, the *Cogadh* author departs considerably from his annalistic sources in this eulogy of Brian and scarcely returns to them in the remainder of his narrative, in what is in effect a long lead-up to the encounter at Clontarf.[134] Central to his pre-battle tale is a quarrel between Brian's son, Murchad, and Máel Mórda, king of Leinster in which one of Brian's wives, Gormlaith, sister of the Leinsterman, played a starring role. This altercation led to military assistance being sought by the peeved Leinster ruler from the Norse of Dublin and their kinsmen overseas, according to the narrative account. This does not correspond to events, as recorded in the chronicles. Nevertheless, certain details in the *Cogadh* are paralleled in annalistic sources. The involvement of Flaithbertach ua Néill in the lead-up to the battle, and in particular his attack on Mide[135] mirrors actual events,[136] as does the description of a raid on Leinster by Murchad, Brian's son.[137] In the same way historical happenings underlie the account in the creative composition of Brian's siege of Dublin 'from the feast of Ciarán at harvest

time to great Christmas' (ó feil Ciaran fogmair co notlaic mor);[138] it may echo
the prolonged plundering of the Leinstermen and their foreign allies, of
which annalistic entries make note.[139] Whereas 'he [Brian] did not make
peace' (ni tuc síd), according to one annalistic source,[140] the Cogadh redac-
tor claims more flamboyantly that both Vikings and Leinstermen failed to
obtain 'a single hostage or a single battle or a single truce' (oen giall, no oen
cath, no oen coma), lack of provisions alone forcing Brian to retire.[141] It was on
his return the following spring that he faced Viking and Leinster forces in
the battle of Clontarf.[142]

A Literary Hero

Brian's career as it has been recorded both in annalistic and narrative sources
bears a colourful hue and while the degree of the tincture may vary, it being
deepest in the version presented in the Cogadh, the distinction between
historical personage and literary hero is frequently blurred. It is most
amorphous in the accounts of Clontarf, Brian's participation in the battle
being regularly enhanced. The part actually played by him in the conflict is
questionable, his advanced age perhaps ensuring that his was more of a
directing role.[143] In any event, the Cogadh depicts him as a wise counsellor
and pious bystander, brutally cut down by a cruel Viking while at prayer.[144]
As well as being endowed with saintly characteristics, Brian acquires many
of the attributes of a sacral king in the narrative. An embodiment of the
social and cosmic order, the rightful ruler ensured the welfare of his people, possessing justice, wisdom and generosity, the all-important fír flathemon
(literally 'prince's truth'), according to an ideology prevalent throughout the
medieval Irish literary corpus.[145] It is precisely in this mould that Brian's loss
is also cast, his death robbing Ireland of her legitimate king, as a result of
which her fertility and prosperity departed; for this reason is the world in
total disarray:[146]

> Ro sceind da ttrian einigh ocus engnama o laochaibh na hErenn le cloistecht
> an sceoil sin. Ro sceind da ttrian connla ocus crabhadh o cleirchibh Erenn
> don scel sin. Do cuaidh a náire ocus a ngeinmnaigecht ó mnaibh Erenn don
> scel cedna … Do cuaidh da ttrian lachta o ceitraibh fos don scel sin.

Two-thirds of the honour and valour of Ireland's heroes vanished on hearing that news [of Brian's death]. Two-thirds of the piety and devotion of Ireland's clerics vanished because of that news. The modesty and chastity of Ireland's women disappeared because of that same news ... In addition, two-thirds of the cattle's milk disappeared because of that news.

In the same way his dynasty, Dál Cais, is presented as the true guardian of Ireland's 'rule and sovereignty' (*follamnas ocus flathemnas*) in our first introduction to them in the tale. Stanzas attributed to the tenth-century Munster king, Cormac mac Cuilennáin, as well as to the Mide poet, Cúan ua Lothcháin (who died as late as 1024), serve to underline its significance. Moreover, along with his brother, Mathgamain, Brian is said to stand at the head of this chosen people, possessing the qualities of ideal kingship in abundance – valorous in battle, being protective of his subjects, as well as spirited and strong.[147]

In life and in death does Brian cut a dramatic dash, this being the dominant impression created by the narrative tale. While not yet Dál Cais ruler, his leadership qualities are nevertheless presented as apparent in the *Cogadh*, a contrast with his older brother being drawn in this regard. When Mathgamain talks peace, Brian is depicted as continuing to make war, a loyal band of fearless followers providing him with unflagging support. Accusing his older sibling of cowardice, he adopts the ultimate heroic line that death in battle is a warrior's duty, whereas meek submission is not. Such is his authority that Dál Cais immediately and unanimously concur and the voice of one hundred was as the voice of one man (*ocus ba guth cet ar bel oenfhir sin*).[148]

His presentation continues in literary mode. Like many an imagined hero, Brian triumphed against the odds, single-handedly killing his enemies (Vikings) 'in pairs, in threes and in fives; in twenties and in hundreds' (*ina dessib ocus ina triaraib ocus ina cuiceraib ocus ina fichtib ocus ina cedaib*).[149] In his metamorphosis into royal ruler, tried and tested tropes are similarly deployed to convey the sense that the legitimate leader now holds sway.[150] His territory is said to have been transformed from a conflict-torn country to one where peace and harmony prevail:[151]

Robi in rigi cathach coccadh congalach inridach airgneach esadal, toseach na rigi sin. Robi, imorro, in rigi sberach sadal somemnach sithemail sona somaineach saidbir fledach fuirigech fothamail fo deoid a dered.

> The beginning of that reign [Brian's] was filled with battle, war and conflict, with attacking, plundering and disquiet. However, its end was bright, pleasant, joyful, peaceful, happy, prosperous and rich, feast-filled, full of plenty and secure.

Moreover, he dealt justly and fairly with 'Ireland's robbers, thieves and plunderers' (*meirleacha ocus bithbenacha ocus foghladha Erenn*), unlike the tragic Conaire Mór, as set out in an earlier tale of kingship, *Togail Bruidne Da Derga* (The Destruction of Da Derga's Hostel), which the *Cogadh* author may conceivably have known.[152] And while the peace that prevailed initially in Conaire's reign dissipated accordingly, Brian's Ireland was such that a treasure-laden lone woman could journey unmolested from one end of the country to the other, as mentioned in passing above.[153]

Battle Tales

Yet in reality it was *cocad* (war) rather than *síd* (peace) that characterised Brian's reign, as indeed the literary depiction of it in the *Cogadh*, with its emphasis on his numerous encounters, makes clear. As well as the conflict at Clontarf, two other battles receive particular attention in the text, one at Sulchóit in 967 in which both Brian and his brother, Mathgamain, were involved, and a later one at Glenn Máma in 999 in which the men of Leinster and Dublin faced Brian in a prequel to the climax at Clontarf. As historical events, both are recorded in chronicles; the earlier encounter being described as a victory by Mathgamain over the Vikings of Limerick after which their settlement was burnt.[154] Glenn Máma was the more significant engagement of the two, Brian defeating there 'the best of Ireland's Vikings' (*formna Gall Herend*), according to the Annals of Inisfallen. Victory was consolidated by burning Dublin at the beginning of the following year.[155]

At the hands of a literary master, both encounters are considerably enhanced, 'a fierce, bloody, red, rough, coarse, implacable, unfriendly battle' (*cath fichda, fuileach, forderg, anmin, agarb, aniarmartach, escardemail*) being fought on both occasions.[156] Victory over Vikings was resounding; the two Norsemen named as having fallen at Glenn Máma, Aralt son of Amlaíb and Cuilén son of Echtigern, are also recorded in chronicle accounts.[157] Poetic celebrations in victory then ensue, according to the *Cogadh* creator, which are particularly elaborate in the case of the eastern fight.[158] Viking settlements are thereafter attacked, the augmented accounts perhaps revealing something of the character of Hiberno-Norse towns. In Limerick jewels and saddles were plundered, as well as gold and silver, and multi-coloured cloths.[159] Dublin treasures secured include precious stones, carbuncle gems, buffalo horns and goblets.[160] On both occasions women and youths are taken captive.[161] Humiliation of the prisoners follows: 'the races of Feradach's son' (*grafaing mic Feradaich*), as described in the Sulchóit account, involved something approaching collective rape.[162] Under Brian's rule, in the *Cogadh* account, they were forced into servitude, tilling the land, grinding corn and washing clothes.[163] By contrast, loyal followers were well rewarded, Mathgamain bestowing on everyone 'his right and proper share' (*a cuit coir comadais*) after Limerick was sacked.[164] Brian's munificence was even greater, no Munsterman being left 'without his appropriate due of gold, silver and variegated clothing, and of every other treasure besides' (*gan adhbar athighedhais leis d'ór ocus d'airccett ocus d'éttach datha, ocus da gach ionnmhass ar chena*). To this, the author affirms, both scholars and those in the know (*lucht fesa ocus senchusa*) attest.[165]

Twelfth-Century Tones

Literary convention, therefore, ensured that Brian's activities were cast in a particular mould and this, combined with the author's wish to create in the Munster king a hero for his own twelfth-century times, means that the 'Life of Brian', as portrayed in the *Cogadh*, is as imaginary as it is real. Annalistic accounts, some of which are no longer extant, lie in part behind the depiction; surviving chronicle sources can thus provide a measuring stick of sorts. Even where events actually occurred, however, the creative composer often imbued them with a topical twist. Thus activities of various years are telescoped to project an impression of unrelenting Viking attacks, as we have seen, the achievement of the Dál Cais ruler in the face of such opposition being perceived as all the greater as a result.[166] The inclusion of yet other of Brian's pursuits may have been deliberately designed to bring more recent actions by his great-grandson, Muirchertach, during whose reign the text was composed, to mind. The earlier king did indeed journey northwards in 1005, specifically to acquire the hostages of the northern territories of Cenél Conaill and Cenél nÉogain. The terms in which that journey is recorded, however, reflect more closely a circuit hosting undertaken by the younger Ua Briain in 1101.[167]

Activities attributed to Brian in the *Cogadh* but not recorded elsewhere
may also serve to cast the older ruler in the young imitator's image. Thus, at
one point in the narrative Brian is hailed for his commitment to learning,
sending forth wise men to teach and having books brought in from overseas to replace those which Vikings had destroyed. That the canny leader
was cognisant of the value of writing is not in doubt, as the title *imperator
Scotorum* in the Book of Armagh suggests. Muirchertach's awareness of the
power of the pen, however, may well have been even more profound, to
judge from his involvement in the production of works such as the *Cogadh*
and a companion volume, *Lebor na Cert* (The Book of Rights).[168] Moreover,
the twelfth-century king had well attested links with ecclesiastics overseas,
particularly in his role as patron of reform. Hence the flow of books 'across
the sea and the great ocean' (*tar muir ocus tar mórfhairrge*), to which Brian's
biography alludes, may signal traffic of a later time.[169]

The Making of Brian

Recreating the past ever mindful of the present, the *Cogadh* author pro-
duces a made-to-measure Brian, putting him in shoes larger than those
worn by the competent but less impressive counterpart that emerges from
a careful sifting of the annalistic sources, as we have seen. That this inflation
could occur bears witness in the first instance to the continued success of
Brian's descendants on the Irish political stage, for in the words of Francis
John Byrne, 'the medieval Irish thought no man deserved a place in history
until the durability of his achievements had been attested by the success
of his great-grandchildren'.[170] Had Brian's great-grandson, Muirchertach,
and his father, Tairdelbach, before him, not striven with considerable success to dominate large tracts of Ireland, a narrative hailing their eponymous
ancestor as the most powerful king in Ireland would scarcely have been warranted. In addition, production of the text demonstrates rigorous control of
all-important centres of learning whence such material emanated, control
first acquired by Brian Boru himself. Thus, as Donnchadh Ó Corráin has
demonstrated, Brian's brother, Marcán, who died in 1010, was abbot not
just of Emly, as has been mentioned, but of Inis Celtra (Holy Island) and
Terryglass as well. He was followed by others with Dál Cais affiliations.[171]
Their continued association with Terryglass, for example, is attested by the

occurrence of the earliest, albeit fragmentary, copy of *Cogadh Gáedhel re Gallaibh* in the twelfth-century manuscript, the Book of Leinster, a scribe of part of which, Áed mac Crimthainn, ruled that monastery. Áed was preceded in the abbacy by Finn Ua Cennétig who died in 1152, grandson of an earlier Dál Cais abbot of Terryglass, Céilechair mac Cennétig, who died in 1081.[172]

As the case of Terryglass demonstrates, Uí Briain maintained some influence there even after it had reverted to what were its original Leinster affiliations. In the same way, they also cultivated connections with other enemy churches, a policy that similarly dates to the reign of Brian Boru. If an entry in the Annals of Inisfallen is to be believed, Brian took the hostages of a trio of formerly Éoganacht churches – Lismore, Cork and Emly – in 987, as we have seen. And while his action may have been designed 'as a guarantee of the banishment of robbers and lawless people' (*fri innarbu foglaide ocus aessa escána*), his descendants skilfully quarried written sources emanating from these centres. Thus, Emly annals have been incorporated into the reworked Annals of Inisfallen,[173] while Lismore documents form part of *Cogadh Gáedhel re Gallaibh*.[174] The latter are no doubt explicable in terms of Muirchertach Ua Briain's close involvement with that monastery; not alone did he retire there in 1116 some time after illness struck, but his son was buried there in 1129.[175]

Uí Néill churches were similarly patronised by Brian, most significantly Armagh, as his famous offering of twenty ounces of gold on Patrick's altar in 1005, already mentioned, shows.[176] Moreover, it was at Armagh, according to the Annals of Inisfallen, that he achieved his first real northern success, in 1007 against Cenél nÉogain, a victory he consolidated in the same place three years later. It may be that the support of this most important northern church gave Brian crucial local assistance. In addition, he may have recognised the benefits of association with an ecclesiastical establishment fast acquiring all-Ireland primacy, as Donnchadh Ó Corráin has suggested.[177] Whatever his motivation, Brian's own connections with Armagh were strong, most evidently manifest in his 'emperor of the Irish' appellation inserted into that church's most famous book at the height of Brian's power.[178]

As Armagh's importance continued to grow in the eleventh century, Brian's descendants were, not surprisingly, keen to capitalise on these connections and it is scarcely a coincidence that it is the Munster annalist who emphasises the Armagh location in Brian's dealings with the king of

Cenél nÉogain.[179] He would have done so against a background of growing
Armagh authority in the south, as indicated by the frequent presence of
Patrician stewards there, termed *maír Pátraic* 'Patrick's stewards' or more
commonly *maír Muman* 'stewards of Munster', in the eleventh and twelfth
centuries.[180] In addition, Muirchertach Ua Briain's dependence on Armagh
is reflected in a replay of his great-grandfather's offering to that church,
almost one hundred years later, leaving eight ounces of gold there (as
opposed to his ancestor's twenty) and promising one hundred and sixty
cows.[181] It can also be seen in his respect for the attempts of the abbot of
Armagh to make peace between him and his northern rival, Domnall Mac
Lochlainn, by wielding that church's most potent relic, *bachall Ísu* 'the staff
of Jesus'.[182] The real reason for his subservience, however, is to be found
in another piece of Uí Briain propaganda, *Lebor na Cert*, also linked with
Muirchertach's reign, as noted above. Not alone is the king of Cashel portrayed as supreme ruler therein but, as Anthony Candon has argued, his
authority is specifically likened to the ecclesiastical primacy of the church
of Armagh.[183] Close co-operation with churches, therefore, was essential to
the progress of Uí Briain.

Uí Néill and the Making of Brian

That Uí Briain should set themselves up as Armagh's secular counterpart
is understandable; what is less comprehensible is that their claims are also
recorded in Uí Néill documents. Thus, in northern kings-lists, Brian Boru is
frequently accorded a place, whereas powerful Munster predecessors, such as
the eighth-century Éoganacht ruler, Cathal mac Finguine, and his ninth-century successor, Feidlimid mac Crimthainn, are not. Similarly, as noted above,
a genealogical tract of Uí Néill provenance is made to claim that 'no king has
taken [the kingship of] Ireland after the death of Patrick apart from the lineage
of Níall, except for two, i.e. Báetán and Brian'. Furthermore, as if to underline
Brian's dominance, the genealogist notes of the Ulaid king 'but some do not
reckon Báetán among the great kings' (*sed tamen alii Báetán non numerant inter
magnos reges*).[184] Are we to suppose, therefore, that northern rulers in a weakened state for much of the eleventh century actually acknowledged southern
supremacy? Or might Munster rulers, as they had gained control of centres of
learning in their own immediate territory, similarly have acquired influence
in policy-making ecclesiastical establishments further from home?

Alternatively, we might see in this accommodation a continuation of what John Kelleher suggested was Uí Néill policy in the tenth century, the rewriting of genealogies of various Munster tribes, including Dál Cais, in an effort to detach them from allegiance to Cashel and to encourage semi-independence under Uí Néill auspices.[185] Such genealogical manipulation is more readily explained, however, by reference to the well-oiled propaganda machine of a confident, burgeoning dynasty seeking to leave its humble origins well and truly behind. In the case of Dál Cais, as we have seen, this involved a name change from the lowly In Déis Tuaiscirt 'The northern vassal' to 'seed of Cas', bringing with it an implication of equality with the long-established ruling Éoganachta whose eponymous ancestor, Éogan, was a brother of Cas.[186] With all due respect to Kelleher, Uí Néill did not in fact make Dál Cais; in some sense, however, they can be said to have made Brian.

In this connection, we may note that much literary activity can be dated to the reign of Brian's Southern Uí Néill counterpart, Máel Sechnaill mac Domnaill, who was unquestionably the most powerful king in Ireland from the time of Brian's death at Clontarf until his own death eight years later in 1022. Significantly, much of this work is focused on Tara and was allegedly composed by Máel Sechnaill's court-poet, Cúán ua Lothcháin, who died two years after his master in 1024. It includes a poem on Tara, belonging to a genre termed *dindshenchas* (lore of famous places), beginning, *Temair toga na tulach/ foatá Ériu indradach* 'Tara noblest of hills, under which is Ireland of the battles',[187] as well as one on the closely associated site of Tailtiu, *A chóemu críche Cuind chain* 'O nobles of the land of comely Conn'.[188] The latter, written in support of Máel Sechnaill who in a conscious declaration of power celebrated the famous *óenach* 'gathering' there in 1006 after a gap of almost eighty years, endorses the monarch as 'the sole champion of Europe' (*oen-milid na hEorapa*), 'the glory of the noble western world' (*ordan íarthair domuin duind*) and, most significantly, as the rightful king of Tara whose rule bestowed peace and plenty on his subjects. In the same way the narrative poem, *Temair Breg, baile na fían* 'Tara of Brega, homestead of the champions',[189] which may also be by ua Lothcháin, furnishes Níall of the nine hostages (Noígíallach) and his descendants, of whom Máel Sechnaill was one, with a patent for the kingship of Tara, serving as the poetic counterpart to the later corresponding prose version, *Echtra mac nEchach Mugmedóin* (The Adventure of the Sons of Eochaid Mugmedón).[190] In addition, *Baile in Scáil* (The Phantom's Frenzy), while not specifically associated with Cúán, may also be a product of Máel Sechnaill's reign, since he is the last in a long line of Uí Néill kings to be listed therein.[191] Imaginative writing flourished, therefore, in Máel Sechnaill's time.

Moreover, this burst of creativity has been attributed by scholars indirectly to Brian, whose unexpected political advance has sometimes been seen as having jolted midland literati out of their complacency.[192] In any event, the renewed focus of medieval northerners on Tara with its attendant symbolism is viewed as a deliberate ploy to reassert the long held rights of Uí Néill to the kingship, in the face of opposition from more recent claimants, Brian Boru in particular. If so, Uí Néill literati, and Cúan ua Lothcháin specifically, had especially well tuned antennae. In the case of Cúan, there is some slender evidence that he may have been versed in Munster lore. In the first place, Cúan's reference to the fictitious *Saltair Temrach* 'the Psalter of Tara' in his poem on Tara, as Pádraig Ó Riain has shown, 'was conjured up in response to the influence of the very real Psalter of Cashel'.[193] A more tenuous connection is perhaps evident in the close similarities between the tale of Níall Noígíallach and his brothers related in verse in *Temair Breg, baile na fían* and that of seven brothers, all called Lugaid, sons of a legendary Munster king, Dáire. Thus, both sets of brothers go hunting and seek water before encountering a hideous hag with whom Níall and Lugaid Laígde sleep, thereby enabling her transformation into the most beautiful of women who bestows kingship upon them. The Munster tale survives only as part of the *dindshenchas* of Carn Máil and in the eleventh- or twelfth-century compilation *Cóir Anmann* (The Fitness of Names), and is difficult to date.[194] Should it go back to an earlier exemplar, however, Cúan could arguably have been influenced by it in the production of his own composition. Finally, Cúan's work was certainly well-known and admired in Munster, so much so that he is cited as an authority in no less a work than *Cogadh Gáedhel re Gallaibh* for the long-held right of Dál Cais to the kingship of Cashel.[195]

Nonetheless, even if Cúan was reasonably familiar with Munster scholarship, he may well have been unusual in Ireland's northern half in this regard.[196] For this reason, we would do well to tread cautiously before investing Brian's northern near contemporaries with the benefit of premature hindsight: it may well have been some time before the reign of the Munster king was seen as the significant innovation it in certain ways was. It is thus a moot question whether the concern with the kingship of Tara, clearly evident in the work of Uí Néill scholars from the beginning of the eleventh century, is explicable solely in terms of a perceived threat from a powerful southern ruler. Whatever their perception of Máel Sechnaill's Munster rival, Brian, it would hardly be unexpected were Uí Néill policy makers to present their own king as a reincarnation of one of the most successful midland kings, conveniently also called Máel Sechnaill. All the more is this the case, since the earlier Máel Sechnaill, a son of Máel Rúanaid, is the first king styled *rí Érenn uile* 'king of all Ireland' in his obit in 862 and was, therefore, crucial in the development of the concept of a national kingship.[197] Prodigious literary production by northern scholars in the years following Brian's death need not simply be a reaction to developments in the south.

Notwithstanding this, Brian's success in extending his sway over the greater part of the country undoubtedly had a bearing on how overlordship was perceived. The concept of all-Ireland kingship continued to be elaborated in eleventh- and twelfth-century texts and it forms the chronological corner stone of *Lebor Gabála Érenn* (The Book of the Taking of Ireland – commonly known as 'The Book of Invasions').[198] Dating perhaps to the late eleventh century originally, this text was elaborated upon in the twelfth century during the reign of the Connacht king, Ruaidrí Ua Conchobair. Moreover its production owes much to Ruaidrí's powerful provincial predecessors, Brian Boru in particular, who were living proof that the kingship of Ireland was not merely an Uí Néill, northern preserve. Leth Cuinn and Leth Moga, the northern and southern parts of Ireland respectively, are deemed to be two equal halves in this complex narrative and the overlordship of Cashel is readily accommodated alongside that of Tara. Brian's descendants can but have benefited from such creative developments claiming their eponymous ancestor as a rightful holder of 'the kingship of Ireland' (*flaithes Érenn*) and they were presumably active in their promotion. The literary manifestation of this doctrine, as it has survived, however, bears a predominantly northern stamp, bound up as it is with the compositions of such northern poets as the Louth historian, Flann Mainistrech, and Gilla Cóemáin. As a result, Uí Néill can be said to have played a part in the making of Brian.

The Vikings and the Making of Brian

Linked to the evolution of a national kingship was the developing sense of Ireland as a political entity and of her people as a single, unified race, although in practice depictions could be remarkably diverse. According to the political schema laid down in *Lebor na Cert*, for example, the Dublin

Norse are the exact equivalent of their Leinster neighbours, no distinction being drawn on the basis of ethnic affiliations. Nevertheless variations could be deliberately stressed when the need arose and another Munster scholar, the creator of *Cogadh Gáedhel re Gallaibh*, working around the same time as the author of *Lebor na Cert*, and like him in the employ of Uí Briain, painted the Vikings as an altogether different beast. Concerned as he was with portraying his hero, Brian Boru, as liberating Ireland from their tyranny, Scandinavian invaders were portrayed by this particular author as an invincible force who inflict indescribable suffering on the Irish. He guarantees that Brian's reputation is assured by depicting him as overthrowing these cruel oppressors; that the Munster king lost his life in the final battle added to his fame. According to this influential rendering, therefore, it was the Vikings who made Brian.

In truth, as we have seen, Brian Boru was far from remarkable in his dealings with the 'heathen foreigners'. That he should come to be primarily identified by his resistance to them is due in no small measure to his presence at the battle of Clontarf, a pivotal contest in terms of the political advancement of the Munster king, but one that was to acquire an added significance when redrawn, in accordance with contemporary tastes, as a pagan-Christian duel. At its head was a holy ruler, who as leader of a mighty struggle against unruly barbarians symbolised the triumph of good over evil that the battle came to entail. And as Clontarf came to define the Irish king, so too did the conflict become 'Brian's battle'.

'Brian's Battle': Conflict at Clontarf

It is with the battle of Clontarf, specifically termed *Brjánsorrosta* (Brian's battle) in the Norse sources,[1] that the fame and fate of Brian Boru is inextricably bound. Fought on Good Friday, 23 April 1014, it was undoubtedly a significant struggle, being the encounter in which the Munster king lost his life after a long and eventful career.[2] The subsequent portrayal of its protagonists as pagan Viking and Christian Irish on two opposing sides, while simplifying the actual circumstances of the battle, also had the effect of augmenting its importance. In the first place, it came to be celebrated as a victory of the forces of good over evil, the 'martyred' King Brian laying down his life for the ultimate Christian cause. In addition, it was accorded a national dimension, Brian being depicted at the head of a unified Irish force that succeeded in defeating the tyranny of Viking rule. Both elements are encapsulated in the description contained in a Classical Irish poem, *Aonar dhuit, a Bhriain Bhanba* (To you alone, Brian of Ireland), attributed to the thirteenth-century professional poet, Muireadhach Albanach Ó Dálaigh:[3]

Aoine cásg do marbadh Brian
ag díon Gaoidhiol na ngiall

mar do marbadh Críost gan coir
ag diodhan chloinne hAdhamh.

On Good Friday Brian was killed, defending the Irish of the hostages, just as
Christ without sin was killed, defending the children of Adam.

They are also implicit in the dramatic image preserved in a seventeenth-century
manuscript copy of *Cogadh Gáedhel re Gallaibh*, of an ageing ruler brutally
slain while fervently praying for victory in the company of a solitary attendant who relayed to him news of the conflict.[4]
    Not least because of the heroic manner of his demise, Brian's reputation
was cemented in death and he quickly became the yardstick against whom
great kings came to be measured. Thus the death-notice of Cathal Crobderg
Ua Conchobair, written little over a century after Clontarf, praises the
Connacht king as 'the best Irishman since Brian Boru in terms of nobility
and honour' (*in t-aen Gaidhel is ferr tainig o Brian Boroma anuas ar uaisli ocus ar
onoir*).[5] In the same way *Aonar dhuit, a Bhriain Bhanba* concludes with a plea
for someone of Brian's ilk to emerge.[6] And while he may not have been of
the stature of the Munster monarch, the fourteenth-century Leinster leader,
Donnchad Caemhánach Mac Murchada, is coupled with Brian in the obituary of him preserved in the Annals of Ulster under the year 1375, because
'no one since Brian Boru's time had destroyed more Danes than he had' (*ní
táinic o Brian Borumha anuas fer is mó do dithaigh do Danuraibh anás*). That the
slaughter of foreigners was deemed central to Brian's reputation was due in
no small way to the gradual evolution of embellished accounts of the battle
of Clontarf.

Chronicle Accounts

Even the most elaborate descriptions, however, retain some semblance of
fact at their core, as an analysis of what may well be contemporary records
of the battle in certain annalistic compilations reveal. Brian's 'home chronicle',
the Annals of Inisfallen, despite its obvious Munster bias, has a relatively
laconic notice of the event in which the Dublin Vikings are portrayed as
that king's principal opponents: *Cocad mór eter Brian ocus Gullu Atha Cliath*
(a great war between Brian and the foreigners of Dublin). Yet that they
were not acting independently is evident from the inclusion of the king

of Leinster, Máel Mórda mac Murchada along with his nobles, and 'the Vikings of the western world' (*gaill iarthair domain*) among the casualties on the opposing side. Brian's allies, on the other hand, were nothing like as geographically diverse, numbering his son, Murchad, grandson, Tairdelbach, and nephew, Conaing, as well as the rulers of two neighbouring Munster kingdoms, Corcu Baiscinn and Ciarraige Luachra, and that of the adjoining southern Connacht territory of Uí Maine.[7]

What may well be a Clonmacnoise chronicle, *Chronicum Scotorum*, agrees with its Munster counterpart in citing Vikings as Brian's chief opponents, although in this case they encompass 'the Vikings of the world such as were of them from Lochlainn westwards' (*gaill an domain do neoch baoí diobh o Lochlain síar*).[8] In the Annals of Ulster, a related northern compilation, the foreigners of Lochlainn similarly appear but are preceded by another pair of enemies closer to home, 'all the Leinstermen ... and the Vikings of Dublin' (*Laighin uile ... ocus Gaill Atha Cliath*).[9] Estimating 1,000 as the size of the overseas Viking contingent, the annalists evidently consider this to be an encounter of some note[10] and its significance is underlined by its depiction as a struggle apart: *cath crodha ... dona frith inntsamail* 'a valiant battle ... the like of which was never encountered'.[11] This hyperbolic turn of phrase, coupled with a much augmented list of casualties in the two accounts, suggest, however, that these particular battle reports are in fact enhanced, reflecting an early stage perhaps in the reshaping of what was to become an increasingly fictionalised fight.

Brian's enlarged retinue is dominated by warriors from his home territory of Munster but it includes the rulers of territories not traditionally loyal to Dál Cais – the Éoganachta, the Déssi and Fir Maige. A second Connacht region, Uí Fhiachrach Aidne, bordering on that of Uí Maine, is also deemed to be on side. To these, the Annals of Ulster adds the name of a lone Scottish supporter, Domnall mac Eimín, 'great steward of Marr in Scotland' (*mórmhaer Marr i nAlbain*), whose isolated inclusion may conceivably bear witness to an actual alliance, though occurring at the end of a list of Brian's troops it is more likely to have been added at a later stage reflecting subsequent connections across the Irish Sea.[12] The trio of additional Leinster rulers among the ranks of Brian's enemies recorded as having been slain are also suspect since one of them at least, Tuathal mac Ugaire, died peacefully more than half a century earlier.[13]

In the same way the names of some of the supplementary vanquished Vikings in the Annals of Ulster do not inspire confidence.[14] While some have recognisably Scandinavian names, including Oittir Dub (Old Norse Óttarr), others such as Grisene and Luimne are pseudo-Norse. Moreover the conspicuous lack of detail concerning the individuals in question points to an author supplementing names merely to pad out his source. This may not always have been the case; one of the six, Amlaíb mac Lagmainn, has been identified as the son of a Hebridean king who died in 989.[15] In addition, Donnchad ua Eruilb has been linked by David Thornton to Donnchad mac Áeda who appears in Clann Eruilb genealogies.[16] Greater information is furnished on a pair of Viking heirs-in-waiting, Dubgall mac Amlaíb and Gilla Ciaráin mac Glúin Iairn whose relatives are also attested elsewhere,[17] as well as on the Orkney earl, Sigurd (Old Norse Sigurðr), and Brian's ultimate slayer, Brodar (Old Norse Bróðir), all of whom feature in both interlinked annalistic accounts. Notwithstanding the inclusion of some who were in all likelihood at the encounter, these enhanced lists of the battle dead mark the entrance of the battle onto a literary stage.

Thus even the earliest annalistic accounts of the battle have been augmented, with the possible exception of the brief record preserved in the Annals of Inisfallen. Furthermore, the depiction in that compilation of the Vikings of Dublin as the principal enemy force accords well with what the chronicles reveal about the general political circumstances prevailing at the time. Already master in the southern part of the country, Brian expended considerable energy in the years leading up to the battle forcing key northern players into submission. By 1012 or thereabouts his authority over the greater part of Ireland was relatively secure. As we have seen, part of this process involved the careful cultivation of links with Armagh which, under Uí Néill patronage, had acquired something of the status of a national Church, as indicated by his pointed request of Máel Sechnaill mac Domnaill to make a raid on the territory of Conaille in revenge for their profanation of Patrick's relics in 1013.[18] Association with the premier ecclesiastical establishment was coupled with active interest in Ireland's economic capital, the Viking-controlled town of Dublin.[19] Having captured and plundered the place after the battle of Glenn Máma in 999,[20] Brian reinstated its rulers the following year[21] but evidently on his own terms since the Dublin Vikings provided military support in many of his later campaigns.[22] Subsequently they shifted their allegiance to the Leinstermen, supporting them in a raid in 1013 in Mide, the home ground of Brian's ally, Máel Sechnaill, in which the latter's son, Flann, was slain.[23] When the Vikings moved further southwards attacking Cork and Clére, Brian was compelled to intervene, spending the last three months of that year 'in Osraige and in Leinster ... attacking Vikings and he did not bring about peace' (*i nOsrugu ocus i lLaignib ... oc gabail fri Gullu ocus ni tuc síd*).[24]

When Brian advanced on Dublin the following year, at the head of 'a great muster of the men of Ireland' (*morthinol fer nErend*),[25] thereby precipitating the battle of Clontarf, what was at stake was his control over its Hiberno-Norse inhabitants and the lucrative trading network over which they held sway.[26] In direct competition with him were the Leinstermen, advantageously positioned adjacent to the Dublin kingdom and whose king, Máel Mórda mac Murchada, Brian had himself a decade earlier enthroned.[27] Any lingering loyalty to his Munster patron had long since dissipated, however, and, immediately prior to the battle, the Leinster king and his people were attacked by Brian's son, Murchad, who burnt 'the entire region' (*in tir uile*).[28] Undaunted, the Leinstermen certainly constituted the Vikings' chief allies at the battle of Clontarf.

Observers Overseas

This Dublin-Leinster partnership, headed by the eastern ruler, Máel Mórda, and his Norse counterpart, Sitric mac Amlaíb, is similarly depicted in the Welsh chronicles as forming a united front against Brian,[29] information that is undoubtedly derived from Irish sources. Whether the sources in question were contemporary with the battle cannot be determined since the Latin original from which all the Welsh texts derive was not compiled until the second half of the thirteenth century.[30] One version of an earlier related Latin compilation, *Annales Cambriae*, contains a brief reference to the battle, suggesting that there was some knowledge of it in Wales not long after its occurrence.[31] Details concerning it survive in the later texts. These note the involvement of Brian's slayer, Brodar, in the battle, depicting him as the leader of, 'ships of armed pirate men' (*llongeidieu o wyr arvauc o ypirate*) hired by Sitric of Dublin to assist the opponents of the Munster king.[32] However, in the Welsh sources, he is the only Viking leader recorded as having been slain.

News of the conflict appears to have reached France relatively quickly, as an entry concerning it in the chronicle of Adémar de Chabannes (989–1034), a contemporary of the participants in the battle, demonstrates.[33] Writing some time around 1025, Adémar's notice is relatively short but it contains significant detail: the conflict is said to have continued for three days, during which time Norse women and children drowned themselves in the sea, while the Norsemen who survived were thrown to wild beasts.[34] The authenticity of this information is questionable, however. The author undoubtedly had access to written sources for some of his material but he also drew extensively on oral matter, particularly when discussing events of his own time.[35] Moreover, he was certainly dependent on oral informants, whom he names, for other material in this section, mainly concerned with Byzantine affairs.[36] Yet he was also a master fabricator, hence we have to be alert to the fact that Adémar's inventive imagination might have manifested itself here.[37]

Nonetheless, he knows something of the Irish, ascribing their conversion correctly to Patrick, claiming that the latter was a Roman. Against this, his description of Latin as the language of Ireland and his reference to the twelve *civitates* of Ireland suggests that he was not overly familiar with the country. Nor was it ruled by a single king, as he purports;[38] but, if his knowledge derived from a partisan of Brian Boru, as seems likely, the Munster leader could well have been presented to Adémar as Ireland's sole sovereign. In addition, his reference to the drowning of Norse women and children is broadly echoed in Irish literary accounts of the battle, the twelfth-century narrative, *Cogadh Gáedhel re Gallaibh*, particularly stressing the number of Viking warriors who were submerged in the sea during the encounter.[39] Moreover, another element in Adémar's account of the battle concerning the release of a Norse captive by an Irish king who recognised him as a Christian slave has been compared with the episode in which Þorsteinn Síðu-Hallsson is granted respite in Norse versions of the encounter;[40] it may be that both can be traced to the same, most likely Irish, source. Whether the overall tenor of Adémar's account, which casts the conflict as a bipolar struggle between Irish and Norse, is also derivative is a moot question. If so, it provides valuable evidence for a subtle shift in the battle's focus within a decade or so of its occurrence.

Furthermore, Brian's piety is highlighted in a reference to his death preserved in another continental source, penned in this instance by a monk from the north of Ireland, Marianus Scotus, who was born in 1028, precisely at the time when Adémar was writing his *Historia*, and who left for Germany in 1056 where he spent time in Cologne and Fulda, dying in Mainz around 1083.[41] His key work is a chronicle extending down almost to the time of his death and containing some matter pertaining to his homeland. Much of this undoubtedly reflects that which he had learned and heard as a young ecclesiastic in Ireland before going into exile.[42] This includes the information he records concerning Patrick, Brigit, Columba and other well-known Irish saints, as well as a king-list of northern rulers ending with Flann son of Máel Sechnaill mac Maíle Ruanaid who died in 916. It is likely that he would have become familiar with some of the circumstances at least surrounding Brian's death while in Ireland, though his knowledge of this and other Irish events may, of course, have been modified or amplified by compatriots whom he encountered overseas. Among these was an ecclesiastic at Fulda who had been banished from the monastery of Inis Celtra, with which Brian himself was closely associated.[43] Hence opportunities would have presented themselves for in-depth discussion of Dál Cais affairs. For whatever reason, Brian's slaying appears twice in Marianus's *Chronicon*, erroneously under the year 1029, according to his system of reckoning, which corresponds to 1007, and in its proper place under 1036 which equates with 1014. Although the battle itself does not feature, the Munster king is said to have been killed during the preparations for Easter 'with his hands and mind directed towards God' (*manibus et mente ad Deum intentus*).[44] As a pious, Christian king, Brian had already been acclaimed.

Embellished Accounts

A more elaborate image of Brian at prayer is preserved in two later Irish chronicles, the Annals of Loch Cé and the Annals of Boyle, which are interconnected.[45] Accompanied by his nephew, Conaing mac Duinn Cuain, this most supreme of kings is said to be 'behind the battalions singing his psalms and performing prayers' (*ar cúl na cath ag cantain a salm ocus ag denam irnaide*) when he was opportunistically stabbed by an unnamed fierce *Danmargach* (Dane). Both Brian and Conaing died as a result, as did their slayer 'in the counter-attack of that fight' (*a bfrithghuin in comhruic sin*).[46] Furthermore, such was Brian's holiness that his body and that of Conaing (alongside those of Brian's son, Murchad, and Mothla, king of the Déssi, according to the Loch Cé annalist) were immediately brought by the abbot of Armagh to Ireland's premier church where they were buried 'nobly, with respect' (*co uasal ormitnech*).[47] As a measure of the honour accorded them, the abbot himself, along with the congregation, spent two nights 'waking the bodies, in accordance with the honour of the king who was laid out' (*ag aire na gcorp propter honorem regis positi*).[48]

As well as being closely related to one another, as certain correspondences in their accounts of this battle reveal, the Annals of Boyle and Loch Cé also contain a great deal of material in common with the Annals of Ulster.[49] This is particularly evident when the catalogue of those slain at Clontarf in the three compilations is compared. While the Annals of Boyle omits the six Viking names added to the northern chronicle, the core of the list is identical in both sources. Furthermore, the roll call as it appears in Loch Cé forms with that in the Annals of Ulster a perfect match, the order of certain names apart. It would appear, therefore, that this trio of chroniclers based their versions of events on the augmented account of the battle preserved in what looks likes its earliest form in the northern compilation. To this the Boyle annalist added a description of Brian's death and burial of which a comparable, though more detailed, retelling is contained in the Annals of Loch Cé.[50]

It was with occurrences immediately prior to the encounter, however, that the Loch Cé annalist was especially concerned. The international allies of the Dublin Vikings are carefully enumerated in his account, including 'the choicest strong men and heroes from the island of Britain' (*tréinfhir thoghaidhe ocus áirsighe innsi Bretan*), as well as 'the best kings and nobles, heroes and warriors, champions and strong men of the northern world, both black and fair foreigners' (*forgla ríogh ocus taoíseach, curadh ocus caithmhílidh, ocus láth ngoile, ocus treinfir thúaiscert in domain, etir Dhubhlochlonnach ocus Fhionnlochlonnach*).[51] Yet some of those specifically named are Norman rather than Norse.[52] Moreover, anachronisms are coupled with a penchant for the Otherworld. No fewer than three supernatural incidents supposed to have happened on the eve of the battle are related, ensuring that the tone of this account is markedly different from that of other chronicle texts.

In tone and in some of its detail, it is with the elaborate, much embellished account of the battle in *Cogadh Gáedhel re Gallaibh*, that the entry in the Loch Cé annals can be most readily compared. The opening of the chronicle account, relating the plundering of Mide and Brega by a combined host of Leinstermen and Vikings, appears in the *Cogadh* as part of a protracted onslaught on the midland leader, Máel Sechnaill mac Domnaill, Brian's primary ally, designed to weaken the Munster king. The individual forays, including that of Flaithbertach, ruler of Ailech, into Mide and that of Ualgarg Ua Ciarda and Ua Ruairc into neighbouring Gailenga, are similarly recorded in other chronicles.[53] What are depicted as independent skirmishes elsewhere, however, have been skilfully linked in the narrative text to convey an atmosphere of ever increasing opposition to Brian. Thus the king of Ailech's attack may in reality have been directed against Máel Sechnaill, but the author of the *Cogadh* manages to redirect the focus on the Munster ruler by specifying that an officer of Brian (himself a Norseman) was slain.[54] The manipulation is not evident in the Loch Cé compilation, since no more than one pre-battle event is recorded and that in less detail than is found in the more expansive *Cogadh* description.[55]

In the same way, although both texts devote considerable attention to the foreign forces who came to support the Dublin–Leinster contingent at Clontarf, enumerating Brodar and Sigurd, Earl of Orkney among their number, many of the other names do not in fact correspond.[56] In addition, while the Loch Cé annalist speaks of '1,000 bold, strong, brave warriors of the black Danes, with shields, targes and many breastplates' (*míle láoch do dhubh Danaroibh dána, róithréna, rochalma, go scíathoibh ocus go stargghaibh ocus co lúirechoibh iomdha*), the *Cogadh* author views the new arrivals in a very different light: 'an assembled host of ignorant, barbarous, stupid, stubborn, anti-social Vikings' (*comtinol sloig buirb, barbarda, dicheillid, dochoisc, dochomaind do Gallaib*).[57] As the opponents of the hero of his story, Brian Boru, they could scarcely have been portrayed otherwise by the Uí Briain insider who put together this dramatic tale.

Dramatic effect is not the sole preserve of the *Cogadh* author. Incorporated into the elaborate entry in the Annals of Loch Cé are a pair of vision tales set on the eve of the encounter, as a result of which the tension and sense of foreboding surrounding the battle are greatly increased.[58] In the first of these, Senán, patron-saint of Inis Cathaig, one of the chief churches in Brian's territory, appears to a servant of that king to reclaim debts due from Brian. The implication is clear: the money may not be forthcoming on the morrow and on being told of the apparition 'his [Brian's] state of mind was the worse for hearing it' (*ba messaide a menma lais a chluinsin*).[59]

The Munster ruler is left in no doubt as to his fate according to the second of the visions, in which Óebinn from the Otherworld mound (*síd*) of Craig Léith came to Brian himself 'and told him that he would fall the following day' (*gur innis do go dtiotfadh ar na bharach*). Concerned with the succession, Brian enquired as to who would be king after him and was told that it would be the first son whom he would see. Anxious that Murchad should succeed him, he called immediately for his second son but it was the oldest, Donnchad, who hearing his father's voice appeared.[60] The animosity revealed towards the elder son in the Annals of Loch Cé, encapsulated in Brian's reaction on seeing him (*is cuma lem … cidh be ní do néis, oir ni dot iarradh robha* 'I don't give a damn … what you do, since it's not you I was looking for'),[61] is less pronounced in the allusion to the same vision preserved in the seventeenth-century copy of *Cogadh Gáedhel re Gallaibh*. Resigned to his fate, the Munster king resists the valiant attempts of his attendant to get him to retreat:[62]

> … uair táinicc Aibhell Craicce Leithe chuccam arair … ocus ro innis damh go muirfidhe mé aniú, ocus adubairt riom an céd mac dom chloinn do chifinn aniú gomadh é do ghebhadh righe tar m'éis, ocus bidh é Donnchadh eisein … ocus mo bheannacht do Donnchadh ar mo cheinnaiti dic tar m'éis.

> … for Aíbell of Craicc Léith appeared to me last night … and she told me that I would be killed today and that the first son I saw today would be king after me, and that was Donnchad … and my blessing upon Donnchad for paying my bequests when I am gone.

Nonetheless, Murchad is clearly the chosen son in the literary narrative also. In the first place, Donnchad is not accorded any part in the actual battle, being dispatched to Leinster before the fight began in earnest and returning only after Brian's killing.[63] Furthermore, it is his younger brother who is depicted as the hero of the hour, the last man of real valour in Ireland 'who would not retreat a single step before the whole of the human race' (*nach berad oen traig teighchid reisin ciniud doenna uli*).[64] The Hector and Hercules of his generation, capable of killing fifty men with his right hand as well as fifty with his left in a single onslaught, he it was who slew in the encounter both Sigurd, Earl of Orkney and a son of the king of Lochlainn.[65] Moreover, Brian himself is confident that the troops will remain courageous and all will be well as long as Murchad's battle-standard remains on high. On hearing of its fall, he laments that 'because of it Ireland has really fallen and no warrior comparable with that warrior will ever come after him' (*do thuit Ere de go fír ocus nocha ticfa tar a éis co bráth aon laoch a ionnsamhail no cosmaileis an laoich sin*).[66]

Underlining Murchad's importance is the ascription to him of a vision in an interpolated passage in the *Cogadh* that is not recorded in the Annals of

Loch Cé.[67] The supernatural visitor on this occasion is Dúnlaing Ua hArtacáin, a courageous champion of Murchad's acquaintance who has returned
from a paradisiacal existence to warn the Munsterman of his own impend-
ing death, as well as that of his father, Brian, son, Tairdelbach, and cousin,
Conaing. Dismayed by the news, Murchad upbraids Dúnlaing for having
related it, implying that he has betrayed his true inheritance for the sake of
Otherworld pleasures.[68] The latter is made to redeem himself by behead-
ing a Viking named Cornablìteoc and slaying the 150 of his followers who
attacked him in the process in one of the three most difficult encounters
fought in Clontarf on that day.[69] Although Dúnlaing was victorious, he too
was slain, as he himself had in fact foretold.[70]

In both the Annals of Loch Cé and the *Cogadh*, therefore, recourse is had
to apparitional interludes to emphasise the auspicious nature of the battle
and to highlight the tension with which it was associated. Thus can the
literary techniques of the two authors in this respect be compared. Not surprisingly, refinement of this particular skill is more advanced in the narrative
composition whose verbose creator took care to present to his audience
a dramatic battle-tale. To this end, in addition to the visions he related, all
manner of birds of carrion and supernatural spirits are said to have hovered
over the battlefield greedily awaiting their prey. In this case, the litany of
creatures cited has a familiar ring, including the war-goddess, Badb, alongside 'goblins, sprites, spirits of the glen, destructive witches, phantoms, old
birds, harmful demons of the air and of the firmament and an inauspicious,
demoniac phantom-host' (*bananaig ocus boccanaig ocus geliti glinni ocus amati
adgaill ocus siabra ocus seneoin ocus demna admílti aeoir ocus firmaminti ocus sia-
barsluag debil demnach*).[71] The appearance of these self-same beings on other
imaginative battlefields indicates that the *Cogadh* author in this instance was
drawing on well-established narrative tradition to produce a tried and tested
literary effect.[72]

It may well be that it was from the same common pool that he and the
Loch Cé annalist derived the story of Brian's vision on the eve of the battle.
In any event, the differences between both depictions make it unlikely that
the two texts are directly related. Information on the aftermath of the battle
preserved in both sources corroborates this. While the *Cogadh* preserves a
detailed account of an altercation between Brian's son, Donnchad, and the
leaders of south Munster, designed to highlight the indomitable courage of
Dál Cais who rose to do battle despite being wounded and maimed, a mere
reference to the encounter is contained in the Annals of Loch Cé which

parallels precisely that in the related compilation, the Annals of Ulster.[73] Furthermore, the other events for the year 1014, which conclude the entry on the battle in the Loch Cé chronicle and for which no equivalent matter is to be found in the *Cogadh*, are also likely to have been drawn from the same source.[74] Not alone do they occur in exactly the same order in the two annalistic compilations, it is with precisely the same formula, 'numerous are the events of this year' (*ad imdha trá airisi na bliadnai sa*), that the entries in both end.[75] This, coupled with the correspondences in the catalogue of the dead in both chronicles, indicates that, despite its literary flourishes, it is to the description of the battle in the Annals of Ulster that the much augmented account in the Annals of Loch Cé is most closely related. Yet as its metaphoric likening of Brian's attack on Dublin to plunging a hand into a griffin's nest demonstrates,[76] the Loch Cé annalist deliberately abandons his predecessor's more prosaic approach. A further stage in the ever-evolving presentation of what is becoming an all-important battle has been reached.

Chronicle Evidence Surveyed

The battle of Clontarf was undoubtedly a crucial conflict by means of which Brian Boru sought to re-impose his authority over the Dublin Vikings and their key Leinster allies, as is evident from what may be a contemporary record of the battle preserved in the Munster chronicle, the Annals of Inisfallen. Almost immediately, it was seized upon as fodder for fertile imaginations, as the augmented list of casualties in the Annals of Ulster in particular reveals. While many of those named may have been present at the battle, the addition of a group of what appear to be fictitious names gives pause for thought. As the importance of the fight was deliberately enhanced, so too were its complexities disregarded, most notably the fact that Irish and Norse fought on both sides. As its Viking-Irish configuration was moved centre-stage, it quickly acquired the status of a contest between indigenous natives and their foreign attackers, at least in the description of the battle recounted by Adémar of Chabannes not much more than a decade after its occurrence. Moreover the two opposing sides came to be differentiated principally on the basis of their beliefs and a battle involving the struggle of good over evil was born. As a symbol of all that is right Brian's persona was nurtured, the holy, ageing king struck down at prayer, as the eleventh-century continental chronicler, Marianus Scotus, and, more specifically, the later compiler of the Annals of Loch Cé make clear. Not surprisingly, further elaboration of what was becoming a battle of the utmost significance followed and the events of its eve, and later aftermath, were carefully cultivated. In so doing, specific emotions concerning the conflict were deliberately engendered, as the sense of tension and foreboding created by the vision-tales that form part of the account in the Loch Cé compilation demonstrates. Such manipulation is far from widespread, however, in what are, for the most part, relatively prosaic chronicle accounts. The situation is markedly different when we turn to literary retellings of the battle of Clontarf.

Poetic Material

The battle is mentioned in passing in a number of texts, including a Munster king-list that specifies that Brian was killed 'at the battle of the weir of Clontarf' (*i cath corad Cluana Tarb*) at the hands of Leinstermen and Vikings.[77] A Danish host (*drong Danar Danmarg*) perpetrated the deed, according to a poem attributed to the eleventh-century poet, Flann Mainistrech.[78] The encounter is also celebrated in other verse, specifically by name as 'the battle of Clontarf of the hosts' (*cath torach Tarbchluana*) in a poem on the deaths of Irish heroes attributed to a tenth-century poet, Cináed ua hArtacáin, but including later material. Máel Mórda, king of Leinster, is specified as Brian's slayer, working in conjunction with 'a strong, victorious Viking host' (*sluag Gall mbrogach mbuada*).[79] While not named, the Leinster ruler is also implicated in an eleventh-century prophetic poem, the Prophecy of Berchán, together with King Sitric of Dublin. Their overseas allies are also alluded to, approaching 'across the placid sea' (*tar muir mall*).[80] Although he praises the Munster ruler (*mochen Éiriu fris-mba rí* 'fortunate is Ireland over which he will be king'), the poet is also careful not to castigate his opponents unduly, Sitric being termed 'the fair, gracious one from Dublin' (*in find co rath ó Duiblind*).[81] Moreover, the contest itself is seen as calamitous for both Irish and Norse.[82]

Cogadh Gáedhel re Gallaibh

For the author of the most detailed depiction of the battle to have survived, that contained in *Cogadh Gáedhel re Gallaibh*, a biography of Brian Boru commissioned by his great-grandson, Muirchertach, in the early years of the twelfth century, as noted above,[83] the Vikings were despicable heathen foes routed by the might of his patron's illustrious ancestor in whose reflected glory his descendants sought to bask. Notwithstanding this, in framing his elaborate narrative this literary partisan of Uí Briain drew on a variety of material at his disposal, including king-lists,[84] genealogies,[85] as well as some of the verses attributed to Berchán.[86] Annalistic entries constitute his main source, however, as indicated by our brief comparison of the text with the Annals of Loch Cé. Structurally the two compositions also share similarities, in that annalistic-style recording is combined with narrative description in each, although the latter is confined to the vision passages just discussed in the chronicle text. In the case of the *Cogadh*, annals form the basis of the early part of the tract cataloguing Viking attacks on Ireland, as well as the resistance to them provided by a variety of Irish rulers, including Brian and his older brother, Mathgamain. When attention is focussed on the siblings in particular, however, a more discursive approach is adopted. This remains the compositional style employed by the author when relating his story of the battle of Clontarf.

Battle Participants

With regard to the main protagonists, the *Cogadh* agrees with the chronicle sources in describing the encounter as 'another great expedition ... to attack Dublin and the Leinstermen' (*mor sluaged ele ... do gabail for Ath Cliath ocus ar Lagin*).[87] Yet the additional details provided portray the conflict as very much more. In the first place, the list of overseas allies, which differs in its particulars from that in the Annals of Loch Cé, as we have seen, transforms the Norse-Leinster confederation into an international force, supplementing it, amongst others, by a pair of Saxon earls, a duo of Cornish barons, and two sons of the king of France. Other supporters form 'an assembled army of ignorant, barbarous, stupid, wild, anti-social Vikings from the Orkney and the Shetland Islands, from the Isle of Man, Skye and Lewis, from Kintyre and Argyll' (*comtinol sloig buirb, barbarda, dicheillid, dochoisc, dochomaind do Gallaib Insi Orc ocus Insi Cat, a Manaind ocus a Sci ocus a Leodus, a Cind Tiri ocus a hAirer Goedel).*[88] Brian's host too is much augmented, encompassing 'the two territories of Munster and Connacht, and the men of Mide' (*da cuiced Muman ocus Connachta ocus fir Midi*).[89] The impression thus created of a conflict between two mighty hosts is reinforced by the catalogue of casualties on the two sides.

To this end, the *Cogadh* author records four of the supplementary suspicious names preserved in the Annals of Ulster, as well as supplying some of his own, including Carlus and Ciarlus, two sons of the king of Lochlainn, as well as Goistilín Gall, all of which give pause for thought. Other additional names are clearly Norman, such as Simon (Simond mac Tuirgéis), Geoffrey (Séfraid mac Suinín) and Bernard (Bernard mac Suainín). This is also the case with Baron Eoin (Eo[i]n *barún*) and Richard (Ricard), whose lack of historicity is underlined by their description as sons of the fictitious *Ingen Ruad* (Red Girl).[90] Nonetheless, the reinforced record of the dead in the Annals of Ulster could well have provided the *Cogadh* creator with his starting point, which was then augmented at a later stage. When precisely is difficult to determine since the final part of the text containing the litany of the slain is missing from the earliest manuscript versions, surviving only in the copy made by Mícheál Ó Cléirigh in the seventeenth century. The Norman flavour may suggest thirteenth-century interpolations or later, though this could represent but a further layer in the recounting of what was to prove a remarkably elastic encounter. Be that as it may, it is obvious that the *Cogadh* author himself was also supplementing his sources in his elaborate account of what he sought to portray as an intensely ferocious battle of Clontarf.[91]

Concerned though he was with augmenting the number of those active in the battle, that author also drew attention to what he was keen to record as notable absences. One of these was the Dublin king, Sitric mac Amlaíb, who was married to Brian's daughter, Sláne. Dramatic altercations between husband and wife as they watched the fight from their vantage point on the town's battlements, revealing their diametrically opposed allegiances in the process, form a colourful part of the narrative. Indeed, on one notable occasion, the pair came to blows.[92] Yet no reason is provided for the inactivity of the Norse king; it is simply noted by means of explanation for the fact that he was not killed.[93] Moreover, that Dublin was not sacked on the day is said to be due to the company he kept, in what is a probable allusion to Sitric's relationship with Brian's daughter.[94]

Greater detail is provided concerning a more culpable battle-avoider, Brian's principal political opponent, the Mide ruler, Máel Sechnaill mac Domnaill, who along with his men had joined the Munster king as preparations for the encounter were under way. With remarkable foresight, Brian knew 'that they would desert him as that battle approached, even though they came to the assembly' (co treicfitis é re hucht in catha sin, ce tancatar isin comthinol). Not surprisingly, therefore, when Brian's troops came together to take counsel, Máel Sechnaill and his followers are depicted as not being in agreement with the rest.[95] Moreover, the Mide ruler refused to line up alongside the other allies, preferring instead to set himself apart as a result of a deal done with Brian's opponents:[96]

> ba hi comarli Gall in aidaich remi dó, clad etorro ocus gaill, ocus mini insaigtis siun Gaill, ni insaigfitis Gaill iatsium, ocus is amlaid sin da ronsat, uair ro bi in drochomarlli etorro.

> This was what the Vikings advised him [Máel Sechnaill] the previous evening: to build a ditch between themselves and the Vikings and that if they did not attack Vikings, Vikings would not attack them. Thus, was it done, since there was evil plotting amongst them.

The ditch in question is specifically mentioned by Máel Sechnaill in an eyewitness account of the battle he is reported to have communicated to his Clann Cholmáin kinsmen.[97] Having recourse to a spectator's view of events is a common literary motif, which served to underline the authority of that being recounted. In addition this particular passage was designed to emphasise the ferocity of the encounter, enhancing its significance in the process. A combat apart, the Mide king claims never to have seen a fight like it, nor to have heard of its equivalent. Indeed, so incomparable was it that in Máel Sechnaill's opinion 'even if an angel of God attempted to describe it, I doubt that he could' (cid angel Dé do berad a tuarascbail is dichreitim lem da fedad).[98] The part played by Máel Sechnaill himself, however, is somewhat ambiguous. He was certainly on the battlefield, though as a bystander rather than as a valiant activist. Yet his inactivity is depicted in the Cogadh as an inevitable outcome of the ferocity of the conflict, rather than as the action of a traitor.[99]

Whether Máel Sechnaill actually participated in the battle is a moot question. He appears as co-leader of the expedition, alongside Brian, in the Annals of Ulster and related chronicles, though as 'king of Tara' he is depicted as subservient to the Munster leader who not alone is named first, but is also hailed as 'king of Ireland'.[100] This unequal relationship is underlined in the *Cogadh*. In the first place, Brian's initial onslaught upon the Leinstermen in the final months of 1013 was undertaken in response to a plea for assistance by Máel Sechnaill who was unable to defend his territory in the face of repeated attacks.[101] In addition, when Brian returned the following spring to fight what was to become known as the battle of Clontarf, he was accompanied by those who were under his command, including the men of Mide.[102] That they should subsequently turn against their heroic defender was a despicable deed, according to the narrative text, and one that more than justified the Munster king's elevated position vis à vis his less noble colleague. More importantly the descendants of this wondrous ruler were by implication exalted, especially in comparison with Máel Sechnaill's successors over whom their ancestor's ignoble act could be deemed to cast a shadow. For Brian's great-grandson, Muirchertach, during whose reign and at whose behest *Cogadh Gáedhel re Gallaibh* was composed, the depiction of his ancestor's counterpart in Ireland's northern half as both ineffectual and perfidious may well have been designed to provide some justification for attempts by the later Ua Briain ruler to extend his power over Mide. At the very least, it bolstered his moral authority over his own northern competitor, Domnall Mac Lochlainn, against whom he was engaged in a long struggle in the early years of the twelfth century when the *Cogadh* was most likely being written.[103]

Other battle vignettes would also have resonated with the text's contemporary audience. According to one version of events, ascribed to Munster historians, Murchad, Brian's chosen son, and his north Munster (Thomond) battalion, took up position alongside his south Munster (Desmond) neighbours, whom both Brian and his descendants sought to control. Such was Murchad's courage that he advanced furthest vowing not to retreat a single step. Furthermore, the nobles of Desmond followed and thus were all killed.[104] The depiction of a contingent from south Munster being led by a Dál Cais opponent and one to whom they were obviously inferior eloquently elucidated Brian's triumph over what had once been the premier Munster dynasty, the Éoganachta, whose heartland of Desmond (Desmumu) remained strong.[105] More significantly, it sent a powerful message to their twelfth-century descendants concerning the continuing efficacy of Uí Briain rule.[106]

The castigation of the men of Desmond is much more pronounced in a passage now preserved solely in the seventeenth-century manuscript version of the *Cogadh* describing the aftermath of the battle of Clontarf. Hoping to take advantage of the depletion of Dál Cais forces, two of their leaders demanded hostages of Donnchad, Brian's son. The latter's spirited reply reminds them that, like Máel Sechnaill, they too were indebted to his father who defended all of Munster when the men of Desmond were in no position to do so. Furthermore, the valorous actions of his Dál Cais men who immediately rose to fight their traitorous neighbours, despite being seriously wounded, shows Brian's descendants, too, to be a race apart. In the face of such courage, the south Munstermen refrain from giving battle, squabbling pettily with each other instead.[107]

This highly negative portrayal of Desmond and its rulers in the final section of the narrative echoes their depiction in the account of the murder of Brian's brother, Mathgamain, at an earlier point in the tale. Indeed Cian, one of the leaders who is said to challenge Donnchad after Clontarf, is the son of Máel Muad mac Brain who is portrayed as the betrayer of Brian's older sibling.[108] It may be, therefore, that it formed part of the original composition, reinforcing an image already well drawn. Muirchertach Ua Briain, great-grandson of Brian, whose controlling hand is perceptible throughout the narrative, had particular reason to emphasise his dominance over his south Munster neighbours, supporters as they were of his recalcitrant half-brother, Diarmait. Hence it is not surprising that the denigration of Desmond should be a recurrent theme.[109]

Order of Battle

Notwithstanding this, the actions of the South Munster battalion at Clontarf are no more than mildly chastised, attention being drawn to their ineptitude in the face of the superior strength and courage of Brian's favoured son.[110] Ireland's own Hector, such was Murchad's skill and valour that he was leader of his father's Dál Cais troop on the battlefield.[111] Since this particular group was placed at the head of the army of the Munster king, and considering Brian's advanced age, Murchad is being depicted as military commander at Clontarf.[112] What that actually entailed was another matter. Like their opponents, Brian's men were arranged in battalions (*catha*). The Viking-Leinster alliance is said to have encompassed seven such formations, although only three are specified.[113] In the van were the overseas allies under Brodar; these were followed by the Dublin Norse, led by Dubgall mac Amlaíb and three other Viking noblemen, while the Leinstermen under their king, Máel Mórda, brought up the rear.[114] The opposing force had at its head Dál Cais, led by Murchad and aided by his son, Tairdelbach, and cousin, Conaing, as we have seen. Behind them was a Munster contingent under the joint command of the kings of the Déssi and Uí Liatháin. The Connachta led by Tadc Ua Cellaig and others also supplied a battalion, while that of Máel Sechnaill of Mide was, as already mentioned, some way apart at the rear.[115] Brian's ten chief stewards 'with their foreign hosts' (cona nGall socraitib) are placed on one side of the army, according to one version of the text, which situates Uí Briúin and the Conmaicne, under Fergal Ua Ruairc, on the other.[116]

The battle is said to have begun by each side striking 'a strong, furious, barbarous blow'(blod beim bailc, bodba, barbarda) against the other[117] and the encounter between Dál Cais specifically and the Vikings (described as Danair and Danmargaig) receives considerable attention.[118] For the most part, however, the assault is depicted as a succession of combats between independent battalions or, more frequently, between individual heroes each at the head of their own particular group of loyal men. Thus the extent to which Brian or his surrogate, Murchad, was perceived as chief commander is questionable. Notwithstanding this, some measure of pre-planning was certainly envisaged, as is indicated by the careful arrangement of the fighting men. Furthermore, as was usual, the Munster king is said to have held counsel with his allies prior to the onslaught, though of their deliberations nothing is recorded.[119] In the heat of the conflict, however, man meets man, the struggle between Domnall mac Eimín, Brian's Scottish supporter, against Plait, son of the king of Lochlainn, being the first described.[120] Others singled out for mention belong to Dál Cais. These include Conaing, Brian's nephew, whose fight with Máel Mórda is briefly recorded; though he slew the Leinster king, he too was slain.[121] Brian's grandson, Tairdelbach, also lost his life, drowned by the incoming tide while he slaughtered Viking foes on either side.[122]

It is Tairdelbach's father, Murchad, however, who is accorded pride of place on the battlefield, being directly equated with Hector and Hercules, as well as with the biblical strongman, Samson, and the omnipotent Irish hero, Lug Lámfhata.[123] In addition, the depiction of his emotional state, his being consumed by 'an intense, enormous anger' (ferg dicra dimor) and 'a vast, increasing vehemence' (bruth borrfadach adbulmor) may well have been designed to bring the greatest of all native warriors, Cú Chulainn, to mind. And where 'a hero's moon' (*lúan láith*) occupied the space over the latter's head, it was 'a bird of valour and courage' (*en gaili ocus gaiscid*) that fluttered above Murchad. Rushing furiously at the Viking battalion, he slew fifty men with his right hand and fifty with his left thrice over, as even his enemies, 'Viking and Leinster historians' (*senchaidi Gall ocus Lagen*), relate.[124] Not content with that onslaught, he later turned on Sigurd, Earl of Orkney killing him with two skilful blows to his neck. His valour is similarly underlined in the description of his combat with Anraid mac Ebric, son of the king of Lochlainn, Murchad succeeding in casting him to the ground and stabbing him with his own sword. Retaining a knife, though wounded, the son of Ebric managed to cut out his attacker's entrails and both died as a result. As befits a Christian hero, however, Murchad lived until the following day, receiving absolution and communion and making confession and a will before his death.[125]

Notwithstanding this focus on Murchad's valiant exploits, it is clear that he is fighting alongside his Dál Cais following. Thus in his initial attack on the *Danair* (Danes) he is supported by 'one hundred and forty kings' sons who were in his household' (*uii fichit meic rig batar ina theglach*).[126] Similarly, his encounters with Earl Sigurd and Ebric's son take place 'in the midst of the Dál Cais battalion' (*ar lar catha Dal Cais*) and 'right in the middle of Dál Cais' (*i certmedon Dal Cais*) respectively. Moreover it is in defence of his loyal men who are being slaughtered by their opponents that Murchad frequently attacks.[127] The bravery of those men is also highlighted in an earlier alliterative passage recounting a battle between[128]

cath dolig, dibergach, durcraideach, duabsech, dian, denmnetach, dasachtach, na nAnmargach ocus in damraid dian, díulaind, direcra ocus gamanraidh glan, gasda, gerata, gar[g]beoda, galach, gnimach, rigda, rathmar, robladach Dal Cais.

the harsh, plundering, hard-hearted, forbidding, stern, impatient, furious battalion of the Danes and the swift, overwhelming, incomparable host and the pure, dexterous, valiant, mettlesome, valorous, active, royal, gracious, very famous band, Dál Cais.

As the first encounter between two named battalions at Clontarf, it emphasises forcefully the crucial role of Brian Boru's own men.[129] Their supportive neighbours also receive a mention, specifically the troops of South Connacht under Tadc Ua Cellaig who advanced against the Dubliners inflicting and suffering great losses as a result. Of their precise nature, however, 'only God knows, since those who might have known fell there on both sides' (*ni mo ina ic Dia ita a fis, uair cach oen is mo ica m[b]iad a fis drocratar and leth ar leth*).[130]

Such literary flourishes are characteristic of what is, after all, a fiction-alised account of an actual event. Thus the description of the order of the troops is supplemented by the remark 'that a four-wheeled chariot could run from one end to the other of the battalions on either side' (*co refed carbat ceterri[a]da on chind coraele don cath cechtarda*), underlining the proximity of the opposing troops.[131] The density of the fighters is further emphasised in a depiction of Murchad's followers 'foot to foot, head to head and skin on skin' (*bond fri bond, ocus cend fri cend, ocus cnes fri cnes*).[132] The image of their hair blowing behind them in the wind 'being cut by heavy, gleaming axes and by shining, flaming swords' (*ar na letrad do thuagaib troma taidlechaib ocus do claidbib lainnerda lasamna*)[133] echoes Máel Sechnaill's complaint that they were prevented from carrying out valorous deeds by hair that had become entangled around their spears.[134] Similarly his comment that such was the volume of blood covering them 'that no member of either battalion could recognise the companion nearest to him, even if it was his son or his brother, unless he could recognise his voice' (*nach tibred duni don da cath achni ar celi, cide a mac no a brathair bad comfagus do, mini thugad aichni ar a guth*)[135] is in accord with the depiction of the aftermath of the battle when 'they buried those of their people whom they could recognise' (*ro adhlaicsiot gach aon ro aithnigedar da muinntir*).[136]

Weaponry

Notwithstanding the narrative's sensationalist style, much of the information concerning the battle broadly rings true. In this regard the range of weapons alluded to is reasonably realistic.[137] Bows and arrows the Vikings may certainly have had, though these had scarcely been dipped 'in the blood of dragons, toads, water-snakes, vipers, scorpions, wild beasts and various venomous snakes as well' (*a fuilib drecon, is loscend, is dobornathrach, uifprec, iscorp is onchon is nathrach aithnemneach, necsamail archena*).[138] Reference to their 'fierce, broad, shining spears' (*laigni lonna, lethanglasa*) and their 'strong, warlike swords' (*claidmi calma, curata*) is also unsurprising: swords of various types, as well as spear- and arrow-heads, along with shield-bosses, constitute the staple finds of Dublin Viking graves.[139] Not surprisingly the Irish were fitted out with similar equipment: 'handsome riveted lances ... warlike, sharp spears' (*slega suarci, semnecha ... bera bodba biraithi*), in addition to 'hard, powerful, pointed, beautiful, well-constructed swords' (*claidmi cruadi, comnerta, colcda, coema, cumdachta*) and significantly 'heavy, shining, strong, powerful, beautiful, sharp, clear, gleaming, broad, sharpened, axes of Lochlainn' (*tuaga troma, taidlecha, trena, tolgda, taitnemacha, gera, gluair, glainidi, lethna, limtha Lochlannacha*).[140]

Nonetheless, the descriptive detail provided is rarely sufficient to enable us to identify a particular weapon sub-type, the doubled-edged axe with which Brodar clove Brian Boru's head being a notable exception: 'a shining, beautiful, trusty battle-axe ... with its handle set in the middle' (*tuagh taidhleach taitneimhach trostánach ... ocus ionnsma na samtaigte ina medhon*).[141] Swords may be hard and straight (*cruaid, colgdiriuch*)[142] and occasionally, as in the case of Murchad's own prestigious example, inlaid with ornament that inconveniently melted in the heat of battle.[143] Yet whether they were of a distinctively Viking type is impossible to determine.[144]

Whatever the precise nature of these and other Irish weapons, however, they are deemed inferior to the armoury with which the Vikings themselves were equipped, the author deliberately stressing the superior art of the enemies' tools of war.[145] Despite the obvious advantage afforded by these, the Irish are presented consistently as overthrowing 'the mail-coated foreigners' (*goill na luireach*),[146] their victory being all the more remarkable as a result. In a vivid scene, the sparks caused by the sharp swords of Brian's own valorous Dál Cais men are visible from Dublin's battlements as they succeed in hacking off the seemingly impregnable protective armour of their opponents.[147] Murchad, too, when advancing on Anraid mac Ebric, son of the king of Lochlainn, 'turned sideways to attack the mail-coated battalion and of those who were mail-clad slew fifteen Vikings with his right hand and fifteen with his left' (*ro impo fiartharsna fo cath na lureach cor marb .u. Gallu dec da deis, ocus i cuic dec da cli donnneoch ima rabi lureach*).[148] Furthermore, in his assault on Sigurd, Earl of Orkney a deftly placed blow removed the elaborate fastenings of the latter's helmet 'and [Murchad] used the sword of the other hand ... to hack and hew him, after his helmet had fallen off' (*ocus tucastair claidium na lama ailli ... da airlech ocus da atchuma, ar toitim a cathbairr ar a cul de*).[149] Use of helmets and mail coats by Irish warriors appears to have been rare in the eleventh and twelfth centuries.[150] Nonetheless, protective armour was highly valued at least by a certain elite.[151] Indeed it is one of the items likely to have been bestowed by Muirchertach Ua Briain, the driving force behind the writing of the *Cogadh*, upon subordinate kings, according to another text composed under his direction, *Lebor na Cert* (The Book of Rights), the Munster ruler receiving refection in return.[152] It hardly suited the purpose of the *Cogadh* author to mention this, however, concerned as he was with emphasising the disadvantaged position of Brian and his men to augment the extent of their achievement, as we have seen.[153]

In one other respect the Irish had certainly adopted Viking custom in their use of *meirgi* (battle standards), the word itself (sg. *meirge*) being a borrowing from Old Norse *merkke*.[154] These are particularly featured in a passage added to the text about the middle of the twelfth century, anachronistically high-lighting the exploits of Fergal ua Ruairc who had died in 964.[155] Surveying his troops, Brian beholds[156]

.x. mergi ocus tri fichit orro, do derg, ocus do buidi, ocus d'uani, ocus do cenel cacha datha mon mergi sithi sarsuachnid, senta, sainemail ruc buaid [cacha] catha ocus cacha cliatha ocus cacha congala, ris ar brised .uii. catha conicci in ninad sin .i. mergi orgranemail Fergail Ua Ruairc, airdri tuath Brefni ocus Conmacni.

seventy battle standards above them, red, yellow, green and of every colour, including the exceedingly illustrious, propitious, distinguished, silken ban-ner which gained victory in every battle, conflict and encounter and which had been successful in seven battles up to then, namely the gold-spangled (?) banner of Fergal ua Ruairc, chief king of the territory of Bréifne and Conmaicne.

The condition of Murchad's banner is cited as the gauge by which Brian measures the success of the entire enterprise, the old king proclaiming:[157]

is maith betit fir Erend ... cen bias in mergi sin na hessum, daig biaid a mesnech fein, ocus a n-engnum in gach duni dib i cen iticerat in mergi sin.

the men of Ireland will be well ... as long as that battle-standard is standing, for each will find his own courage and valour as long as he sees that standard.

Thus all is truly lost when he hears that his son's standard had fallen, the honour and valour of Ireland being depleted as a result: "'by my word'", said

he, "the honour and valour of Ireland fell when that battle-standard fell;
Ireland really fell on account of that'" (*"dar mo breithir" ar se "do thuit eineach
ocus engnam Erenn an tan do thuit an meirge sin, ocus do thuit Ere de go fir"*) .[158]

Battle Terrain

By way of confirmation, the *Cogadh* describes how a short time later Brian
himself was slain by Brodar in his place of prayer.[159] Where exactly the
Munster king was located is not specified, although it cannot have been too
far removed from the battle, since his attendant, Latean, could see and report
on the action.[160] His Norse slayer is said to have come upon the ageing ruler
almost by accident when retreating from the incoming sea,[161] in which many
of his allies were submerged.[162] Following them into the water, Tairdelbach,
Brian's grandson, was cast against the weir of Clontarf and was drowned 'with
a Viking under him and one in his right hand and another in his left, and the
weir's stake through him' (*ocus Gall fae ocus Gall ina deis ocus Gall ina c[h]le ocus
cualli na carad trit*).[163] It was at Clontarf that the battle reached its zenith, the
fast flowing tide having carried off the enemy's ships. Prevented from reaching the River Liffey's main crossing point, *drochat Dubgaill* (Dubgall's bridge),
presumably by their Irish opponents, and hemmed in by Tomar's wood (*caill
Tamair*) to the north,[164] the *gaill* were forced to stand their ground and fight or,
as very many of them did, retreat in haste into the sea.[165]

It appears to have been on the north of the bay that the fighting also
began; reacting to the plundering of Fine Gall and Benn Étair (Howth)
by Brian's men, the *gaill* opposed them at Mag nElta, the plain in which
Clontarf was located.[166] This may also be the plain (*mag*) upon which the
Connacht men attacked the Dublin Norse, pursuing the twenty or so who
escaped as far as Dubgall's bridge.[167] Indeed a reference to 'the great battle of
Mag nElta' (*cath mór Muige hEalta*) in the *Cogadh* may conceivably be to the
battle of Clontarf. Preserved in a poetic celebration of the battle of Glenn
Máma and presented as much less significant than that earlier encounter,[168]
it may well be, however, that the author of the narrative did not identify it as
such. He himself refers to Clontarf on only one occasion, in the description
of Tairdelbach's drowning, as we have seen.[169]

If the main action took place north of the bay, it was on 'the green of
Áth Cliath' (*faithche Áth Cliath*), some way south of the river's main crossing
point, that Brian's troops first assembled and where the Munster king took

counsel before the fighting began.[170] Not surprisingly, therefore, it was upon the same 'green' that they gathered together in the aftermath of the battle, slaughtering captured oxen in full sight of their Norse owners who sent messages from their defended settlement of Áth Cliath (Dublin).[171] It was from this protected vantage point that Norse bystanders had also observed the raging battle, Amlaíb's son, Sitric, being 'on the battlements of his own chamber watching it' (*ar scemled a grianan fein aca fegad*).[172] Such topographical detail is not a feature of the early chronicle accounts, Brian depicted as simply marching to Áth Cliath.[173] Hence Clontarf, which has come to be so intimately associated with the encounter, may only gradually have moved centre stage.[174]

The Philosophy of War

Difficult though it may be for us to reconstruct exactly the practicalities of the battle at Clontarf, as depicted in the *Cogadh*, these must surely have borne some relationship to the actual military experience of a twelfth-century audience, many of whom were familiar with Dublin's terrain. In the same way, the moral justification provided for the vicious encounter resonated with contemporary thinking on the philosophy of war.

Among the ideas informing the text may have been those associated with the promotion of the peace of God which from relatively modest beginnings in Burgundy and Acquitaine around the end of the tenth century gradually spread throughout France and beyond.[175] Concerned with establishing a coherent morality of warfare, a succession of councils that form the corner stone of this movement set out the circumstances in which war was justifiable, the Council of Narbonne in 1054 in effect rejecting violence between Christians.[176] By contrast, war against God's enemies was not only legitimate but holy, an ideology that achieved its practical manifestation in the Crusades, the first of which was set in train by a Church council at Piacenza presided over by Pope Urban II in 1095.[177] The Church, therefore, had given its blessing to war against the heathen and by so doing did much to fuse Christianity and martial ideals.[178] Furthermore, it fostered a new type of ruler imbued with reformist ideals who recognised that successful governance was to a large extent dependent upon proper moral conduct.[179]

As depicted in the *Cogadh*, King Brian precisely fitted that mould. Very much concerned with the welfare of his subjects, Ireland under his leadership was undoubtedly a Christian society (*societas Christiana*) as advocated by reformers. Thus the normal state of affairs was total harmony and, as befitted a Christian ruler, Brian revered the Church as well as its primary vocation, learning. To this end, he had various ecclesiastical establishments built and repaired, and also concerned himself with the state of other structures. And as a reward almost, his reign was 'prosperous and peaceful' (*co sona, sitha-mail*) not least because of his manner, which was 'venerable and holy, with chastity, devotion and probity, and with clerical rules' (*co conaich cadusach, co ngenmnadeacht, ocus co crabud, ocus co rrecht, ocus co riaglaib ic clerchib*).[180] When plundering pagans sought to destroy his rightful rule, therefore, Brian is depicted as going on the offensive with the might of all of Christendom behind him. Clontarf had taken on the character of a holy war.

Presented as a military engagement of defence, the Clontarf encounter had in Brian a tenacious protector of territory, as well as a courageous Christian valiantly opposing what was in part at least a heathen host. In this he had worthy predecessors, both King Alfred and Æthelred in England having waged defensive wars against morally reprehensible foes.[181] Like Brian, they too had the Church on their side. Indeed Clontarf's portrayal in the *Cogadh* exemplifies what Matthew Strickland has described as 'the [well-known] theme of battle as a judicial duel on a grand scale, a collective ordeal in which God bestowed victory upon the side whose cause was most just'.[182] Inspired by the Bible, the ultimate account of a conflict between good and evil and one depicting God as actively involved in human affairs,[183] prayer and fasting, together with an appeal to relics and saints, became part of the scene of combat, as Brian's chanting of the psalms while the battle raged around him clearly shows.[184]

In the context of the Crusades such symbols acquired added significance, tangible demonstrations of Christianity's might. The narrative's emphasis on single combats might also be viewed against this background: while long a common mode of warfare in literature, it became increasingly dominant in crusading texts, the overthrowing by Christian champions of Muslim opponents encapsulating the triumph of Christendom as a whole, as Matthew Strickland has noted.[185] As footsoldiers in Brian's 'crusading' army, therefore, the individual heroes in the *Cogadh* each had their part to play in banishing an encroaching pagan foe. In the same way, the identification of the Irish with the Franks and the Israelites is significant in this regard,[186] as is the comparison drawn between Brian and a trio of biblical giants, Solomon, David and Moses,[187] on the one hand, and between his chosen son, Murchad, and

Samson, on the other.[188] By contrast, the lack of reverence shown by Brian's opponents 'either to God or man, to church or to sanctuary' (*do Dia no da duni, do cill no do nemead*) is repeatedly underlined.[189]

Brennu-Njáls saga

The most detailed Norse account of the battle, in 'Njáll's saga' (*Brennu-Njáls saga* 'The Saga of Burnt Njáll'), one of the most significant of Icelandic sagas, portrays the encounter in similar terms. In this connection, Richard Allen has drawn attention to the function of the Clontarf episode in the tale, as a final judgement on the surviving men who had attacked Njáll.[190] Similarly, Lars Lönnroth has noted the emphasis placed on God's control over the course of events, linking it to an Augustinian perspective prevalent down through the Middle Ages. It is through divine power that the Irish king triumphs; God's justice is seen to prevail.[191]

The place of Clontarf in the Norse saga itself, however, has been debated, its positioning in the narrative according it something of epilogue status. Indeed scholars in the past considered the account of the battle to be an interpolation.[192] Concerned with the fate of the burners of the saga's main protagonist, Njáll, who joined the expedition of the earl of the Orkneys, Sigurd (Norse Sigurðr), to Dublin, losing their lives there, the episode, though 'largely digressive' as John Hines has noted,[193] can be taken as an integral part of the tale. Lars Lönnroth has identified many correspondences in style and narrative technique between the Clontarf episode and the rest of the composition.[194] Moreover, its emphasis on the triumph of good over evil with its overtones of Christian morality, as we have seen, accords well with the main thematic concerns of the story of Njáll.[195] Drawing on an existing account of the battle, therefore, a thirteenth-century Icelandic author wove it skilfully and effectively into his comprehensive family history of Burnt Njáll.

The precise nature of the now lost source (or sources) drawn on by the author must perforce remain speculative; whether it took the form of a saga of Brian (*Brjáns saga*) remains far from clear. Long since postulated,[196] this putative composition has been discussed by Donnchadh Ó Corráin and Benjamin Hudson who suggest that it lies behind the Norse descriptions of the battle of Clontarf.[197] If so, it has left few direct traces in the extant literature: a possible reference to a saga of Brian in *Þorsteins saga Síðu-Hallssonar* (Þorsteinn Síðu-Hallsson's saga) is ambiguous and may equally refer to *Njáls saga* itself or a saga of the Orkney earl, Sigurd, as has previously been noted.[198] Should 'Sigurd's saga' denote a version of *Orkneyinga saga* (The History of the Earls of Orkney), as Hudson has suggested, it may well have been this text on which the later author of *Njáls saga* drew.[199]

As it has come down to us, however, *Orkneyinga saga* mentions Sigurd only briefly and is remarkably reticent about the battle of Clontarf. Thus, while its description of the encounter is in substantial agreement with that preserved in *Njáls saga*, the author of the latter must have had access to a source markedly different from *Orkneyinga saga*, as it has survived.[200] Recourse to other texts might also account for the differences, including some emanating in Ireland itself. Following Sophus Bugge, both Ó Corráin and Hudson situate 'Brian's saga' in Dublin,[201] Hudson arguing for transmission to Iceland via an ecclesiastical route.[202] There is nothing inherently implausible in this: the Hiberno-Norse in all likelihood preserved written records, the author of the *Cogadh* referring in passing to *senchaidi na nGall* 'Viking chroniclers'.[203] Moreover, Irish names have been rendered reasonably into Old Norse, suggesting a certain familiarity with the language, as Sayers and Ó Corráin have noted.[204] However, since *Brjáns saga*, should it ever have existed, has not in fact survived, what its contents might have entailed is simply unknowable. Thus it seems safest to conclude, with Hudson, that material written in Ireland, whatever its form, provided but one possible strand of information for Icelandic authors on the battle of Clontarf.[205]

Their records of the conflict frequently differ from those of their Irish literary counterparts in perspective and tone, as well as in some details, being the products of another time and space. In the case of *Njáls saga*, a thirteenth-century Icelandic family saga, the description of Clontarf forms part of the pursuit of revenge for the burning of the main character, Njáll, led by his son-in-law, Kári. A feud with the chief burner, Flosi, brought him to the Orkney Islands when King Sitric (Norse Sigtryggr) of Dublin was at the earl of Orkney's court seeking support for his conflict against Brian. Having acquired agreement to participate from Earl Sigurd, on promising him his mother's hand in marriage and the kingship of Ireland, Sitric journeyed to the Isle of Man to enlist the aid of the formidable Viking pair, Óspakr and Brodar (Norse Bróðir).[206] The heathen, Óspakr, said 'that he did not wish to fight against so good a king' (*eigi vilja berjask í móti svá góðum konungi*) and in fact went over to Brian's side.[207] The apostate, Brodar, on the other hand, in return for the self-same gifts (*konungdómi ok móður sinni* 'the kingdom and his mother') was persuaded to take a stand against Brian.[208]

The account of the battle itself is relatively brief. Having assembled with his forces in Dublin some time earlier, Brodar took the decision to engage in combat on Good Friday, since it had been prophesied that Brian would gain victory but lose his life if the conflict were fought on that day.[209] The Viking heathen, together with Sitric and Sigurd, lined up in three columns to oppose Brian's men led by the Munster king's brother, Úlfr Hræða, the convert, Óspakr, fighting alongside Brian's own sons, and Kerþjálfaðr, his beloved foster-son. 'The armies clashed; bitter was the fighting' (*Fallask þá at fylkingar; varð þá orrosta allhǫrð*);[210] as in the Irish literary sources, however, the focus is on individual combats, in this case between Brodar and Úlfr Hræða, Sigurd and Kerþjálfaðr, and Óspakr who outlived Brian's pair of sons to face the Dublin king, Sitric.[211] As the Norse fled, pursued by the victorious Irish forces, Brodar attacked Brian whose defenders had for the most part joined the fight. Despite a valiant attempt by his youngest son, Tadc (Norse Taðkr), to save him, the Munster king was killed by a deft blow of the Viking's sword that simultaneously removed both his head and his son's protecting arm. Revenge was swift and fierce: Brodar was slit open and disembowelled before he and his entire retinue were slain. Justice of sorts, is thus seen to be done for the murder of a magnificent martyr whose dying blood healed his son's arm and whose severed head and body became miraculously reattached.[212]

Brian's exalted status, therefore, is a feature of both Norse and Irish accounts, his holiness being particularly emphasised in *Cogadh Gáedhel re Gallaibh*, and in the Annals of Loch Cé, both of which portray him as having been slain at prayer, as well as in the somewhat later Icelandic text, *Njáls saga*, as we have seen. In the latter, the Irish king is presented in direct contrast to his wicked ex-wife, Gormlaith (Norse Kormlǫð), whose beautiful appearance concealed an evil, duplicitous mind.[213] Brian, on the other hand, is explicitly described as the most accomplished of all kings (*hann var allra konunga bezt at sér*),[214] willing to forgive a man the same crime three times,[215] and capable of adopting the son of an enemy as his own.[216] Such was his reputation for goodness that the heathen, Óspakr, 'the shrewdest of all men' (*allra manna vitrastr*) chose to convert to Christianity and follow Brian.[217]

That a twelfth-century Irish author and particularly a partisan of Brian's descendants, Uí Briain, should present a renowned ancestor in such a positive light is unsurprising. The occurrence of an equally affirmative portrayal in a body of literature in which disdain for the Irish is a frequent feature, is worthy of note. Moreover, as Haki Antonsson has remarked, Brian's saintly characteristics are in fact augmented in the Icelandic text: the king's refusal to fight on Good Friday is explicitly stated and his posthumous pair of miracles underlines his martyred state.[218] In the absence of any tradition of royal martyrdom in Ireland in the early medieval period, in marked contrast with its prevalence in Scandinavia at the time, Haki Antonsson has suggested that it is at the hands of a Norse author that the martyring of King Brian takes place.[219] If so, he was certainly put on the road to martyrdom by the author of the Irish literary text. Moreover, since that author, like his learned contemporaries, was familiar with ideas emanating from the Gregorian reform movement that was influential in European intellectual circles in the eleventh and twelfth centuries, he is unlikely to have been unaware of the increased emphasis on martyrdom current at the time.[220] This was initially propagated by Pope Gregory VII but was taken up by subsequent reformers and adopted enthusiastically by those associated with the Crusades.[221] In presenting his royal hero as a holy ruler, therefore, the Irish author could certainly have been mindful of portrayals of fighting men attacking the enemies of Christianity elsewhere overseas and fully aware of the spiritual rewards that thereby ensued.

This is made even more apparent in a poem dependent on the *Cogadh*, *Aonar dhuit, a Bhriain Banba*, 'To you alone, Brian of Ireland', attributed to the thirteenth-century poet, Muireadhach Albanach Ó Dálaigh, and even if not by him, conceivably of his time.[222] The good king's soul has now become sinless (*anam Bhriain gan iomarbhas*), his body blemish-free (*a chorp gan chol*).[223] Furthermore, his sainthood is underlined through his coupling with the greatest of Ireland's saints, Patrick, as one of two pairs of men who most came to Ireland's aid.[224] Brian's death on Good Friday is similarly highlighted, the parallel with Christ, no more than implied in *Njáls saga*, being unambiguously invoked: *Aoine Cásg do marbhadh Brian ... mar do marbadh Chríost gan choir* (Brian was killed on Good Friday ... just as sinless Christ was killed).[225] In view of Brian's increasingly exalted state, it is scarcely surprising that 'angels from Paradise' (*aingil a bParthas*)[226] bear off his body, according to the later poem. They replace the ecclesiastics charged with conveying the pious king's body via a series of churches to the chief church of Armagh, in Brian's careful planning of his own funeral arrangements, as set out in the *Cogadh*.[227] Thus the saint-like reputation of the Munster ruler continued to grow, thirteenth-century Irish and Norse writers augmenting his sacred nature in subtle but significantly different ways. It is as a pious, godly figure of authority that Brian is presented in the earliest extended literary portrayal of him to have survived, *Cogadh Gáedhel re Gallaibh*, to which the later composer of *Aonar dhuit* certainly had access. Whether the Norse author of *Njáls saga* was also familiar with the Irish narrative is another matter.

Brennu-Njáls saga and *Cogadh Gáedhel re Gallaibh* Compared

Other differences between the accounts of the battle of Clontarf preserved in the *Cogadh* and in *Njáls saga* suggest that the author of the latter was not drawing directly on the Irish text, as it has survived. Key elements may be paralleled in both; nonetheless, their presentation displays considerable variety in the two texts.[228] The role of Gormlaith in inciting the conflict is common to both narratives. Though dramatic, her intervention is brief in the Irish tale. Described as Brian's wife and mother of his eldest son, Donnchad, and located in the Dál Cais stronghold of Cenn Corad, she allies nevertheless with her paternal kin, the Leinstermen, taunting her brother, the king of Leinster and Brian's arch-enemy, Máel Mórda, for submitting to the Munster ruler. Ostentatiously casting a gift given to her brother by her husband into the fire, goading him for his subservience in the process, she causes him to flounce off.[229] It was a quarrel with another son of Brian, Murchad, the following morning, however, that led the Leinsterman to take the decisive step of seeking allies to march against Brian.[230]

By contrast, her words are decisive in *Njáls saga*, where she acts in conjunction not with her brother, but with her son by the Hiberno-Norse king of Dublin, Amlaíb Cuarán, Sitric. Furthermore, her relationship with Brian is specifically stated to have terminated and indeed her anger at him is depicted as her motivating force.[231] Urging her son to seek military reinforcements for a battle against her ex-husband, she implicitly pre-approves his duplicitous decision to offer his mother and the kingdom as inducement to a succession of warriors by categorically stating that Sitric should spare nothing in his attempts to amass a fighting force.[232] From her vantage point, most likely Dublin,[233] Gormlaith is thus presented as the all-controlling force, an evil, vengeful queen whose role as instigator of the calamitous conflict is intentionally underlined.[234] In this, she is comparable with other women

in the tale, specifically with Hildigunnr, a similar inciter of violence, as well
as two widows, Gunnhildr, and the much more prominent Hallgerðr, the
threatening nature of whose power is also highlighted.[235] It is in the context
of the overall thematic concerns of Njáls saga, therefore, that Gormlaith's
enhanced role in the Norse narrative is to be viewed, a thirteenth-century
author deliberately manipulating a character who may already have had
negative connotations in his source or sources. This is certainly the case in
the Irish material concerning her. Indeed so pronounced were her scheming
traits in the Cogadh that writers drawing on the text also sought to cast her
as the villain of the piece in later accounts of the battle, specifically coupling Máel Mórda's decision to seek battle allies with the effect of his sister's
taunt.[236] Their twelfth-century forbear, however, affords her a kinder touch.

Of greater surprise perhaps is the fact that the Cogadh author is also not
unduly harsh on Brian's slayer, Brodar, at least when his depiction therein
is compared with that in the Norse text.[237] He remains a relatively shadowy
figure in the Irish account, one of two earls asked by the Vikings to join
them on Brian's renewed advance against Dublin in the spring of 1014.[238]
As in Njáls saga, his contempt for God is noted, his being 'without respect,
acknowledgement, honour, or protection, for either God or man, church or
sanctuary' (can chagill, can aititin, can chadus, can comarci do Dia no da duni, do cill
no do nemead).[239] Jointly commanding a significant force of 2,000 men,[240] he
is not accorded any part in the battle until, along with two other warriors,
he stumbles upon the ageing ruler. Not noticing him initially, Brodar has to
be persuaded that the old man he takes to be a 'noble priest' (sagart uasal) is
in fact the great King Brian (an rí mór Brian). Wielding his axe he split the
king's head, but not before Brian had cut off his two legs with his sword. We
must assume that he died from his wounds,[241] the text explicitly specifying
only that one of Brodar's companions was killed by Brian.[242]

According to Njáls saga, on the other hand, the Viking's action was much
more meditated, Brodar deliberately seizing the moment when he noted
that the majority of Brian's defenders were in pursuit of the Norse. Despite
the valiant counter-attack of Tadc, son of the Irish ruler, he succeeded in
slaying the king but was immediately tortured and killed by Úlfr Hræða, as
detailed above.[243] His cruel fate would have been perceived to be no more
than he deserved by an audience already cognisant of the essential nature of
Brodar's being. Once a Christian and indeed a 'mass-deacon' (messudjákn),
he had since turned his back on the true faith 'and sacrificed to heathen
spirits and was the most skilled in magic of all men' (ok blótaði heiðnar vættir

ok var allra manna fjǫlkunnigastr). Despite his impenetrable armour, however, he could not protect himself from the portents of doom that caused boiling blood to pour down upon himself and his men, their weapons to turn upon them and ravens to attack.[244] He had to seek the help of his erstwhile ally, Óspakr, who had refused to fight against the good King Brian, to glean the significance of these terrible events. Learning that he and his retinue were soon to die, Brodar determined to kill the messenger. Wise Óspakr managed to escape, heading with his men straight to Brian's court where he received baptism from the holy king himself.[245]

As Brodar's direct antithesis, Óspakr serves to underline the inherently evil nature of his 'foster-brother' (*fóstbróðir*) and it is as a contrasting pair that they are deliberately presented in the tale. Our first encounter with them is as a couple (*heitir annarr Óspakr, en annarr Bróðir* 'one is called Óspakr, the other Brodar'), an invincible duo whose fame is such that Gormlaith sends her son, Sitric, to acquire their assistance whatever their reaction might be.[246] In the event, both respond very differently to the approach of the Dublin king and, notwithstanding their shared past, their paths completely diverge. It is in Óspakr's depiction as a heathen, in contrast to that of Brodar's as a lapsed Christian, that the true nature of their differences is seen to lie.[247] As a well-intentioned pagan who has not yet encountered Christianity, Óspakr can still hope to be saved and indeed he does come to receive baptism, as we have seen. In his deliberate renunciation of his faith, Brodar, on the other hand, has shown himself to be far worse than the ignorant but virtuous heathen. It is his apostasy that is being specifically condemned.

It is significant in this regard that Sigurd, Earl of Orkney the other overseas ally recruited by Sitric, is also a lapsed Christian.[248] He, too, is seen to be unwise: despite the explicit advice of his fighting men he joins the expedition and is killed.[249] Óspakr has a close counterpart in the person of Brian's erstwhile enemy, King Kylfir. While not specifically designated a pagan, his many battles against the Munster king were certainly the act of one. On entering a monastery, however, he and Brian were immediately reconciled, the holy, forgiving ruler adopting his son, Kerþjálfaðr, whom he came to love 'more than his own sons' (*meira en sínum sonum*).[250] What is repeatedly reinforced, therefore, is the message that those who embrace Christianity are rewarded, while those who have deliberately turned their back on it are truly damned.

In this way, the author of *Njáls saga* displays a more nuanced approach to religious divisions than his Irish counterpart, whose portrayal is of a native-Viking conflict couched in terms of a mighty struggle between Christian royal saviour and implacable heathen foe. As the holy leader of a righteous Christian army emerging triumphant over a ferocious barbarian foe, Brian's depiction in the *Cogadh* reflects an awareness of the crusading spirit prevalent elsewhere in the early twelfth century when the text was being composed.[251] The Norse writer, too, is mindful of the divine direction of events, seeing in Clontarf an illustration of how God's great plan unfolds, as already noted. Yet his creator has a compassionate side, allowing for acceptance and conversion of well-meaning non-believers; those who reject Christianity, however, are immediately cast adrift.

The extension of salvation to clean-living pagans is an idea found in much European religious writing in the twelfth century, surfacing occasionally in secular narratives as well. Connected with the reform movement of the time, it epitomises the gradual replacement of a distant, omnipotent God by a more loving figure whose human incarnation, Jesus, devout Christians could hope to emulate. This more lenient, tolerant leader could find a place for a variety of virtuous beings in his growing gallery of saved souls, including those who had been good pagans who managed to convert.[252] Echoes of it here in the Norse narrative parallel its occurrence in Irish compositions roughly contemporary with the *Cogadh*.[253] The Fragmentary Annals of Ireland, for example, was written perhaps half a century before the Dál Cais text and is thematically related to it in its partisan portrayal of the trials of Cerball mac Dúnlainge, king of Osraige, against a powerful Viking foe.[254] Nonetheless, while heathenism is practised by many of Cerball's Scandinavian enemies, others among them have converted; thus the Danes 'abstained from meat and women for a time, for the sake of piety' (*gabhaid sealad fri fheóil ocus fri mhnáibh ar chrabhudh*).[255]

Furthermore, relinquishment of one's faith is also roundly condemned therein, those who do so being associated with Vikings:[256]

Isin bliadain si dno ro treigsiot sochaide a mbaitis Críostaidhachta ocus tangattar malle risna Lochlannachaib, gur airgsiot Ard Macha, ocus go rugsat a maithius as. Sed quidam ex ipsis poenitentiam egere, et uenerunt ad satisfactionem.

In that year, moreover, many abandoned their Christian baptism and joined the Scandinavians, and they plundered Armagh, and took out its riches. But some of them did penance, and came to make reparation.

In what appear to be later insertions into the text, the term Gall-Gaídil (Scandinavian-Irish), used in contemporary annalistic material for a group of mixed descent,[257] is adopted for the Irish apostates and a fanciful explanation is given of the term:[258]

ro bo thuidheachta do mharbadh an ro marbadh do Ghall-Ghaoidhealaibh ann, úair daoíne ar ttregadh a mbaiste iad-saidhe, ocus adbertais Normannaigh fríu, uair bés Normannach aca, ocus a n-altrum forra, ocus ger bó olc na Normannaigh bunaidh dona heaglaisibh, bá measa go mór iad-saidhe, .i. an lucht sa, gach conair fo Eirinn a mbidís.

For it was worth coming to kill those Gall-Gaídil who were slain there, for those were people who had forsaken their baptism and they used to be called Northmen, for they had the customs of the Northmen, and they had been reared by them; and though the original Northmen had perpetrated evil on the churches, these were much worse, i.e. this group, wherever in Ireland they were

This parallels an earlier reference to Gall-Gaídil in the narrative into which a later gloss has been incorporated:[259]

Cath do thabhairt d'Aodh, do rígh Ailigh, .i. don righ as fearr eangnamh 'na aimsir, do loingius na nGall nGaoidheal, .i. Scuit íad, ocus daltai do Normainnoibh íad ocus tan ann adbearar cidh Normainnigh friu.

Áed, king of Ailech, the most able king in his time, waged battle against the fleet of the Gall-Gaídil, i.e. they were Irish and pupils of the Northmen and sometimes they are even called Northmen.

The term used for the Vikings in these passages, *Normannaigh*, is unusual in this regard, occurring on only three other occasions in the narrative in entries that are not paralleled in other sources.[260] It, too, may be indicative of the late date of the passages in question, *Normannaigh* being most frequently used in conjunction with the Anglo-Normans after their arrival in Ireland in 1169, though as the vernacular equivalent of the Latin term *Nordmanni* 'Northmen' it was used for Vikings at an earlier date. The date of this supplementary material is difficult to determine, therefore; nevertheless, it could conceivably have been inserted around the time *Njáls saga* was being composed or some time earlier. Linguistic differences between these passages and the remainder of the text are not pronounced.[261]

Retrograde Christians, therefore, also constitute a theme in Irish writing where they are specifically associated with Vikings. Moreover, they are prominent in a narrative, thematically related to the *Cogadh*, in passages inserted into the text perhaps in the same century as the Munster tract was composed. The Fragmentary Annals appear to have been well known in Iceland;[262] apostates, however, do not appear to have been prominent in the Irish account of Clontarf that formed part of the source material upon which the author of *Njáls saga* drew. As he developed the character of Gormlaith, denigrating her further in the process, so too he enlarged upon the person of Brian's slayer, Brodar, making him the villain of the day. In this elaboration, the implicit contrast with Óspakr is important, just as Gormlaith's wicked actions are emphasised by reference to her ex-husband's very different kinds of deed.

As the kernel of Gormlaith's personality is perceptible in the Irish composition, common elements in the accounts of Brian's slaying also occur. In the first place, both refer to very similar battle terrain. In the Norse narrative, Brodar flees the battle to the woods from where he later emerges to attack the king.[263] While the Irish text is less specific, Earl Brodar and his retinue simply approaching Brian from the distance,[264] reference to a wood, *caill Tomair* (Tomar's wood), directly to the north of the battlefield is found elsewhere in the account.[265] In the same way, Brian is served by a single lone attendant in both Irish and Norse compositions, to which a crucial, albeit very different role, is assigned. Laitean in the *Cogadh* conveys news of the battle to his master, while in *Njáls saga*, Brian's son, Tadc, assumes the mantle of his father's protector, in the absence of what had been a shield of armed men.[266] The fatal blow is applied in a very different manner, as we have seen, however, and this, together with the detailed focus on Brodar's character that is absent from the Irish text, suggests that the relationship between *Njáls saga* and the earlier *Cogadh* is far from direct.

Other significant differences between the two texts support this view. Gormlaith's enhanced role in *Njáls saga* focuses attention on her son, Sitric, who is presented as her mouthpiece in the lead-up to the encounter. He is also at the head of one of three ranks of fighting men when the battle begins, facing Óspakr and Brian's sons.[267] When he flees, so too does the whole army, implying that he, in fact, is the supreme commander.[268]

By contrast, the Dublin king is conspicuously inactive in the Irish narrative, cheering on his kinsmen from the relative safety of the town's battlements to the annoyance of his wife, Brian's daughter, Sláine, as mentioned above. That he did not die at Clontarf is indicated by his active career subsequently which included going on pilgrimage to Rome in 1028.[269] He died peacefully in 1042.[270] It is in an attempt to explain his survival on that fateful day that the author of the *Cogadh* removes him from the action, since no Viking of any rank present at the encounter escaped alive.[271] As well as emphasising the carnage and hence augmenting the Irish victory, as is this writer's wont, he also removes from Brian's son-in-law the ignominy of having left a battlefield in flight.

Another notable absentee in the heat of the battle, according to the Irish literary account, was Máel Sechnaill, king of Mide, as we have seen, one version of the text alluding to an agreement he had come to with the Vikings on the eve of the battle.[272] This has led to the suggestion that he can be identified with the unnamed rider carrying a javelin said to have conversed with Brodar and Gormlaith for a long time on the day before the fight in *Njáls saga*.[273] The details are not sufficient, however, to confirm the identification and the mysterious man 'on the dapple-grey horse' (*á apalgrám hesti*) constitutes another divergence between the two texts.

Anecdotes concerning Norse warriors in the battle rout that are characteristic of *Njáls saga* are also unparalleled in the Irish account. These include Earl Sigurd's lively exchange with Hrafn the Red regarding who should act as fated standard-bearer; recognising that the buck does indeed stop with him, Sigurd stuffs the flag under his clothing and is killed.[274] Equally dramatic is the pregnant pause of Þorsteinn Hallson who bent down to tie his shoelace while in flight. A question put by Kerþjálfaðr, Brian's foster-son, as to why he was no longer running away elicited this celebrated comment in response: "'Because', said Þorsteinn, "I cannot reach home tonight, since my home is out in Iceland'" (*"Því", sagði Þorsteinn, "at ek tek eigi heim í kveld, þar sem ek á heima út á Íslandi"*). He was spared, as a result.[275]

This section of *Njáls saga* also details the death and revenge of Brian that are also deviant from the relevant passages in the *Cogadh*, as we have seen. In particular, the part accorded to the Norse-named Úlfr Hræda, brother of Brian, as the slayer of Brodar and thus avenger of the king, is worthy of note. Although lacking a direct parallel in the Irish text, William Sayers has drawn attention to the connection between the meaning of his name 'troublesome wolf' and that of Cú Duilig (*cú* 'hound' and *duilig* 'hard, intractible'), one of three designated protectors of Brian, all of whom died in the battle according to the *Cogadh*.[276] Significantly he is therein described as 'son of Cennétig', making him also a brother of Brian. The correspondence is certainly striking and, while the appellation in itself is one that could have been independently allocated to any number of Irish and Norse heroes, the fact that it is Brian's brother who is so named in both traditions suggests in this instance a palpable link between the two.

That the author of *Njáls saga* had access to an earlier account of the battle of Clontarf is clear. Furthermore, a comparison between his version of events with that preserved in the earliest lengthy Irish description of the battle, *Cogadh Gáedhel re Gallaibh*, brings a number of similarities to light. Thus the place and date of the battle are identical in both; key characters are also common to the two texts, though their precise depiction often varies, as we have seen. Nonetheless, the role of Gormlaith in particular and the circumstances surrounding Brian's slaying suggest that the same rough outline of the battle lies behind both works. That this description originated in a milieu partisan to Brian seems apparent. It may have been circulated in written form. The Norse calque on Cú Duilig suggested by Sayers points to a learned environment in which some degree of bilingualism prevailed, as do some of the correspondences between Norse and Irish personal names noted by Ó Corráin. Thus 'Kerþjálfaðr' for Irish 'Tairdelbach' (Brian's grandson rather than his foster-son) and 'Kantaraborg' for 'Kankaraborg', the *borg* or fort of Cenn Corad, point to confusion of insular 'c' (Old Norse 'k') and 't'.[277] That written account, in conjunction with numerous oral retellings of the battle, gradually made its way north. Whatever its precise form, however, it certainly differed significantly from the elaborate story of the conflict preserved in the *Cogadh*, as our comparison between the two texts has shown.

It could hardly have been otherwise: the partisan Irish source set up Brian as an illustrious model for his own people and as a reminder to their neighbours of Munster's past – and by implication present – might. To this end, he becomes the triumphant leader of a climactic conflict, overcoming his heathen enemies while being 'martyred' for the cause. By contrast, Brian's provenance is of little interest to the Norse writer; he knows a martyr in the making when he sees one, however, and Brian, the moral and just king, precisely fits this mould. By weaving the Clontarf story into his complex family narrative of the doomed Njáll, he provides a further dramatic example of how, through the actions of rightful rulers, divine justice always prevails.

Darraðarljóð

If the account of the battle in *Njáls saga* has a predominantly optimistic note, the tenor of *Darraðarljóð* 'Dǫrruðr's song', an independent poem of eleven stanzas appended to it, has a very different feel. Cast in the mould of vatic verse, valkyries are presented as weaving a bloody web, a catastrophic encounter in which the Irish are vanquished being alluded to in the process:[278]

> Ok munu Írar
> angr um bíða,
> þat er aldri mun
> ýtum fyrnask.

And Irishmen will experience grief which will never depart from men.

The poet's allegiance, however, is with the victors:[279]

> Þeir munu lýðir
> lǫndum ráða,
> er útskaga
> áðr of byggðu.

Those who previously dwelt on an exposed cape will rule the lands.

> Vel kváðu vér
> um konung ungan
> sigrhljóða fjǫlð,
> syngjum heilar!

We have spoken well about the young king; let us, unscathed, sing a multitude of victory-songs!

As well as the unnamed young king who survives the battle, reference is made to a great king who is destined to die, as well as to an earl (*jarlmaðr*) who is in fact slain.[280] The lack of specific detail in the poem, however, makes it uncertain as to which exact event is being commemorated. The author of *Njáls saga* undoubtedly identified it with Clontarf, stating that

Dǫrruðr's vision of the weaving women that gave rise to the poem happened on the Good Friday morning of the battle.[281]

The indications are that he was correct in doing so, as John Hines has
shown.[282] Thus the young ruler is King Sitric of Dublin, the slain earl, his
ally, Sigurd of Orkney, and the mighty king for whom the norns proclaim
death, none other than Brian. Of concern to the poet is the reason for
Sitric's survival, also a feature of *Cogadh Gáedhel re Gallaibh*, as we have seen.
Not surprisingly, *Darraðarljóð* interprets his escape from death much more
positively than does the Irish text, Sitric being the one the valkyries chose
to protect. Sitric himself or his immediate descendants had most to gain
from this reading of events and Hines's suggestion that the poem may have
come into being in a time and place close to Sitric has much to commend
it.[283]

If so, *Njáls saga* embodies two opposing views of the battle, the prose
presenting it as a triumph for the good and holy Brian, while the more
subdued metrical *Darraðarljóð* recounts a victory for his young Norse opponent. This marked discrepancy has led Russell Poole amongst others to seek
a different context for the work, situating it in the Viking-Irish struggles of
a century earlier and taking the cataclysmic encounter to be the battle of
Dublin fought in 919, in which another Sitric defeated the most powerful
king of Ireland in his day, Niall Glúndub of Uí Néill.[284] The absence of an
earl in other records of the tenth-century encounter is scarcely decisive,[285]
and Poole adduces evidence to show that the poem might also be read as a
commentary on the earlier event. Such is the vagueness of *Darraðarljóð* itself,
however, that any Norse-Irish conflict of note might reasonably be considered as its subject matter. For a thirteenth-century Icelandic writer at any
rate, the feud being described was the battle of Clontarf.

Furthermore, unlike the tenth-century battle of Dublin that constituted
an unambiguous Viking victory,[286] the success of Brian's troops at Clontarf
might be seen to be a much more muted affair. Though they won the day,
their powerful leader was slain and such was the extent of their losses that
only a skeleton host under the king's son, Donnchad, returned home.[287]
Indeed this is the tenor of the account preserved in the eleventh-century
Prophecy of Berchán; both Viking and Irish are worse off in the wake of the
encounter.[288] Moreover, both sides receive some measure of praise, the high-
king Brian being opposed by a gracious, fair one,[289] just as in *Darraðarljóð*
Sitric's contender is 'a mighty king' (*ríkr gramr*).[290] In the eleventh century,
even Brian's followers may have regarded their success as bitter-sweet. In this

climate, it would not have been difficult for a pro-Norse author to attempt to salvage something in defeat, rewriting history in the process. After all, the downfall of Ireland's greatest king did indeed constitute a victory of sorts. One might argue that the emphasis on the 'young king' (*konungr ungr*) in the first place was born out of a desire to whitewash his far from heroic actions on the day and that the overdone protestation that forms part of *Darraðarljóð* could have been read as the elaborate excuse it, at least in part, was.

If this is how the author of *Njáls saga* interpreted the poetic composition, inclusion of it in his complex family narrative would have been far less contradictory than might now appear. In addition, how he employed the poem in his work suggests that, for him, *Darraðarljóð* did not revolve around the simple matter of victory and defeat. The eleven stanzas serve above all as an indicator of the extraordinary nature of the encounter, as made manifest in the valkyries' supernatural weaving of a spear-woven cloth:[291]

Sjá er orpinn vefr
ýta þǫrmum
ok harðkléaðr
hǫfðum manna;
eru dreyrrekin
dǫrr at skǫptum,
járnvarðr yllir,
en ǫrum hrælaðr.

The cloth is wrapped with men's guts and weighted hard with human heads; bloodstained spears are the shafts; ironclad the beam and pegged with arrows.[292]

The process is irreversible, the refrain of *vindum, vindum* 'let us weave, let us weave', with which three consecutive stanzas begin,[293] underlining the certainty of a catastrophic end: 'the death-tales of men will fare through the land' (*munu um lǫnd fara/ læspjǫll*).[294]

The immediately succeeding prose passages add to this sense of Clontarf as a battle apart. Strange occurrences on Good Friday are depicted: at Svínafell in south-east Iceland, a drop of blood appears on a priest's stole; elsewhere in Iceland, at Þváttá in Álftafjörður, also in the south-east, a colleague sees a deep, terrible ocean beside his altar and is unable to say mass. In Orkney, too, Háreki encounters the ghost of Earl Sigurd, riding into a hill with him, never to be seen again.[295] The sequence ends, as it begins, with a poetic vision, attributed this time to Earl Gilli in the Hebrides to whom a man called Herfiðr, returning from Ireland, appeared bearing news of a ferocious battle in which he took part:[296]

Sigurðr fell í dyn vigra;
áðr téði ben bloeða;
Bríann fell ok helt velli.

Sigurd fell in the storm of spears; wounds bled freely; Brian fell but conquered.

It is in conjunction with this other related material that *Darraðarljóð* should be interpreted, suggesting that it is as a comment on the battle, rather than as a mere description of it, that the poem was intended to be read.[297]

In composing his account of the conflict at Clontarf as part of his broader narrative on the family of Njáll, the author of *Njáls saga* had access to an earlier poem, *Darraðarljóð*, which, whatever the original circumstances of its composition, was certainly taken by him to refer to the battle fought outside Dublin in 1014, as we have seen. Its focus on the calamitous nature of the event accorded well with how that writer sought to portray the encounter, even if its sympathies with Sitric, rather than Brian, were at variance with his own. The identification of the eleven stanzas with the Dublin king suggests that they emanate from a milieu different from that of the other material on the battle to which the author had access. It is one that may also be detected in another divinatory poetic composition, the eleventh-century Prophecy of Berchán. A compilatory work, the authors of that Prophecy drew on both Irish and Scottish material in their elaborate versified king-list and it could have been in either territory that the final poem took shape. In this connection, we may note that the prose introduction to *Darraðarljóð* places Dǫrruðr's dream in Caithness, and it concludes with a reference to a similar vision being experienced by Brandr Gneistason on the Faroe Islands,[298] leading Anne Holtsmark to suggest that it was written perhaps in Caithness or Orkney.[299] The poem's lack of detail means that its place of origin cannot be postulated with any certainty, though the Scottish Isles and Orkney in particular may have been central in the transmission of such material northwards, as Michael Chesnutt has claimed.[300] It was at some distance from

Ireland that the somewhat sombre note evident in the two metrical works was also likely to prevail. In the light of these considerations, therefore, it is tempting to speculate, that both Berchán's Prophecy and *Darraðarljóð*, represent the same geographical strand of the Clontarf tradition and one that is at some considerable remove from that preserved in much more triumphant tones in the pair of prose narratives, *Cogadh Gáedhel re Gallaibh* and the saga of Njáll.

Orkneyinga saga

Measured triumphalism, however, is a feature of one text indirectly linking Orkney and Clontarf, *Orkneyinga saga* (The History of the Earls of Orkney), which contains a brief mention of the battle. Composed in Iceland possibly as early as 1200[301] and thus a century or so earlier in date than *Njáls saga*, all the information it contains is also found in the later tale. Focusing on Earl Sigurd, it relates how he went to Ireland to aid King Sitric in his battle against the king of the Irish (*Írakonungr*), Brian. The date of the battle, Good Friday, is specified, though its year, the fifth year after the battle of Svöld that was fought in 1000, is incorrectly given. The outcome is succinctly expressed: 'King Sitric fled; King Brian fell in victory and triumph' (*Sigtryggr konungr flýði; Brjánn konungr fell með sigri ok gagni*).[302]

A passing reference made to the earl's altercation concerning a battle standard is the only detail of note preserved in the text: 'no-one would carry the raven-banner, so the earl himself did and fell there' (*þá varð engi til at bera hrafnsmerkit, ok bar jarl sjálfr ok fell þar*). The magical banner in question was made by Sigurd's mother, an Irish sorceress (*margkunnig*) called Ethne (Norse Eðna) daughter of Cerball (Norse Kjarvalr), who can be identified with Cerball mac Dúnlainge, hero of the Fragmentary Annals. Of its properties, she is made to claim in an earlier passage 'that it will bring victory to the one before whom it is carried, but death to the one who carries it' (*at sigrsælt myni verða þeim, er fyrir er borit, en banvænt þeim, er berr*).[303] This explains the more elaborate account of an altercation concerning the earl's banner on the battlefield preserved in *Njáls saga* alone. After two of his standard bearers had been killed, Sigurd ordered Þorsteinn Hallsson to take the banner, but the latter is warned by Ámundi the White of the lethal consequences of the action. Taunted by Hrafn the Red (*"Ber þú sjálfr fjanda þinn"* "Carry your own fiend yourself"), the earl stuffs it under his clothing and is killed, as mentioned in passing above.[304] That the audience of *Njáls saga* would have been familiar with the supernatural nature of the banner must, therefore, be assumed. Whether the author was necessarily drawing his information specifically from *Orkneyinga saga*, as Benjamin Hudson has proposed,[305] is another matter. The Clontarf episode, as told in *Orkneyinga saga*, is simply too brief to enable any firm conclusions on the matter to be drawn.

Þorsteins saga Síðu-Hallssonar

The supernatural standard also features in another Norse account of the Clontarf conflict, preserved in the fourteenth-century narrative, *Þorsteins saga Síðu-Hallssonar* (Þorsteinn Síðu-Hallsson's saga).[306] In it Þorsteinn is not dependent on anyone else to protect him from the banner, retorting when asked by his commander, Sigurd, to bear it, "'carry your own crow, Earl!'" (*"ber sjálfr krák þinn, jarl!"*). This the Orkney man does, in a move reminiscent of *Njáls saga*, tucking it into his clothes.[307] The verbal correspondences between the two accounts are such as to suggest that *Þorsteins saga* is drawing on the earlier text, and *Njáls saga* is in fact mentioned by name in the younger work directly before events at Clontarf are related.[308]

Notwithstanding this, there are differences between the two versions suggesting additional access to another tradition: thus, on concealment of his banner, Sigurd is not immediately killed, according to *Þorsteins saga*, but is addressed by a celestial voice advising him that, if he wants victory, 'let him make for Dumazbakki with his men' (*þá sæki hann á Dumazbakka með lið sitt*).[309] Often explained as a compound of Irish *duma* 'mound' or *dumach* 'sandbank' and the Norse doublet *bakki* 'bank', the mysterious Dumazbakki represented the relative safety of the tidal flats or river bank, it has sometimes been claimed.[310] Wherever precisely is envisaged, Sigurd appears not to retreat there, for he was killed 'in that attack' (*í þeiri atlǫgu*), presumably at Clontarf.[311] In addition the disembowelment of Brodar avenging Brian's death is carried out not by Úlfr Hræða, the king's brother, as in *Njáls saga*, but by Óspakr. When the focus returns to Þorsteinn, however, echoes of *Njáls saga* reappear: the young twenty-year-old standing motionless near an unnamed wood in the aftermath of the battle displays the same laconic humour he is made to exhibit in the earlier tale, bemoaning the fact that he

1 Brian Boru, as he
was depicted by a
later artist.

2 An imaginative portrayal of Brian Boru at the battle of Clontarf (WH Holbrooke).

3 Opening page of a twelfth-century literary account of Brian Boru's life, *Cogadh Gáedhel re Gallaibh* (The Viking-Irish Conflict) from the Book of Leinster (Trinity College Dublin, manuscript 1339, p.309a).

4 The round tower at Inis Celtra (Holy Island), Co. Clare. Brian Boru had his brother, Marcán, appointed as abbot there; he also held office in a number of other monasteries.

5 The early church at Killaloe, Co. Clare.

6 A stone slab from Killaloe, Co. Clare, which contains a runic inscription on one side (shown) and an ogam inscription on the other side.

7 How Dublin might have looked in Brian Boru's time. This reconstruction of about the year 1000 is based on the evidence of archaeological excavations there.

8*a* Cashel, Co. Tipperary, the seat of Munster kingship. It was donated to the Church by Muirchertach Ua Briain, Brian Boru's great-grandson in 1101.

8*b* Cashel, Co. Tipperary and surrounding countryside.

9 Tenth-century, Wooden Gaming Board, Ballinderry, Co. Westmeath; gaming pieces belonging to boards like this have been discovered in excavations of Viking Dublin. A dispute over a game such as this, between Brian Boru's son, Murchad, and the Leinster king, Máel Mórda, is said to have been one of the factors leading to the Battle of Clontarf, according to the twelfth-century literary narrative, *Cogadh Gáedhel re Gallaibh* (The Viking-Irish Conflict).

10 Ninth-century Viking sword, Ballinderry, Co. Westmeath, carrying the name of its maker, Ulfbehrt, and originating in the Rhineland. Swords like these were the principal weapon of Vikings.

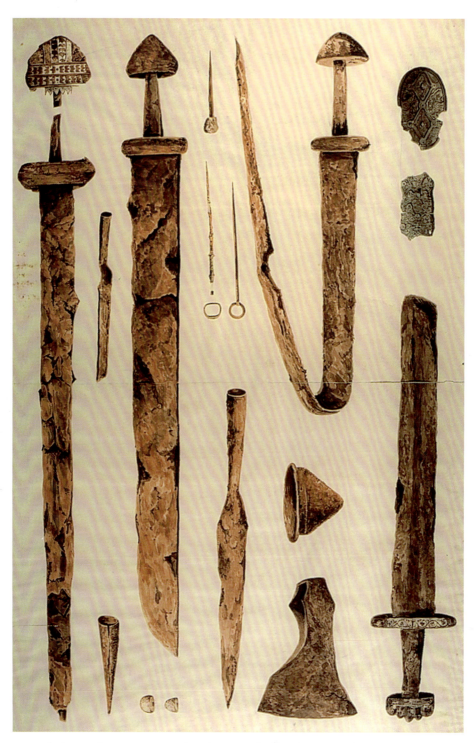

11 A nineteenth-century watercolour by James Plunkett depicting Viking weapons and other artefacts from the Viking cemeteries at Kilmainham and Islandbridge, Co. Dublin.

12 Tenth- and eleventh-century silver ornaments, including bossed penannular and thistle brooches, produced from coins which had been melted down and indicative of increased access to important trade-routes in the wake of the arrival of the Vikings.

Top, left: 13 Coin of King Sitric Silkenbeard, Brian Boru's son-in-law; he established the first mint in Ireland.

Middle: 14 Wooden toy Viking ship, found at Winetavern St, Dublin, a replica of a Viking longboat.

Bottom: 15 The surviving parts of the Viking ship, Skuldelev 2, as it is exhibited in the Viking Ship Museum, Roskilde, Denmark. This enormous ship (30 metres in length and about 4 metres wide) was built in Dublin around the year 1040.

16a The reconstruction of Skuldelev 2, 'The Sea Stallion of Glendalough', under sail.

16b The reconstruction of Skuldelev 2, 'The Sea Stallion of Glendalough', under sail.

17 An imaginative portrayal of the battle of Clontarf (WH Holbrooke).

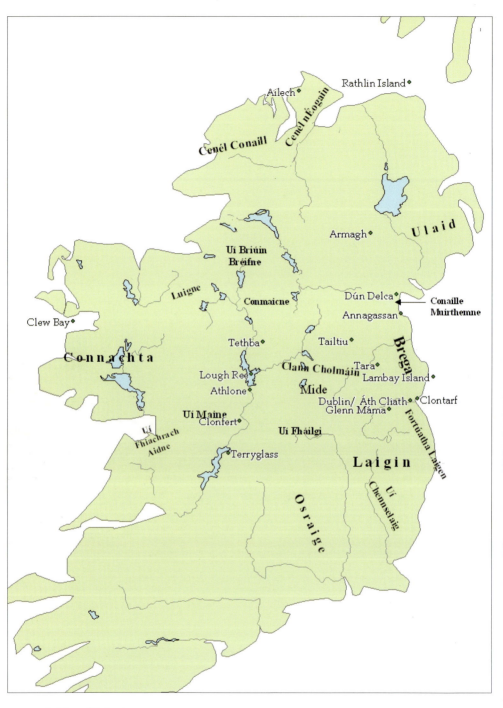

18 Map of Ireland.

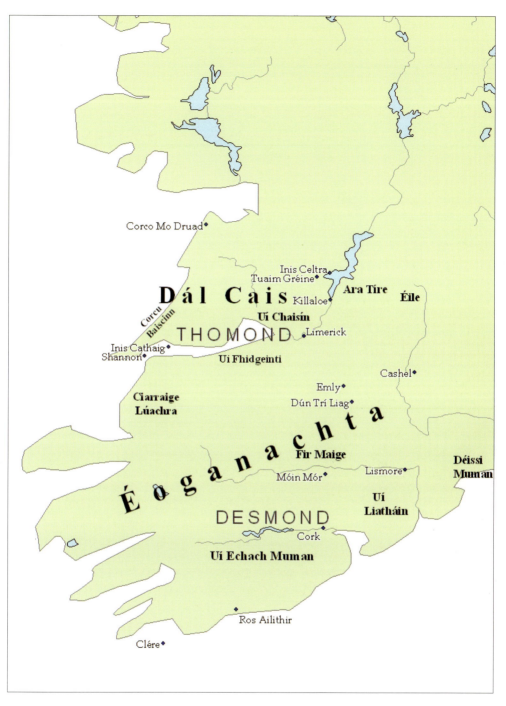

19 Map of Munster.

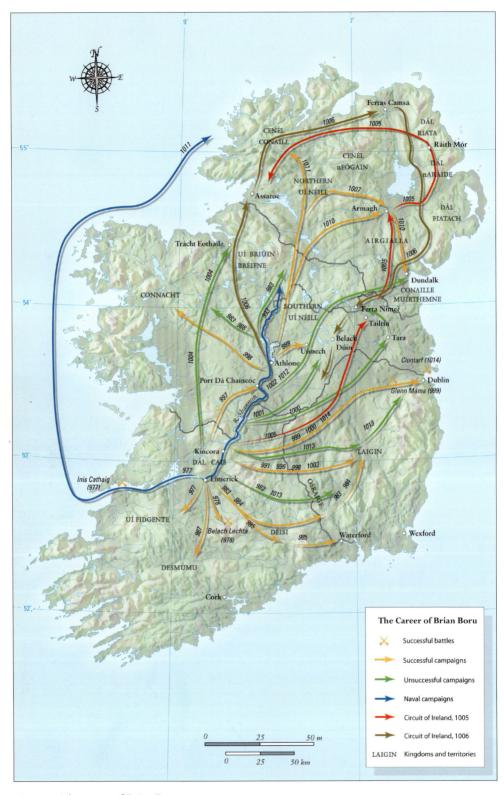

The Career of Brian Boru

✗   Successful battles

→   Successful campaigns

→   Unsuccessful campaigns

→   Naval campaigns

→   Circuit of Ireland, 1005

→   Circuit of Ireland, 1006

LAIGIN   Kingdoms and territories

20 The career of Brian Boru.

cannot get home tonight. Moreover, in *Þorsteins saga*, too, his quick retort spares him.[312] While he is not heard of again in the earlier text, according to his own saga, he returns to the Orkneys and goes from there to Norway, returning to Iceland after a sojourn abroad of three years.[313]

By the time the author of *Þorsteins saga* was writing, the battle of Clontarf had become well known and not just in the west (i.e. Ireland and Britain), as he suggests, but in the Scandinavian world as well. Its fame is attributed by him to the large number of participants therein and to the many (unspecified) events of importance that happened there.[314] The popularity of *Njáls saga*, to which he certainly had access, also had a role to play in the growing fame of *Brjánsorrosta* 'Brian's battle', as it came to be known.[315] It is as such referred to in Snorri Sturluson's *Óláfs saga helga* in *Heimskringla*, in a passing reference to Earl Sigurd's death at Clontarf.[316] In Norse writing, therefore, the battle has a long literary history, as our examination of the various, often interlinked sources concerning it has shown. The earliest accounts undoubtedly emanated in Ireland, travelling from there to the Hebrides, the Orkneys and beyond, the Irish battle becoming less localised in the process. *Írakonungr* ('king of the Irish') Brian may have been, but his Norse incarnation, *Brjánn*, was the mighty monarch to have fought against if one's descendants wanted stories to tell. Additionally, transcending all boundaries, he came to symbolise proper Christian kingship, a righteous ruler for an ever-changing age. Clontarf was essential to the evolution of our king.

Literature and History Surveyed

Annalistic accounts of the battle, written in all likelihood before some of those wounded had fully recovered, show clear signs of revisionism, as we have seen. Many of those self-same compilations served as source material for other authors whose imaginative outpourings were not in any sense constrained by the form and content of a chronicle page. With specific stories to tell and particular personages to whom to pander, a series of often interlinked narratives came into being, forming a kaleidoscopic Clontarf-collage that alters depending on the light. Analysis of the perspective of each artist is crucial in any attempt to make of the colourful conflation a functional frieze.

Its first image might be that of Berchán, the 'prophet' to whom four short stanzas on the battle are ascribed, written not long after the actual event. Their focus is undoubtedly Brian, the ruler being commemorated in this section of his elaborate king-list, yet the note he strikes is realistic: this was a conflict that both Viking and Irish lost. His fellow 'prophet', whose battle-picture is painted in the Norse poem *Darraðarljóð*, stands closer to his chosen subject, the Dublin king, Sitric, than Berchán does to the latter's opponent, Brian. Nonetheless, he, too, depicts grief on both sides; the calamitous nature of the account is underlined. It was this that may have drawn the author of *Njáls saga* to the work, since Dǫrruðr's vision forms part of a series of interlinked incidents in his Clontarf narrative designed to mark it out as a battle apart. Brian (Brjánn), not Sitric, is his hero, though as a righteous and pious ruler martyred in death for his contribution to the Christian cause. In this way, he is perceptibly different from his heathen-hating counterpart, Brian, of *Cogadh Gáedhel re Gallaibh*, whose war is similarly just but whose opponents are not merely pagan but Viking, thus imbuing the text with a xenophobic slant. It was as saviour of the Irish more than of the 'holy Roman Empire' that Brian's twelfth-century descendents venerated and basked in the glory of their very own saint.

Their phenomenal success is apparent, as the later celebration of Brian's feast-day attests.[317] Clontarf, according to the *Cogadh*, soon acquired canonical status, as later retellings of the battle reveal.[318] What began with 'a great battle' (*cocad mór*) between Brian at the head of a host from Munster and southern Connacht and a combined force of Leinstermen and the Dublin Norse was transformed into the triumph of Christianity over heathendom and of the Irish against the Vikings of the western and northern world. That Brian himself was killed there is incontrovertible, but his slayer is not identified in all the chronicle accounts. The presence of Máel Mórda, king of Leinster, as one of Brian's chief opponents also seems assured; the role played by the Dublin king, Sitric, in the encounter is far from clear. That he obviously survived – if indeed he did partake – caused a certain embarrassment to literary authors obliged to provide an explanation for this state of affairs. Yet his complete absence from the historical record is worthy of note. The name of Brian's opposing ally, Máel Sechnaill, by contrast, does occur in one list of participants; as Brian's successor as Ireland's greatest king, the midland ruler stood to gain most from the demise of his Munster rival. His support would surely have been more conditional than real as the *Cogadh* indeed intimates, ascribing to him treacherous motives whilst in the fray.

In this, poetic licence may have a part to play, as it did in the composition of the litany of overseas kinsmen who allegedly came to assist the Dublin-Leinster alliance. How large the roll-call of the dead may in reality have been is impossible to say.

If those present on the actual battlefield cannot always be precisely determined, we can be reasonably sure about where the battle took place. Describing similar terrain, both Irish and Norse sources indicate that the main fighting took place on the north side of Dublin Bay and that the rising tide brought havoc in its wake. Termed the battle of Mag nElta in a number of sources, the plain in which Clontarf was situated, as *cath torach Tarbchluana* and the like, it gradually came to be universally known. That it was a spring encounter is likely, Brian returning to complete unfinished business that had been interrupted by winter weather. Its association with Good Friday, on the other hand, is perhaps best viewed as part of the beatification of Brian that led to his depiction as a warrior at prayer. Old age rather than piety may have been the real reason for his inactivity on the battlefield. As a martyr in the making, however, the parallel with Christ presented itself and is a common feature of Irish and Norse sources.

That the two linguistic traditions are intertwined is apparent even if the precise relationship between the various narratives cannot always be established. Nonetheless, common elements can be perceived. As written accounts of Brian's battle circulated, often in bilingual company, oral versions continued to be told. While oral tales permeated cultural boundaries in various ways, the literary texts were most likely transported by ecclesiastical routes, as has previously been claimed. For Clontarf's allure was enduring: an important battle in its time, it soon had added significance bestowed on it by imaginative authors who appropriated it for various reasons and in all kinds of ways. It was as Brian's battle, however, that it acquired its fame.

'The Like of Brian'?: Succeeding Generations

Brian's descendants stood to gain most from their forefather's glorification and their touch is palpable in various ways on his literary presentation, as we have seen. Casting him as their eponymous ancestor, Uí Briain (descendants of Brian), as they became known, lived comfortably in his significant shadow, wishing that their contemporary leaders could be 'the like of Brian' (*samhail Briain*).[1]

Donnchad mac Briain

Brian's eldest son and successor, Donnchad, did not live up to the billing. Even his role in the battle that became so intimately associated with his father's name is ambiguous. Not mentioned in connection with the Clontarf encounter in annalistic accounts, later narrative sources claim that he was sent by his father to attack Leinster as preparations for the conflict were under way, implying that he was not actually involved in the fray.[2] Brian himself assumes that his son will survive the encounter, according to *Cogadh*

Gáedhel re Gallaibh, since it is Donnchad who is to implement the terms of the great king's will.[3] This he does, organising Brian's transposition to Armagh for burial. He was also involved in burying the dead on the battle-field, on which occasion he taunted the Dublin Norse by slaughtering their oxen in front of their own eyes. Afraid of rising to the challenge, 'the Vikings refused battle for fear of Donnchad and the Dál Cais' (*ro eimgedar na Goill an cath ar eccla Donnchaidh ocus Dal cCais*).[4]

The bravery of the Munster men is similarly highlighted in a subsequent encounter with the men of Desmond, who demand hostages of Donnchad as his men are recovering from the Clontarf fight. Rather than submit to their neighbours, the wounded and the maimed arose and 'stuffed moss into their wounds and seized their swords and weapons' (*ro chuiredar caonnach ina ccréchtaibh ocus do ghabhadar a ccloidhmhe ocus a n-armu archena*).[5] As the new leader of this courageous group, Donnchad's glory is enhanced. He it is who secures stakes for the injured against which they might rest and thus remain standing against the Osraige who challenge the Munstermen to battle on their journey homewards.[6] According to this portrayal, however, it is from his association with such heroes that his significance primarily stems. The narrative in question, *Cogadh Gáedhel re Gallaibh*, was composed almost a century after Clontarf, as we have seen. It was produced at the behest of Muirchertach, the ruling Ua Briain at the time, who was not a direct descendant of Donnchad, but rather of his half-brother, Tadc, whom Donnchad had slain by the Éile in 1023.[7] That the author may not have been favourably disposed towards Brian's eldest son is possible; in actual fact, however, his presentation therein is more sympathetic than in other sources in which his father's wish that Murchad, rather than Donnchad, succeed him is made explicit.[8]

In comparison with Brian's successful reign, Donnchad's tenure as king was certainly inauspicious.[9] His succession appears to have been contested, since he fought against and was defeated by his half-brother, Tadc, in the same year as the battle of Clontarf. The people of Ara on the boundary between Limerick and Tipperary were allied with Donnchad on this occasion, their king, Ruaidrí ua Donnacáin, being slain.[10] Support from other Munster territories was not forthcoming; indeed Donnchad had killed Cathal, king of Uí Echach, in the same year.[11] One year later, Cathal's father, Domnall, sought to avenge his son's slaying but he, too, was killed by Donnchad mac Briain.[12] According to some annalistic sources, he and Tadc stood side by side on this occasion.[13] If so, their co-operation was short-lived: a member of the Dál Cais segment of Uí Chaisín, whom John Ryan speculated may have been acting at Tadc's behest, made an attempt on Donnchad's life in 1019, cutting off his right hand with a sword.[14] Whoever was the instigator of the incident, Donnchad certainly used henchmen himself when he had his brother murdered by the Éile in 1023, *Chronicum Scotorum* specifying that the treacherous murder was 'at the request of Donnchad mac Briain' (*iar na eráil do Donnchadh mac Briain*).[15] Almost a decade after Clontarf, Brian's son may have hoped to have dispelled internal opposition to his rule by means of this dramatic act. In actual fact, however, he merely silenced it for a period, Tadc's son, Tairdelbach, taking the ultimate revenge some forty years later by deposing his uncle.[16]

Not that those forty years were without their difficulties for Donnchad, despite the fact that Máel Sechnaill mac Domnaill, his father's main rival and most powerful king in Ireland after Brian's death, died about the time that Brian's son had his brother slain.[17] The Munster compilation, the Annals of Inisfallen, suggests that Donnchad had in fact challenged the midland king on a hosting to Lough Ree a number of years previously 'and he plundered Inis Clothrand and Inis Bó Finne and brought away the boats of Máel Sechnaill and of the northern part of Ireland [Leth Cuind]' (*coro ort Inis Clothrand ocus Inis Bó Finne ocus co tuc ethru Mail Shechnaill ocus Lethe Cuind*).[18] The southern king had opponents closer to home, however, his base at Killaloe being plundered by the men of Connacht in precisely the same year.[19] Moreover Donnchad formed part of Máel Sechnaill's retinue when the Mide ruler acquired the hostages of the Connachta in 1020, a year after the Munster king had been wounded by a kinsman.[20]

Yet Máel Sechnaill's death in 1022 could have given him a temporary lease of life. In 1026, at what may well have been the height of his power, he succeeded in taking the hostages of Mide and Brega as well as of the Dublin Norse, Leinster and Osraige.[21] The Annals of Inisfallen claim that he camped at Áth Cliath without opposition,[22] a return visit twelve years after the battle of Clontarf. Furthermore, the king of Osraige, together with the abbot of Armagh, were at his headquarters in Cenn Corad later in the same year, in recognition perhaps of Donnchad's burgeoning authority.[23] His growing power is also reflected in the description of him as 'king of Ireland' in an inscription on the shrine of the Stowe Missal that Pádraig Ó Riain, on the evidence of this political activity, has dated to around the same time.[24]

His inroads into Osraige were not looked upon favourably by his main Munster rival, the Éoganacht ruler, Mac Raith mac Donnchada, commemorated as 'king of Cashel' on the same shrine, who united with the Osraige king to attack some of Donnchad's retinue when he was on a hosting in Osraige the following year in 1027.[25] Donnchad mac Gilla Pátraic, ruler of Osraige in this period, is unlikely to have been subservient to an Éoganacht master either, concerned as he was with forging for himself his own significant niche. In 1033 he assumed the kingship of Leinster,[26] having dealt a blow to Donnchad two years previously by killing his *rechtaire* (steward) at Dún na Sciath, near Cashel. Nor did the Munster ruler succeed in avenging the insult: despite acquiring booty and cattle on a hosting to Osraige immediately afterwards, Donnchad mac Briain suffered considerable losses of men: 'and a slaughter was inflicted three times on the men of Munster there' (*coro lad ár for Mumain fo thrí and*).[27] He ravaged Osraige three years later and defeated the men of Bréifne at Clonfert in 1035.[28] These successes apart, however, mac Gilla Pátraic was the more powerful ruler down to his death in 1039.[29]

The demise of mac Gilla Pátraic was not to provide Donnchad with an opportunity to extend his dominion since he was beset by attacks by Osraige's allies, the Éoganachta. The Éoganacht-Osraige combination struck in 1043, plundering Donnchad's strategic fort at Dún na Sciath, though their success may have been limited and they were defeated by a kinsman, Carthach mac Sáerbrethaig.[30] This is likely to indicate internal dissension among the Éoganachta rather than support of one branch for Brian's son, particularly as Carthach himself was slain by Dál Cais two years later.[31] Not in control in his own Munster territory, Donnchad was in no position to ward off incursions by his near neighbours to the north, the Connachta, nor by a rejuvenated Leinster under their ambitious ruler, Diarmait mac Maíl na mBó.

Donnchad made intermittent advances: in 1048, for example, he acquired the hostages of Leinster and subdued the Dublin Norse.[32] The Leinster ruler may have retaliated by plundering the Déssi;[33] if so, Donnchad returned the following year to claim the hostages of both Leinster and Osraige.[34] His success was short-lived: the following year, Áed Ua Conchobair, king of Connacht, killed Domnall Bán, Donnchad's son, and in a very public display of his authority destroyed *bile Maige Adair*, the sacred tree of Dál Cais.[35] Worse was to come: the Connachta attacked again in 1053, the Inisfallen annalist pronouncing the encounter 'a great war' (*cocad mór*), while Donnchad was also besieged by his own nephew, Tairdelbach, son of the murdered Tadc.[36] He managed to fight back by allying with

Conchobar Ua Maíl Shechnaill of Mide and marching into the newly acquired Dublin territory of Diarmait mac Maíl na mBó to seize hostages.[37] In the long run, however, he was powerless to withstand frequent assaults from Leinster and Connacht, more often than not working in tandem with his wily kinsman, Tairdelbach. A raid by the king of Connacht into Donnchad's North Munster base in 1054 was followed both by an attack by Tairdelbach in the same territory and by a more penetrating assault by Leinster, Osraige and the Norse of Dublin, as far south as Emly and Dún Trí Liag.[38] Tairdelbach himself led a similar alliance, alongside mac Maíl na mBó, four years later 'to plunder Brian's son' (do insaigid ar mc. mBriain), Limerick being burned in the process in what some sources call the battle of Sliab Crot.[39]

Donnchad was to all intents and purposes now a spent force and was helpless to prevent the destruction of three of Munster's forts by mac Maíl na mBó the following year in 1059.[40] He submitted to the Connacht king,[41] but one year later turned instead to the Leinster ruler 'and he gave him treasure and much wealth' (co tuc seoit ocus maine imda dó).[42] None too pleased the western ruler, Áed Ua Conchobair, plundered the monastery of Killaloe and Donnchad's homestead, Cenn Corad.[43] Donnchad could not rely on the support of his new master either, since the latter, alongside Tairdelbach ua Briain, killed some of Donnchad's retinue in Munster a year later.[44] This was the prelude to a much more substantial defeat by the same allied pair in 1063, as a result of which Donnchad appears to have been deposed.[45] Brian's son retired to Rome where he died the following year.[46]

Thus, half a century after the battle of Clontarf, a descendant of Brian Boru was king of Munster but with the support of an ambitious outsider, the Leinster ruler, Diarmait mac Maíl na mBó, whose nurturing of Tairdelbach was designed to further his own political ends. His involvement in southern affairs was made possible by dissension within Brian's own dynasty and this kin rivalry sets Donnchad's reign apart from that of his father whose control over his own family was absolute. In other ways, Brian's son had learnt much from his immediate ancestor. Brian Boru drew on the support of the Vikings of Waterford at various points during his career[47] and, perhaps as a result of this, he forged an alliance with the sons of Haraldr of the Isles, as indicated by a reference to 'a great naval expedition of the Haraldssons' (muirfholud mór na macc nArailt) at Waterford in 984 when hostages with Brian were exchanged.[48] According to Colmán Etchingham this union endured, since Ragnall, son of Guðrøðr Haraldsson, died in Munster in 1004,

evidently seeking the protection of the Munster king.[49] Donnchad actively
pursued a similar policy. His marriage in 1032 to 'Ragnall's daughter' (*ingen
Regnaild*)[50] may represent a re-establishment of the link with Waterford, if his
wife was the daughter of the king there, Ragnall ua Ímair. This Ragnall was
killed in Dublin by Donnchad's uterine brother, Sitric mac Amlaíb, three
years later.[51] If, however, her father was the grandson of Haraldr of the Isles
who died in Munster in 1004 when she was presumably a very young child,
as Etchingham has speculated, the marital alliance attests to even greater
ambition on the part of Donnchad. His eyes, like those of his father before
him, would have been firmly fixed upon the Irish Sea.[52] In support of this
interpretation is Donnchad's association with Echmarcach mac Ragnaill,
sometime ruler of Dublin until his deposition in 1052 by Diarmait mac
Maíl na mBó.[53] Unlikely to be connected with Waterford, this king both of
Man and of the Rhinns of Galloway was most probably a son of Ragnall,
son of Gothraid (Norse Guðrøðr).[54] The enemy he and Donnchad mac
Briain shared ultimately subjugated them both and they went together on
pilgrimage to Rome where, according to the eleventh-century chronicler
Marianus Scotus, the two men died.[55]

In his association with particular groups of Vikings, therefore, Donnchad's
approach owed much to his father. Other elements of Brian's political
philosophy are also detectable in his eldest son's career. Acute awareness of
the continuing significance of the church of Armagh is reflected in the visit
paid to Donnchad by Amalgaid, abbot of Armagh, 'with his venerable clerics' (*cona sruithib*) in 1026.[56] It was an occasion of which his church-focused
father would have been proud. And just as Brian cleverly manipulated the
Church for his own purposes, so too may Donnchad's promulgation of
'a law and ordinance … such as was not enacted in Ireland from Patrick's time'
(*cáin ocus rechtge … innas na dernad ó ré Patraicc i nHérind*) have been designed to
bolster his own authority. The enhanced sense of law and order ensuing from
the prohibition of the *cáin* in question of certain activities on Sundays[57] would
have created the impression of a king in complete control.[58]

In actual fact, however, Donnchad's influence was constantly waver-
ing, despite recourse to the usual political methods to keep it on track.
Marital arrangements, for example, were intertwined with military matters.
His marriage to Gormlaith, daughter of Ua Donnacáin, king of Ara Tíre[59]
reflects perhaps a period of close co-operation with his near Munster neighbours who supported him for a time in his struggle against his half-brother,
Tadc.[60] In this way is the union resonant of Brian's first marriage to the

daughter of his close neighbour, Eiden, of Uí Fhiachrach Aidni, in southern Connacht. Nor did the partnerships of Brian's daughters remain aloof from political manoeuvring, that of Sláine to Sitric of Dublin being designed to cement an alliance that the Munster king may have hoped would endure. In a similar spirit might Donnchad have offered his daughter, Derbforgaill, in marriage to Diarmait mac Maíl na mBó.[61] The union thereby forged was similarly ineffectual and failed to prevent the subsequent meshing of the interests of the Leinster king with those of Donnchad's internal rival, Tairdelbach.

Ever-shifting patterns formed the nature of the political fabric and on this variegated material Brian's son, too, made his mark. A short-lived alliance with Ua Maíl Shechnaill, king of Mide, in 1053 was designed to undermine Leinster's hold on Dublin, as a result of which Donnchad secured Diarmait mac Maíl na mBó's hostages for a time.[62] In the end, however, the power base on which Brian's son might confidently rely was not sufficiently secure to enable him to consolidate any gains. Nor did it enable him to withstand simultaneous attacks by an ambitious Ua Conchobair king immediately to the north and a skilful Leinster ruler who, by supporting Donnchad's nephew, had identified the crucial chink in his armour. Donnchad's ultimate undoing was the enemy within.

Tairdelbach ua Briain

The enemy in question, Donnchad's nephew, Tairdelbach, was undoubtedly more successful than his uncle, not least in the fact that it was his descendants who were to dominate the Uí Briain ruling line for some time. As a result, their version of history was propagated and it may be that Donnchad's deeds were deliberately downplayed.[63] The contemporary Munster record preserved in the Annals of Inisfallen notes a number of his achievements, but Tairdelbach's persistent attacks on him are also afforded space.[64] As Donnchad's son, Murchad, is described as *rigdamna Herend* 'royal heir of Ireland' and as *mac ríg Hérend* 'son of the king of Ireland' when he was killed by the men of Tethba in 1068, it may be that this Munster compilation is following a carefully neutral line.[65] Murchad's demise five years into Tairdelbach's reign ensured that the new king of Munster, unlike his predecessor, did not have to contend with internal opposition for long.

His Leinster master retained some measure of control: Tairdelbach received treasures from him, including Brian Boru's sword and the standard of Edward the Confessor, in the year of Murchad's death.[66] Two years later, in 1070, however, the Munster king seized Leinster hostages.[67] In the same year he acquired the submission of the Osraige ruler,[68] an audacious act if performed without the agreement of Diarmait. There is no indication of dissension between the two rulers the following year, Tairdelbach dutifully handing over Leinster and Mide hostages to Diarmait and accompanying the Leinster king on a hosting in Munster.[69] Notwithstanding this, the Annals of Inisfallen claim that Tairdelbach did in fact bite the hand that fed him in 1072, allying with Conchobar Ua Maíl Shechnaill of Mide against Diarmait in the battle of Odba in which the Leinster king was slain.[70] Other sources name the Mide ruler as the sole perpetrator.[71]

Whether Tairdelbach was involved or not in his maker's demise, he moved quickly to assert his authority in Diarmait's domain, burning the latter's home territory of Uí Chennselaig and securing the hostages of the men of Leinster and Osraige in the year of Diarmait's death. Moreover, the albeit biased chronicle, the Annals of Inisfallen, claims that Mide and the Norse of Dublin also submitted to him 'and they gave recognition and the high-kingship to Tairdelbach' (*co tucsat attitin ocus ardrige do Thairdelbach*).[72] If so, the Munster king had already achieved a position approximating that secured by his grandfather more than twenty years into his kingship when, as a result of an agreement with Máel Sechnaill of Mide, Brian became king of Ireland's southern half (Leth Moga).[73]

Victory may not have come quite so easily as the Munster source suggests, however, since Tairdelbach was forced to march into Mide, Gailenga and Brega the following year, though with some success since 'the hostages of the men of Mide came to him then to his house' (*geill fer Mide iar sein do thorachtain dó coa thech*).[74] Despite the claim of the Munster annalist that the Norse had bestowed the kingship of Dublin (*ríge Átha Cliath*) upon Tairdelbach in 1072, he was forced to banish its ruler, Gofraid ua Ragnaill, three years later, after which the grandson of his old master, Diarmait, became king.[75] Donnchadh Ó Corráin has suggested that the appointment of the latter was instigated by the Munster king, in a skilful attempt to keep Leinster divided between Diarmait's kinsmen and those of his brother, Domnall Remar, who were ruling the home territory of Uí Chennselaig.[76] If so, Domnall's death later that year necessitated a change of plan and Tairdelbach granted the kingship to his own able son, Muirchertach, in his stead.[77] That Dublin became an

Uí Briain centre is indicated by the renewed submission of the men of Mide to Tairdelbach there some four years after his son had assumed control.[78]

If Tairdelbach's authority in the eastern part of Ireland was relatively secure, his influence in Connacht was much less so, despite employment of similar tactics in both areas. As the king of Uí Chennselaig was taken prisoner in a show of might by the Munster ruler in 1077,[79] his western number, Ruaidrí Ua Conchobair, had one year earlier suffered the same fate.[80] The action had the desired effect since the Connacht ruler submitted to Tairdelbach in his house.[81] Three years later, the Munster king marched against Ua Conchobair once more, plundering the islands in Clew Bay (Inis Mod).[82] As the western leader had previously slain a rival for the kingship, Áed Ua Flaithbertaig, Tairdelbach may have been attempting to limit Ua Conchobair's control.[83]

Ua Conchobair's main contender, however, was his increasingly powerful midland neighbour, Donnchad Ua Ruairc, whose focus was directed eastwards towards Mide as well as westwards. The Munster king was not slow to react, reasserting his authority over the eastern regions in 1080 'and he brought Ua Maíl Shechnaill, king of Mide, with him to Limerick' (co tuc lais Hua Mail Shechnaill, ríg Mide, co Luimnech).[84] In addition Tairdelbach had made some advances in the north, since the king of the Ulaid, Donn Sléibe Ua hEochada, came southwards 'and reached Tairdelbach ua Briain's house' (co toracht tech Tairdelbaich Hui Briain) after his re-accession to the kingship in 1081.[85] That he and Tairdelbach were still allies two years later is suggested by the enforced drowning in Limerick of Donn Sléibe's deposer, Áed Meránach.[86] None of this can have pleased Ua Ruairc, who issued a challenge to the Munster ruler by marching with the forces of eastern Connacht, Cairpre and Gailenga into Leinster in 1084, according to some sources.[87] Uí Briain were ready, Tairdelbach's son, Muirchertach, at the head of a host of the men of Munster, Leinster and Dublin, defeating him decisively at Móin Cruinneóige. Ua Ruairc himself was slain, alongside members of Tairdelbach's estranged kin, grandchildren of his despised uncle, Donnchad, who had established themselves far from the remit of their relative's power in Telach Óc, taking this opportunity to seek to settle an old score.[88]

Twenty-one years after his assumption of the kingship, the encounter at Móin Cruinneóige did indeed signal Tairdelbach's coming of age, marking him out as Ireland's greatest king. As his ageing grandfather took a back seat at the battle of Clontarf, so too did Tairdelbach, who was in his sixties or older in 1084, refrain from active participation in the conflict, his son, Muirchertach, assuming military control. The older ua Briain did not enjoy his success for long: struck down by a mysterious illness the following year,[89] he died in 1086, universally acclaimed as king of Ireland (*rí Érend*)[90] and as secure in this position as Brian was three-quarters of a century or so earlier. In many ways Tairdelbach was his grandfather's mirror-image, having absolute control in Munster but, unlike his ancestor, with a solid grip on Leinster, Brian wielding greater authority in Connacht than his descendant. Neither ruler acquired a firm footing in the north, though Tairdelbach's governance of Dublin in the person of his son, Muirchertach, arguably gave him the edge his grandfather never had, providing him with a pivotal base from which to venture forth. Control of the Norse town brought with it access to Dublin's insular dominions. As Seán Duffy has noted, it can hardly be coincidence that two of Brian's grandsons were killed in the Isle of Man, alongside Sitric mac Amlaíb, in 1073, a year after Tairdelbach assumed authority in Dublin:[91] Uí Briain sights were set further afield.

Tairdelbach's outward focus is similarly evident in extant correspondence between him and successive archbishops of Canterbury – Lanfranc and Anselm – as well as Pope Gregory VII.[92] In the eyes of these foreign ecclesiastics, it was he who was 'king of Ireland', Lanfranc addressing him as *magnifico Hibernie regi Terdeluaco*,[93] and it was to him they turned to garner support for the burgeoning cause of ecclesiastical reform. That the Munster ruler, like his grandfather and uncle before him, took a keen and opportune interest in Church politics can be deduced from his involvement in the appointment of Gilla Pátraic and Donngus Ua hAingli as bishops of Dublin in 1074 and 1085 respectively, both of whose connections were with English monasteries.[94] As Benjamin Hudson has noted, Lanfranc was closely associated with William the Conqueror, with whom Tairdelbach may also have had links. Both had a shared interest in encouraging trade across the Irish Sea and there are indications that they were successful in this.[95] In this connection, we may note the visitation to Tairdelbach in 1079 by a group of five Jews who may have had commercial interests: for whatever reason they and their gifts were repudiated; in the cryptic words of the Munster annalist, 'they were sent back again across the sea' (*a ndíchor doridisi dar muir*).[96]

Muirchertach Ua Briain

Whether this was an error of judgement, as has been speculated, is another matter. In the course of a long and active political career, however, Tairdelbach demonstrated skill and sagacity, regaining for Munster the pre-eminent position it had enjoyed during his grandfather's rule. If a mistake was made, it was in his failure to ensure the succession of his chosen son, Muirchertach.[97] Instead internal rivalry was guaranteed by the threefold division of Munster between Muirchertach and his brothers, Tadc and Diarmait, on Tairdelbach's death.[98] Muirchertach, who may have been serving as *de facto* king of Munster at his father's right hand according to Anthony Candon,[99] had a sufficient powerbase to enable him to banish Diarmait after Tadc's unexpected death the following month.[100]

It was scarcely an auspicious start and during the early part of his reign he faced frequent opposition from Tadc's sons and from his remaining half-brother. Diarmait may have marched against Muirchertach at Ráith Étair near Dublin in 1087 in support of the Leinster king, Donnchad mac Domnaill Remair, but was defeated.[101] At the head of a naval force, he plundered along the coast of Cork the following year, but again success was limited, two hundred of his people being slain.[102] Muirchertach's kinsmen finally accepted the inevitable: Tadc's sons came to terms with him in 1091 though the peace was not to last.[103] Diarmait submitted to him in an elaborate ceremony at Cashel and Lismore two years later that marked the beginning of a period of relatively stable relations between the siblings.[104] Establishing his authority in his home base, however, was Muirchertach's premier concern, as it had been of his great-uncle, Donnchad, who some three-quarters of a century previously had inherited the mantle of power from Brian himself.

Unlike Donnchad, who appears to have been in the shadow of his more famous father, Muirchertach had been given a degree of political autonomy at an early stage, being appointed governor of Dublin by his father, Tairdelbach, in 1075, as we have seen. Seán Duffy has suggested that his travails in Munster led to his losing control of his eastern capital, the Leinstermen being recorded as defenders of Dublin not long after Tairdelbach's death.[105] In his dealings with his Leinster rivals, Muirchertach proved himself to be very much his father's son, ensuring that the various factions within Uí Chennselaig remained divided. Thus, when Donnchad mac Domnaill Remair was defeated by a rival kinsman, Énna, son of Diarmait mac Maíl na mBó, in 1088, Énna had the support of a force from South Munster, presumably acting at Muirchertach's behest.[106] Donnchad was killed the following year by Muirchertach himself according to one source,[107] by Ua Conchobair Fháilgi according to another.[108] Yet Énna's hour had not come, since Muirchertach immediately had him imprisoned, seizing the kingship of Leinster and of Dublin according to the Annals of Inisfallen.[109] On Énna's death at the hands of his own kinsmen three years later, Muirchertach seized the opportunity to reassert his authority in Leinster once more, acquiring the submission of Ua Conchobair Fháilgi in the process.[110] The latter, too, was imprisoned by the Munster ruler in 1094, in which year he marched to Dublin to wrest control from the Manx ruler, Gofraid Méránach.[111]

As in the case of his father, Muirchertach's encounters with Connacht were less successful, at least initially, confronted as he frequently was by the powerful partnership of the western leader, Ruaidrí Ua Conchobair, and Domnall Ua Maíl Shechnaill of Mide. In 1088 they were additionally supported by the northern ruler, Domnall Mac Lochlainn, who marched into Munster, destroying Muirchertach's fort at Cenn Corad.[112] The Munster king sought revenge the following year, plundering the churches of Lough Ree. Ua Conchobair repulsed him and on his retreat to Athlone, Ua Maíl Shechnaill attacked. There was worse to come since Muirchertach's opponents next turned their ferocious attention to Cashel, one annalist doubting whether they left a beast or a human being in all that space (*conidh anbecht ma dofhacsat mil na duine in aired sin uile*).[113] Ua Briain had no option but to submit to Mac Lochlainn.[114] His subservience was not to last and in 1090 and 1091 he marched to Lough Ree again and invaded Mide, only to have his home base attacked by the Connachtmen later that year.[115] The following year, however, his luck turned: Ua Conchobair was blinded by a rival dynast, Ua Flaithbertaig, and Muirchertach quickly seized the opportunity to install Gilla na Náem Ua hEidin in the kingship.[116] The latter fell from favour and he, too, was imprisoned.[117] In his dealings with Connacht, the Munster king was careful to preserve the southernmost territories of the region, Uí Fhiachrach Aidne and Uí Maine for himself.[118] His authority in the west was increasingly secure.

Muirchertach's dramatic intervention in Mide politics, slaying its king[119] and appointing his favoured candidate, Conchobar, son of Máel Sechnaill Bán, in his stead on the occasion of which he also reasserted control in Dublin,[120] ensured that less than a decade into his reign dominance of the southern part of Ireland, at the very least, was paramount. This he achieved by constant engagement with his enemies both among his own kin and else-where, re-emerging quickly after defeat and consolidating success by further attacks. This suggests significant military capacity, reinforced undoubtedly by access to retinues of subjugated rulers whose loyalty, however, might not always be assumed. As his violent removal of Domnall, king of Mide, from the political scene in 1094 demonstrates, Muirchertach could be brutally ruthless in dealing with his foes. In this he was a descendant of his father and great-grandfather, having also inherited much of their acumen and skill. Tairdelbach's attempts to keep the two main Leinster lines divided were replicated during the reign of Muirchertach who extended the policy of divide and rule to incorporate Mide as well. Conchobar, his chosen ruler, was given control of the eastern part of the territory alone, a kinsman, Donnchad, being made king in the west.[121] This had the desired result of setting the two at war with one another, ensuring that Muirchertach retained the upper hand.

When Conchobar was slain by Uí Briúin Bréifne more than a decade later, the Munster king was quick to intervene to prevent Donnchad assuming greater control.[122] His death the following year is attributed to Munstermen in certain sources.[123] Muirchertach's king-making propensity is also noth-ing new, Brian Boru himself bestowing sovereignty on Máel Mórda of Leinster just over one hundred years before.[124] As his own creation, the king of Leinster opposed Brian at Clontarf, and as Brian's grandson, Tairdelbach, turned upon his moulder, Diarmait mac Maíl na mBó, so too was one of Muirchertach's made men, Tairdelbach Ua Conchobair, to play a part in his demise.[125]

At the height of his powers in the first decade of the twelfth century, the Munster king would not have thought of decline. Concerned with consoli-dation and further expansion, he looked to the future with an eye on the past. As the successor of his glorious great-grandfather, Muirchertach may well have been increasingly mindful of his illustrious forbear, anxious to suggest that one hundred years later Brian Boru's reincarnation was now at the helm. To this end, some of his actions may have been in deliberate imitation of those of his famous ancestor; in any event, as noted above, the compari-son was certainly implied in Brian's literary biography, *Cogadh Gáedhel re Gallaibh*, consciously commissioned about this very time.

Certain similarities in the career paths of the two relatives were less welcome, particularly the failure of both to make headway in the north. Like Brian, Muirchertach had his northern nemesis in the person of Domnall Mac Lochlainn, who ensured, as Máel Sechnaill of Mide had done during his great-grandfather's reign, that southern authority was never to hold sway overall. The younger Ua Briain was as determined as his forefather had been, regularly marching northwards in an attempt to force Mac Lochlainn to give way. In truth, however, his advances were frequently halted not by the military might of his northern counterpart but by the negotiating tactics of his ecclesiastical ally, the abbot of Armagh. Thus, on six separate occasions between 1097 and 1113 when the Munster king marched northwards, *comarba Pátraic* (Patrick's successor) intervened to make peace.[126] The abbot travelled to Dublin to meet the two rulers in 1105 to the same end.[127] In their relatively rare encounters on the battlefield, on the other hand, both were equally matched, Muirchertach emerging victorious in 1101, having demolished Domnall's fortress at Ailech,[128] while the northern king was triumphant two years later at the battle of Mag Coba.[129] Despite suffering heavy losses, Ua Briain was back in the north the following year, though he failed to make significant inroads into Mac Lochlainn's territory.[130]

Whether Muirchertach was supported in the disastrous battle of Mag Coba by his new-found ally, Magnus Barelegs, is not clear. The Norse ruler had first journeyed to Ireland six years previously,[131] concerned perhaps by the extension of the influence of the Munster king beyond Ireland into the Isles. This is evidenced most clearly in an entry in the Manx Chronicle in the 1090s, recording a request by the inhabitants of the Isle of Man that Muirchertach send them a suitable leader.[132] All changed in 1102 when Magnus and his Irish counterpart agreed a truce[133] symbolised by the marriage of the Norse king's nine-year-old son, Sigurd, to the Munsterman's five-year-old daughter, called Bladmynja in the saga of Magnus Barelegs. According to this literary source, having overwintered together, the two kings marched northwards and gained many victories in battle.[134] What is certain, however, is that Magnus was killed while in the north in 1103 by the Ulaid, allies of Muirchertach's, which, as Seán Duffy has suggested, may indicate that the two rulers had experienced 'a parting of the ways'.[135] About the same time, another of Muirchertach's daughters was married to Arnulf de Montgomery, brother of Robert de Bellême, Earl of Shrewsbury, who sought the assistance of the Munster king in his rebellion against Henry I.[136] That Muirchertach was involved is indicated by a letter written by him to Anselm of Canterbury, in which he gives thanks to the archbishop for interceding with the king on his son-in-law's behalf. Henry's displeasure was such that he imposed a trade embargo with Ireland as a result of the betrayal, Ua Briain being sufficiently skilful to negotiate its removal.[137]

To a greater degree than his great-grandfather, therefore, Muirchertach appears to have been a key player in the European politics of his day, as his frequent dealings with contemporary rulers serve to underline. Although the precise circumstances of the gift are not known, King Edgar of Scotland bestowed upon him a camel in 1105.[138] A number of Welsh rulers had reason to be grateful to him for continuous support. These included Cadwgan ap Bleddyn, king of Powys, and his son, Owain, who fled to Ireland in the late 1090s,[139] while Owain sought refuge again with Muirchertach eleven years later.[140] Similarly the king of Deheubarth, Rhys ap Tewdwr, along with his son, Gruffudd, were offered protection by him, with Gruffudd remaining in Ireland until 1113.[141]

It is in the ecclesiastical sphere, rather than the secular one, however, that his connections with the outside world are most significant, since, following his father, he engaged in correspondence with Anselm and became the major Irish patron of Gregorian reform.[142] Already in 1096, his reformist credentials were evident in his choice, along with his brother, Diarmait, of a Winchester monk, Máel Isu Ua hAnmire, as bishop of Waterford.[143] His interest in episcopal appointments continued and he was involved in the installation of Gilla Espaig as bishop of Limerick in 1106,[144] and of Cellach as bishop of Armagh in the same year.[145] Of greater importance was his role at two pivotal reforming synods, at Cashel in 1101, during which he granted the symbolic Rock there associated in former times with his Munster rivals, the Éoganachta, to the Church,[146] and at Ráith Bressail a decade later at which the diocesan organisation of the country based on the twin pillars of Cashel and Armagh was firmly laid down.[147] As an ambitious, expansionist ruler, Muirchertach's involvement in Church affairs, like that of Brian before him, was politically motivated, his munificent donation of Cashel in 1101, for example, setting out clearly Uí Briain possession of that important site.[148] In addition his deference towards Armagh, as indicated by his meek acceptance of repeated interventions in his struggle with Mac Lochlainn by its abbot, was born of his desire, synonymous with that of his great-grandfather one hundred years earlier, for legitimisation of his power by the one true national Church.[149]

It was the Church, too, that was to provide him with a refuge when, on falling ill in 1114, Muirchertach was banished by his ever-recalcitrant brother, Diarmait, and though he made a come-back of sorts the following year, he was forced to retire one year later to Lismore.[150] Diarmait's long sought for success was not to last and he died, perhaps unexpectedly,

in 1118, and is accorded the title *rí Lethe Moga* 'king of the southern part of
Ireland' in some annalistic compilations.[151] Muirchertach was nominally in
control again, but a shadow of his former self as his power had all but disappeared. Nonetheless, he is termed 'king of Ireland' (*rí Érenn*) and described
as 'the tower of the honour and dignity of the western world' (*tuir ordain
ocus airechais iarthair in domain*) in the Annals of Ulster on his death the
following year.[152]

If the centenary of the battle at Clontarf was commemorated among
Brian Boru's admirers five years earlier, it may be that it marked a turn-
ing point in Muirchertach's reign. At Easter time in 1114 the prosperous
Munster ruler could have been basking in the glory of a successful hosting to Armagh the previous year.[153] By mid-summer, however, illness had
struck, the tone of the Munster annalist, following well-established literary
tradition, suggesting that the end of the world (almost) was nigh.[154] From
a southern perspective, all was to change utterly; Muirchertach's mantle of
authority, like that of his great-grandfather, could not simply be passed on.
Just as Brian's son, Donnchad, dissipated much power in internecine strife,
so too did internal feuding in the dying years of Muirchertach's reign enable
the up and coming Connacht ruler, Tairdelbach Ua Conchobair, applying a
lesson well-observed in the politics of his Munster master, to partition the
southern territory to ensure subservience to his rule.[155]

Hard Times

Ua Conchobair's intervention was to mark the beginning of a long era of
western dominance in which Uí Briain were never to regain the exten-
sive authority first acquired by their eponymous ancestor, Brian Boru,
regained by his grandson, Tairdelbach, and consolidated by the latter's son,
Muirchertach. Deliberately pitched by the Connacht king against their
Munster neighbours, Meic Carthaig (the McCarthys) – descendants of
the Éoganachta, the established southern dynasty usurped by Brian's Dál
Cais – even their pre-eminence in Munster was a thing of the past.[156] In
an effort to stave off western domination, the leading Uí Briain, sons of
Muirchertach's estranged brother, Diarmait, pragmatically agreed to
co-operate with their erstwhile southern rivals, making Cormac Mac
Carthaig, whom they brought out of retirement in Lismore in 1127, consensus

king of Munster.[157] Furnished with a deed of ancestry, *Caithréim Chellacháin Chaisil* (Cellachán of Cashel's Battle-triumph), extolling their own esteemed forefather, Cellachán of Cashel, and specifically modelled on Brian Boru's literary biography, *Cogadh Gáedhel re Gallaibh*, as Donnchadh Ó Corráin has shown,[158] it was the southern Munster chieftains who were Brian's rightful inheritors, or so their propaganda implied. In addition they laid claim again to Cashel, building Cormac's chapel there about the same time.[159]

In the year of the chapel's consecration,[160] the southern alliance fell apart, Diarmait Ua Briain's sons asserting themselves once more, occasionally with Leinster support.[161] Emboldened, one of the the sons in question, Tairdelbach Ua Briain treacherously slew the Mac Carthaig leader the following year, paving the way for his own brother, Conchobar, to assume the kingship of Munster.[162] Conchobar's unexpected death in 1142 cut short his reign, after which Tairdelbach himself assumed control.[163] Grandson of the earlier Tairdelbach and a great-great grandson of Brian, he achieved nothing of his ancestors' greatness, despite a relatively auspicious start. Two years after his rule began, his great Connacht rival, Tairdelbach Ua Conchobair, negotiated a truce with him at Terryglass, witnessed by clerics and laymen. Though allegedly to hold 'for as long as they should live' (*oired nobedis 'na mbethaidh*),[164] the agreement was nullified the following year, the leaders engaging in hostilities with one another, as they were to do with increasing frequency in the coming years.[165]

Tairdelbach was also beset by difficulties from another quarter, since the northern ruler, Muirchertach Mac Lochlainn, seemed intent on extending his authority southwards. At what was perhaps the high-point of Ua Briain's career, he led a successful hosting northwards to Gailenga, forcing the Dublin Norse to submit to him in the process.[166] His success was not to last; rival elements within his own dynasty, long since active, and a resurgence in the power of Meic Carthaig effectively put an end to his ambitions. The year 1151 in particular proved catastrophic. Deposed by his son, Muirchertach, his brother, Tadc, also turned against him, acquiring the ready support of Tairdelbach Ua Conchobair. Taking advantage of Ua Briain's misfortunes, Meic Carthaig, too, revived under a new and vibrant leader, Diarmait, and similarly allied with the Connacht king.[167] Thus encouraged, Ua Conchobair marched into Munster and divided it between Mac Carthaig and the besieged Tairdelbach. He returned some months later, supported by Mac Murchada of Leinster, Ua Ruairc of Bréifne and Ua Maíl Shechnaill of Mide. Ua Briain stood not a chance, suffering a calamitous defeat at Móin Mór near Fermoy in which his losses were immeasurable (*co ndechaidh tar airem a n-esbadha*). Fleeing to Limerick, he was forced to divide up among his Connacht enemies 'two hundred ounces of gold and sixty jewels, including Brian Boru's drinking horn' (.*x. fichit uinge d'ór ocus .lx. set im chorn Bríain Boraime*).[168] His great-great grandfather's inheritance had truly been spoiled.

Although Tairdelbach was restored to power in 1153 by Muirchertach Mac Lochlainn, anxious to curtail the advances of the Connacht king, he never really recovered.[169] Three years later he submitted to Ua Conchobair and after the latter's death later that year, he eventually offered his son and successor, Ruaidrí, renewed submission.[170] The northern king also turned against him and was involved in Ua Briain's deposition in 1157.[171] Although he was reinstated the following year, he lost the kingship six years later to his son, Muirchertach, whose supporters included both Meic Carthaig and the Connacht king.[172] Notwithstanding this, he is termed 'king of Munster and of the southern half of Ireland' (*rí Muman ocus Lethi Mogha*) on his death in 1167,[173] although in reality his power had long since disappeared.

An Anglo-Norman New World

As Tairdelbach lay dying, Diarmait Mac Murchada arrived back in Ireland having sought assistance from the English king, Henry II, to regain his Leinster kingdom. The Leinster ruler had crossed the Irish Sea after his alliance with the northern king, Mac Lochlainn, against the Connacht leader, Ruaidrí Ua Conchobair, had perforce ended on Mac Lochlainn's death in 1066. Diarmait was forced to look for aid further afield.[174] The Anglo-Norman troops he brought back with him were to be followed by others, including most famously Richard fitz Gilbert de Clare, otherwise known as Strongbow, who was married to Mac Murchada's daughter, Aífe, and who gained control of Leinster on his father-in-law's death soon after his arrival in Ireland in 1171.[175] Henry II himself crossed the Irish Sea shortly afterwards and received the submission of a number of Irish kings. These included Tairdelbach Ua Briain's son, Domnall Mór,[176] who had succeeded his father and who was married to Diarmait Mac Murchada's daughter.[177] As Marie Therese Flanagan has noted, their public allegiance to Henry was in fact a repudiation of the authority of Ruaidrí Ua Conchobair who had presented himself as an all-Ireland king.[178]

The Treaty of Windsor, negotiated in 1175, made the Connacht ruler overlord of large tracts of the country, including Munster. Domnall Mór Ua Briain soon felt the brunt of his new-found power, being deposed by Ua Conchobair as the Treaty (*sith na hErenn* 'Ireland's peace') was being brought across the Irish Sea. Limerick itself was also plundered 'and the Connachtmen burnt the greater part of Thomond on this expedition' (*cor loisced Connachta urmór Tuadhmuman don turus sin*). Not surprisingly, hostages were proffered by Ua Briain.[179] While Ua Conchobair's power was not to last, the glory days of Uí Briain were well and truly at an end. Relatively successful in maintaining control of Limerick in his lifetime, of which he styled himself king in contemporary charters,[180] Domnall Mór's north Munster domain was but a shadow of its former self. Focused on defeating one another, his three sons were in no position to enhance Uí Briain fortunes on their father's death in 1194,[181] some two hundred years after his great-great-great grandfather, Brian, was well on the road to becoming Ireland's greatest king.

Notwithstanding their much reduced kingdom and nominal adherence at least to English rule, Brian Boru's descendants continued to cultivate his image, espousing the ideal that his like would come again to restore their past prestige. *Aonar dhuit, a Bhriain Bhanbha* (To you alone, Brian of Ireland), ascribed to the thirteenth-century poet, Muireadhach Albanach Ó Dálaigh, comprises a poetic account of Brian's achievements, based in large part on his literary biography, *Cogadh Gáedhel re Gallaibh*, as we have seen. The impetus for its production is evident from its final stanzas, in which the author bewails the fact that, since Strongbow came, Ireland is again overrun with foreigners:[182]

Ón ló tháinic an t-iarla
tig loingeas Gall gach bliagain,
gur ghabhsad Banba na mbeann,
aca atá an chríoch go coitchend.

From the day the Earl came a fleet of foreigners comes every year, they seized Ireland of the peaks, they have possession of the whole country.

The obvious question, when will the like of Brian come (*cuin thucfas shamhail Briain*) is then posed; a saviour who will save the Irish 'as he alone saved them' (*mar do fhóir sion a n-aonar*) is sought.[183] In a micro-context, Domnall

Mór Ua Briain might be said to fit the bill, defending Limerick vigorously against the Anglo-Normans, setting fire to it on one occasion, according to Gerald of Wales, rather than let the settlement fall into their hands.[184] His son, Donnchad Cairprech, who eventually triumphed over his siblings, appears to have had closer relations with his Anglo-Norman neighbours. Knighted by King John in 1210,[185] he may have been married to a daughter of William de Burgh.[186] Had the poem been composed in his day, it might have been read as a reproach to the current ruler whose actions presented a sharp contrast to those of Brian Boru, defender of Ireland, in the work.[187] In two other compositions ascribed to Muireadhach Albanach, however, Donnchad Cairprech is warmly praised and indeed the poet claims that 'his blow will be in every foreigner' (*a bhuille biaidh i ngach Gall*).[188]

In reality that was not the case, though Donnchad's non-confrontational approach did not yield results. During the reign of his son, Conchobar, who succeeded him in 1242, Anglo-Normans were granted by royal decree large tracts of Uí Briain lands, shrinking the already much reduced kingdom of Thomond further.[189] Conchobar's sons, Tadc and Brian Ruad in turn, valiantly defended their lands, attacking their Anglo-Norman neighbours continuously.[190] Their efforts were weakened considerably when Tadc's son, Tairdelbach, turned against his uncle, Brian Ruad, as a result of which the latter sought the assistance of Thomas de Clare who had been granted Thomond by King Edward I in 1276.[191] Civil war ensued, culminating in two major battles at Corcumroe Abbey in 1317 and at Dysert O'Dea the following year, from which Tadc's descendants emerged victorious.[192]

A Literary Legacy

The outline of the conflict can be traced in contemporary annalistic sources that record many of its major incidents. A more detailed account is preserved in a fourteenth-century literary narrative, *Caithréim Thoirdhealbhaigh* (Tairdelbach's Battle-triumph), written by a partisan of Tadc's family (Clann Taidc), Tairdelbach of the title being Tadc's son.[193] Significantly, in seeking to praise one branch of the dynasty at the expense of another, Brian Boru, their eponymous ancestor, is brought to the fore, Clann Taidc being presented as his rightful heirs.[194] In so doing, particular emphasis is placed on the perfidy of Brian Ruad's English supporters, the de Clares, similarity between the actions of Tadc's descendants and the earlier deliverance from foreigners by

Brian Boru being deliberately implied. In composing his text, the Uí Briain author had an account of Brian's activities to hand, specifically the embellished narrative, *Cogadh Gáedhel re Gallaibh*, first composed in the twelfth century but of which a fourteenth-century copy, and perhaps a fragment of another, also survives.[195] Whether it was either of these particular versions upon which the writer drew, we cannot know; however, he was dependent on the *Cogadh* in matters of content, structure and style.[196]

Battle descriptions in *Caithréim Thoirdhealbhaigh* contain verbal echoes of the earlier work. Some may represent stock phrases but in other instances the parallels are such as to suggest direct borrowing on the part of the later author. In addition the number of similarities indicates familiarity with the twelfth-century tract. In both the *Cogadh* and the later text, the troops meet in counsel and take a democratic decision to advance.[197] Poets exhort the hosts to battle[198] while prophets predict the outcome.[199] Attention is given to the arrangement of the forces, as well as to their position in the encounter.[200] The battle itself entails a series of single combats[201] and at its height, though he is standing next to him, a man could not recognise his dearest friend.[202] The slain are enumerated and the injured lauded for continuing to fight, irrespective of their wounds.[203]

More specifically, following a battle victory, Tairdelbach is inaugurated in triumph, as Mathgamain was, after overcoming his Viking foes at Sulchóit in the *Cogadh*.[204] As Mathgamain undertook joint-expeditions with Brian Boru, according to the earlier text, so too do Tairdelbach and his brother, Domnall, march hand-in-hand in *Caithréim Thoirdhealbhaigh*.[205] Brian assumed the reins of power on his older brother's death and the formula used on that occasion is repeated on the election of a ruler of specific Clann Taidc allies in the fourteenth-century work.[206] Brian Boru built bridges and patronised schools and monasteries; among Tairdelbach's constructions were bridges and monasteries, according to his own tale.[207]

Recourse to the *Cogadh* casts light upon a number of specific passages in the *Caithréim*. The loyal support proffered to Clann Taidc by Uí Chellaig of Connacht is explained in the later text with reference to the close ties between Tadc Ua Cellaig and Brian Boru himself.[208] In addition the victory in battle by Clann Taidc at Corcumroe Abbey in 1317, is described as one of a trio of triumphs, the other two being Brian's victory at Clontarf and that of his son, Donnchad, against the Osraige when returning from that famous battle.[209] Both these encounters are set out in the twelfth-century *Cogadh*. The presentation of the Clontarf episode in that text, as a duel in which noble natives were opposed by a foreign foe, notwithstanding the presence of Irish on both sides, may also have influenced the later author who chose to recast his story of a conflict between Uí Briain kinsmen as one in which *allmúraig* (foreigners) and *Danair* (Danes) are the real villains of the piece. In fact, de Clare is accused of inflaming internal dissension within Uí Briain for his own ends.[210]

Notwithstanding the political reality of their own time in which life under English rule was the order of the day, Brian Boru's thirteenth- and fourteenth-century descendants chose to cultivate an image of their exalted eponymous ancestor as a warrior-king who, by expelling tyrannical foreigners, proved himself to be Ireland's rightful ruler. In this respect, the picture elaborately drawn in *Cogadh Gáedhel re Gallaibh* was to have an enduring appeal. For two sons of the Tairdelbach Ua Briain celebrated in the title of *Caithréim Thoirdhealbhaigh*, Brian was also the ideal to which they must espouse. In the case of one of these, Muirchertach, who died in 1343, he is urged in a contemporary poem, *Abair riomh a Éire, a ógh* (Tell me, O pure Ireland), to march forth and claim his inheritance, the kingship of Ireland, since he is a 'descendant of Brian Boru'. Indeed, as Katharine Simms has noted, the poet, Máel Muire Bacach Mac Craith, asks him therein to fight another *cogadh gall re gaoidhealaibh* 'war between the foreigners and the Irish' in a deliberate echo of Brian's influential 'Life'.[211] While no specific reference to the *Cogadh* occurs in another poem, *A toigh bheag tiaghar a tteagh mór* (From a small house one goes into a big one), written by Gofraidh Fionn Ó Dálaigh for Muirchertach's successor, his brother Diarmait, the latter is hailed as his ancestor's equal.[212] Like Brian, he too should be 'the greatest of Ireland's kings'.[213]

Brian's Descendants Surveyed

More than four hundred years after his birth, therefore, Brian continued to be held up as a shining example, an inspirational figure to whose glory his descendants should, at least notionally, aspire. He has retained something of this sheen down to our own times. In this regard, his story was given a new lease of life in the seventeenth century by Geoffrey Keating, whose history of Ireland, *Foras Feasa ar Éirinn*, played a crucial role in the development of the Clontarf-narrative in the eighteenth and nineteenth centuries, as Meidhbhín

Ní Úrdail has shown.[214] She has also highlighted the extent to which Keating was influenced by English accounts of the battle, his greatest debt, however, being to the twelfth-century *Cogadh* which he names as his authority for his information on the Vikings.[215] The earlier tract was also drawn on by a contemporary of Keating, An Dubhaltach Mac Fhirbhisigh, whose genealogical text, 'Concerning the Fomoiri and the Vikings' (*Do Fhomhórchuibh agus do Lochlannachuibh*), chronicles the arrival of Scandinavian invaders in terms reminiscent of the earlier narrative.[216] A later chronicle account of Brian's battles, as well as those of his son, Donnchad, *Leabhar Oiris* (The Book of Chronicles), may also be dependent on the tale.[217]

In the development of Brian's persona, the composition of the *Cogadh* was pivotal and the period of its production is a key epoch in the history of Uí Briain. Their ruler at the time, Brian's great-grandson, Muirchertach, was in many ways his ancestor's equal, a powerful, opportunistic leader who built upon the legacy of his father, Tairdelbach. Reversing the slight dip in their family's fortunes experienced during the reign of Brian's son, Donnchad, Tairdelbach and Muirchertach regained for Munster the pre-eminent position it had enjoyed in Brian's own day. The southern king became once more a leading figure in Ireland's political scene. It was not to last and Uí Briain were forced to give way to their Munster neighbours, the Meic Carthaig, as the twelfth century progressed. The end of that century heralded a new political environment, characterised by the involvement of Anglo-Normans and English kings. Uí Briain rulers became increasingly confined to Thomond, their kingdom much reduced. In straitened circumstances, comfort could be taken from reference to an illustrious past; thus, his descendants continued to cultivate the figure of Brian. As his legend became more developed, so too did the gap between story and history become more marked; 'the like of Brian' had become an almost mythical being.

6

Assessing Brian

Brian's image-makers ensured that he would not languish in obscurity; for him name recognition is assured. He is, in the words of one contemporary historian, 'assuredly the best-known medieval Irish king on record',[1] while the military encounter in which Brian was slain in 1014 was described by another as 'perhaps the most vivid image in the otherwise hazy modern conception of medieval Irish history'.[2] Fame brings with it its own transformations and the plain Brian mac Cennétig who was killed in what is admittedly 'a great war' (*cocad mór*) in the Annals of Inisfallen had become the yardstick against whom all later great kings were measured a mere two hundred years later.[3] Similarly the poetic composition, *Aonar dhuit, a Bhriain Banba*, written about the same time, placed Brian in the most exalted of company: alongside the deity, Lugh, the mythological Finn and holy Patrick, he formed the quartet 'who most helped Ireland' (*as mó do fhóir Éirinn*).[4]

Small wonder, therefore, that he was hailed as one of the leaders of the Irish Resistance movement less than fifty years ago.[5] And while others had been more circumspect previously, John Ryan maintaining, for example, that 'Brian was not a man of new ideas ... he was just a great Irish king',[6] the towering figure of this Munster monarch continues to dominate discussions of the history of this period, popular and scholarly alike. What exactly he achieved continues to be debated. While he may not have created 'a national monarchy or the institutions of such a monarchy', in the words of Donnchadh Ó Corráin, nonetheless 'he did contribute greatly to advancing the idea of a kingship of the whole island'.[7] In the same way, in the opinion of Thomas Charles-Edwards, Brian demonstrated 'the fragility of Uí Néill hegemony' and thereby dangled 'the prospect of domination before his own province and also the other provinces of Leinster and Connacht',[8] echoing Francis John Byrne's view that 'he showed that any provincial king might make himself king of Ireland by force of arms'.[9]

Brian's Career in Perspective

Having due regard to Brian's posthumous reputation and in the light of our assessment of the sources from which our knowledge of his reign derives, it remains to re-evaluate briefly his actual achievements. His skill as a military commander is not in doubt. Although we are dependent for the most part on a Munster source, the Annals of Inisfallen, written very much in his favour, for information concerning the early part of his reign, the general upward trajectory was real enough. Other annalists take an interest as his power is enhanced and specifically when he presents to his counterpart in the northern part of the country, Máel Sechnaill mac Domnaill, a realistic threat. To achieve this commanding position he employed a range of abilities, overcoming his opponents in a variety of ways. Casual raids (*crecha*) in which slaughter was inflicted are recorded, alongside battles (*catha*) in which relatively large numbers fell.[10] Land attacks resulting in the removal of great prey (*preit mór*) are undertaken, as well as strategic naval raids (*crechlonga*).[11] Both are often used on the same expedition, as when Brian took a large fleet (*coblach mór*) into Connacht, some of his retinue going on further 'by land' (*iar tír*).[12] Defence was likewise a priority and he fortified key structures at various points in his career.[13]

Coupled with his proven abilities as a warrior-leader was undoubted political acumen and cunning. He may have plundered the Vikings of Limerick immediately after his succession to power,[14] yet seven years later he allied with the Haraldssons at Waterford.[15] That there had previously been hostilities between the Limerick and Waterford kinsmen may have contributed to their common cause. The hosting to Dublin, on the other hand, as Colmán Etchingham has noted, was directed against the Mide king, Máel Sechnaill mac Domnaill, whose uterine brother, Glún Iairn, was in control there.[16] In his pursuit of power, therefore, Brian entered into a plethora of opportunistic allegiances that are also reflected in his marital alliances. Furthermore, he intervened decisively in other kingdoms' affairs, deposing the king of Leinster in 1003 to appoint his own candidate, Máel Mórda mac Murchada, in his stead.[17]

His intervention in the business of the Church is also noteworthy, his relatives occupying key positions therein, as has been shown by Donnchadh Ó Corráin.[18] Brief references to Brian's ransoming of a Norse captive, a church official of Ros Ailithir, Co. Cork,[19] and to his capture of the head (*comarba*) of the northern monastery of Mag Bile,[20] similarly hint at this ecclesiastical dimension to his political affairs. This is also seen in his seduction of Armagh, most clearly evident in his gift of twenty ounces of gold to that establishment in 1005.[21] This served to undermine his northern rivals, Uí Néill, and specifically to link his own all-Ireland aspirations to the well-established concept of a national Church. That Brian's ambition extended further may be suggested in the title *imperator Scotorum* accorded him about the same time, as Colmán Etchingham has suggested;[22] in any event, his enterprise certainly knew no bounds.

Central to his approach was recourse to records in which his version of events was to the fore. While In Déis Tuaiscirt had been reincarnated genealogically as 'the seed of Cas' before Brian's time, he too deliberately cultivated the written word. The Annals of Inisfallen remain the most obvious testament to this, being a partisan account of Dál Cais activities, at least from Brian's time. Munster annals later drawn on by the author of his own literary 'Life', *Cogadh Gáedhel re Gallaibh*, may also have been produced within his remit, reinforcing the story he very much wanted told. To this end, control of individual churches was significant, since it was in ecclesiastical establishments that reputations were made. Brian's title 'Emperor' was recorded for posterity in Armagh's most valuable book; of this fact the ambitious ruler was very much aware.

The partiality of the sources notwithstanding, there is a sense of real progression throughout Brian's reign, as well as of a skilful ruler growing into the job. Different challenges presented themselves at various times; Brian's response was for the most part appropriate for the task in hand. That he should first choose to avenge his brother's killers ensured that his standing among his own people remained secure. We may assume that he retained a firm hand on his own kingdom, a nephew, Áed son of Mathgamain, being imprisoned by him ten years into his reign in 986.[23] Perseverance was also his hallmark, the territory of Osraige being attacked by him three years in a row. A raid into the territory in 982 was followed by a return visit the following year in which hostages were secured by Brian. To drive the point home, he devastated the region one year later, in a demonstration of his authority, laying waste its churches in the process.[24] A sense of caution is also in evidence, his focus being very much on the southern part of Ireland in the first decade or so of his reign. Yet opportunities presented were seized, as the capture of Dublin after victory at Glenn Máma attests.[25] When he did venture northwards, he demonstrated the same tenacious approach. Having been rebuffed by Cenél nÉogain in 1002 and again in 1004,[26] he adopted a statesmanlike pose the following year when undertaking a grand journey to Armagh. The tactic bore fruit: he returned home 'bringing the pledges of the men of Ireland' (*luid for a culu co n-etire fer nErenn laiss*).[27]

Dependent as we are for information on Brian's reign upon a source-genre that is dominated by battles and death-notices, it is fortunate indeed that echoes can be detected in the record of a range of responses on his part. That these were even more varied in reality can be expected; we are, after all, viewing the period through a single, coloured lens. Occasional glimpses are also afforded of real life. Mention in passing of Brian's officials (*suatrich*) suggests a well-ordered house. It could hardly have been otherwise: running an increasingly large ship, Brian had to be in a position to exercise control over his vassals upon whom he relied in all manner of ways. Frequently absent on military campaigns, he was equally dependent on key personages to maintain control and social order. His descendants entrusted such business, at least partially, to their children: Brian's grandson, Tairdelbach, granted his sons, Muirchertach and Diarmait, authority in Dublin and Waterford respectively, as we have seen. What Brian's precise arrangements were in such matters is uncertain; it seems clear, however, that he ruled with an iron grip. Only by so doing could he have become and remained in his own day, Ireland's greatest king.

Royal Role Models

In its own terms, therefore, Brian's reign was an outstanding success, his status and that of his Munster kingdom considerably enhanced by its end. He was not the first southern ruler to have great expectations, nor was he the first to force the dominant northern dynasty, Uí Néill, to come to terms. We know less about his precocious predecessors, including the eighth-century Munster king, Cathal mac Finguine, and his ninth- and tenth-century sucessors, Feidlimid mac Crimthainn and Cormac mac Cuilennáin, and it may be that there is less to be known. Their era is more sparsely documented, however, and while bias in their favour is also detectable in the southern-based chronicle, the Annals of Inisfallen, it provides no more than an outline of their careers, making it difficult to assess their actual effect.

Yet in the case of Cathal, a later Uí Briain spindoctor was sufficiently impressed with his record to associate him directly with Brian Boru, in an addition made to an entry recording the earlier king's harrying of Brega in 721. Including Feidlimid mac Crimthainn also in the exalted company, these were three of only five Munster kings who ruled Ireland 'after the introduction of the Faith' (iar cretim).[28] Feidlimid, of whom more detail is preserved, anticipated Brian in a number of respects.[29] His interest in Armagh displays an awareness of the significance of this increasingly important church,[30] while persistent raiding by him ensured that successive Uí Néill kings agreed to negotiate with him at a formal meeting (dál).[31] As both king and bishop, he had direct control of all-important scriptoria, and Donnchadh Ó Corráin has suggested that a document setting out Munster's claim to all-Ireland kingship was produced in his time.[32] The Annals of Ulster may not celebrate him on his death in such expansive terms as they do Brian, some one hundred and fifty years later; nonetheless as 'king of Munster' (rex Muman), in the opinion of the chronicler, he is 'the best of the Irish' (optimus Scotorum).[33]

From these kings, Brian's Éoganacht predecessors, lessons may well have been learnt. He would also have absorbed policies implemented by Uí Néill rulers to good effect. Of these, the ninth-century king, Máel Sechnaill mac Maíle Ruanaid (Máel Sechnaill I), appears to have been as successful as Brian. His victories against Vikings may have enhanced his position.[34] Like the Munster king more than a century later, however, he also allied with them in turn, drawing on the military support of a group of Gall-Gaídil 'Scandinavian-Irish' for a number of years.[35] Máel Sechnaill too had propaganda writers, though the traces they have left us are fainter than those made by Brian's writing men. Nonetheless, they may be detectable in a fragmentary narrative concerning the drowning by Máel Sechnaill of a Viking leader, Tuirgéis. The event is recorded prosaically in contemporary annals,

'Tuirgéis was taken prisoner by Máel Sechnaill and afterwards drowned in Loch Uair' (*Turges du ergabhail la Mael Sechnaill ocus badudh Turges i lLoch Uair iaram*).[36] In later material, however, Tuirgéis has been accorded almost super-human might.[37] This is the guise in which he features in Brian's literary biography, *Cogadh Gáedhel re Gallaibh*, as well as in the twelfth-century 'Topography of Ireland' by Gerald of Wales.[38] By separating the account of the audacious activities of Tuirgéis and his wife, who colonise Armagh and Clonmacnoise respectively, from the notice of Máel Sechnaill's killing of the Viking tyrant, the author of the *Cogadh* minimises the heroism of the Uí Néill king. It was in the latter's interest that the original tale is likely to have been composed, however; Máel Sechnaill or his successors were equally cognisant of propaganda's power.

Ecclesiastical support was similarly important to the Uí Néill ruler who sealed his authority over the northern part of Ireland with a royal assembly (*rígdál*) in Armagh in 851. Its participants included the nobles of Leth Cuinn, together with both the abbot and the bishop of Armagh as well as the abbot of Clonard in Mide.[39] As Brian was to direct his energies northwards in pursuit of power, so had the earlier ruler to focus attention on Munster. This he did with a determination equal to that of the southern king in his dealings with Máel Sechnaill's descendants at a later time. And as Brian's efforts bore fruit so, too, did the earlier activities of Máel Sechnaill I meet with success.[40] He could draw on Munster assistance when attacked in 860 by his northern kinsmen, Áed Finnliath and Flann mac Conaing.[41] That raid, and others like it,[42] reveal the chink in Máel Sechnaill's armour; his control over his immediate neighbours was less than secure. Nonetheless, on his death two years later, his overall position was strong and he is the first ruler to be termed 'king of all Ireland' (*ri Herenn uile*) in contemporary sources.[43] It was a title to which later leaders continually aspired.

A desire to be deemed 'king of all Ireland' underlies the rivalry between Brian and his contemporary in Ireland's northern half, also named Máel Sechnaill, as we have seen. In many ways, Máel Sechnaill II, was the southern ruler's equal, achieving considerable successes in the eighteen short years of his significant reign. By contrast, Brian was at the helm for just short of forty years, during which he could implement his policy at a more leisurely pace. Powerful and for a lengthy period at that; the duration of Brian's governance may also have contributed to the enduring impact he was to make.

Anglo-Saxon Angles

Not that longevity was always beneficial. Brian's almost exact contemporary in England, Æthelred the Unready, who succeeded his brother, Edward the Martyr, two years after Brian had taken over the reins of power from his sibling, Mathgamain,[44] and died two years after Brian's fall at Clontarf, has acquired a dismal reputation and did so almost immediately after his death.[45] Comparison between his posthumous fate and that of the Irish ruler is instructive, since similar situations produce spectacularly different results. In both cases Vikings are key, although the threat they posed to Æthelred was much greater than to the Munster king. Nonetheless, Scandinavian prowess is dramatised in literary texts concerning both leaders. The sources in question are roughly comparable, each drawing on earlier annals to tell what is essentially a discursive tale. While Brian Boru's twelfth-century biography employs its focus on ferocious foreigners to exalt its revered subject, his victory being all the greater for overcoming such oppressive foes, the explicit contrast with the Vikings is designed to ridicule the English in the account of an anonymous eleventh-century chronicler, writing in the years immediately following Æthelred's death.[46] And while the author may not have been critical of the English king in particular, he 'supplies the fuel for subsequent accusations against [him]', as Simon Keynes has noted.[47] That fuel was ignited not long after Brian's 'Life', Cogadh Gáedhel re Gallaibh, was composed; in the work of William of Malmesbury in particular, Æthelred's fate is well and truly sealed.[48]

Comparison with his English contemporary, therefore, casts Brian in an excellent light, though this has much to do with the focus of their respective chroniclers, as we have seen. It is with an earlier Anglo-Saxon king, Alfred the Great (871–99), that the Irish ruler can be more readily compared, not least in the fact that the West Saxon too was celebrated in a Life, though in one written in Latin by his scholar-friend and tutor, Asser, during his own time. In a passing remark, A.J. Goedheer drew attention to what he considered to be a similar passage in the two texts, recounting the suffering imposed by Viking on both men.[49] In his view, the putative parallel provided evidence for a story having travelled orally across the Irish Sea.[50] Donnchadh Ó Corráin, on the other hand, suggested that the Uí Briain composition was in fact modelled on Asser's Life.[51]

That there are points of comparison between the two passages can scarcely be denied; as literary responses to similar situations, however, the resonances may be more by accident than design. Brian and Æthelred, like Alfred before them, were born into turbulent times that ensured that engagement with Vikings, to a greater or lesser extent, punctuated their respective careers. As the anonymous recorders of the activities of Brian and Æthelred were later to do, Asser also placed heavy emphasis on Alfred's dealings with Scandinavians. He, too, dramatised their deeds: 'like wolves they burst out of all the gates and joined battle with all their might' (*lupino more, totis portis erumpentes, totis viribus bellum perquirunt*).[52] His reason for doing so had much in common with the motives of the anonymous Irish author more than two centuries later; contrary to Æthelred's chronicler, Asser and Brian's descendant really did consider their subjects to be great. As defenders against heathen hosts, the superiority of both heroes is underlined, in Brian's case to magnify his ruling descendants, while in Alfred's to persuade a contemporary audience of the sagacity and skill of their king.[53]

In consciously moulding their subjects in a particular image, both authors had recourse to solid annalistic evidence and in this regard the structure of the two narratives can also be compared. Brian's designer considerably embellished the chronicle record at his disposal, as we have seen. He borrowed liberally from literary traditions of the kind seemingly eschewed by his Anglo-Saxon counterpart. The flowery account of the battle of Clontarf in which Brian met his death, for example, is not comparable with anything in Asser's composition. That biography appears to have survived only in draft, however, making it difficult to speculate on the precise nature of a putative 'finished' Life.[54]

In portraying their perfect rulers, both authors may also have had in mind a genre known as 'mirror for princes' (*speculum principum*), setting out for prospective leaders an ideal way of life.[55] As Anton Scharer has shown, Asser drew on a specific example of such a text, the ninth-century work, The Book of Christian Rulers (*Liber de rectoribus Christianis*), written by an Irishman, Sedulius Scottus, possibly for the Frankish king, Charles the Bald. The emphasis on wisdom in the two sources is particularly striking, Alfred being a virtual Solomon in this regard.[56] Brian shares similar features. Directly compared with Solomon, as well as David and Moses, on one occasion,[57] his sagacity is acknowledged by his people who invariably agree unanimously with his pronouncements.[58] Scharer has suggested that Asser's emphasis on Alfred's suffering may also be dependent on Sedulius, in particular on his notion that the chosen ones must endure pain.[59] This theme links what Goedheer proposed were parallel passages in Alfred's Life and the *Cogadh*, as we have seen. In the absence of any evidence for widespread circulation of Asser's work,[60] it may be that we should consider the possibility that the ninth-century Welsh composer of Alfred's Life and his twelfth-century Irish successor were influenced independently by a single source. That the author of the work in question was a continental-based ninth-century Irishman lends credence to the suggestion.

Continental Comparisons

Alfred's Welsh creator also drew on another ninth-century work, a royal biography, the Life of Charlemagne (*Vita Karoli*), composed between 829 and 836 by Einhard, a subject of that king.[61] Their portrayal of both rulers as ideal Christian monarchs is one with which Brian's presentation in the *Cogadh* may also be compared. The hagiographical tone of the continental work may have informed the quasi-religious tenor of Asser's narrative; this also accords well with the overall sentiment of the Irish work. We may speculate, therefore, whether Einhard's *Vita* would have been known to the Irish author. Its wide dissemination on the Continent and the preservation of manuscript copies in foundations with strong Irish connections would certainly provide a context in which an eleventh- or twelfth-century Irish man of letters could have become acquainted with the popular work.

All this must remain uncertain, although we can be sure that Brian Boru would have applauded any link made between himself and great kings of the outside world, since his gaze was similarly directed in his own time. This is most strikingly attested in the appellation, *Imperator Scotorum*, given to him by his confessor, Máel Suthain, in 1005, which has been connected with the title *Imperator Romanorum* adopted by the Ottonion royal house during the Irish king's lifetime, as we have seen.[62] Brian himself could well have cultivated the comparison. The activities of his contemporary, Otto III, whose period of active rule between 994 and 1002 corresponded precisely with Brian's ascendancy, were presumably related in Ireland by returning clerics who had been based in Irish monasteries in East Francia during his energetic rule.

There was much in Otto's philosophy with which the ambitious Irishman would have concurred and even more to which he might aspire. Otto's incontrovertible belief in a divinely sanctioned kingship that lay behind his policy of renewal of the Roman Empire (*renovatio imperii Romanorum*) bestowed on him an authority that Brian could dearly have cherished. His control over Church affairs may have seemed to the Irish king the ideal state.[63] Equally attractive might have been Otto's florid title, as the unmistakable label of a man on the make. Tenth-century Anglo-Saxon kings are also termed *imperator*, at the hands of draftsmen concerned with enhancing their subjects' fame.[64] Brian's 'stylistic flourish'[65] was part of the same tradition; Marie Therese Flanagan has suggested that its impetus came from the West Saxon royal house.[66] For our purposes, the exact source scarcely matters; the application to the Irish ruler of a high-flown term resonant of Ottonian imperialism, even if mediated through English channels, is indicative of the confidence that marked out his reign. For Máel Suthain, reiterating no doubt the view of his master, Brian was indeed imperial, towering over all.

Posterity

The 'Empire' that he rejuvenated did not survive him, his son, Donnchad, being much less imperial in deed. And while his great-grandson, Muirchertach, was equally tower-like, circumstances ultimately contrived against Brian's descendants and they were forced to retreat to their Clare heartland once more. They did so extolling their ancestor, tales of whose extraordinary achievements continued to serve them well and in whose persona fact and fiction became inexorably intertwined. Deliberate blurring of boundaries is detectable in Brian's own time; early grooming in which he himself was actively engaged. Loyal kinsmen continued the make-over; care was taken to make their ruler truly great. The powerful persona bears eloquent testimony to their success and, if the historical person has been obscured in the process, that is as Brian himself would have wished. A skilful leader, at the forefront of a newly established dynasty, he carved out for himself a position of power to rival that of the greatest of his predecessors. That these had all been northerners emanating from a long ruling tradition adds to his success. Where this Munster man had ventured, Connacht men followed, attributing to his reign a significance of which his contemporaries could not have been aware.

No more apparent to them was the extent to which Brian embodies and personifies the spirit of his age. At a time when territorial power was expanding, this Munster man sought to control the largest land unit of all, Ireland itself. Nor did the surrounding sea contain his ambition entirely: Brian was a ruler acutely aware of the benefits afforded by an outward look. Imperial ambition inspired him; Anglo-Saxon advances could also have left their mark. Viking foes he may have battled, their naval manoevres, however, soon became his own. Moreover, the enemy was adopted as friend when political need arose. In an era of shifting allegiances, Brian became the greatest mover and shaker of them all, directing developments in neighbouring kingdoms with an audacity that had not yet become commonplace. His dealings with the Church reflect a confidence that later rulers were also to emulate.

His control over particular products emanating from ecclesiastical scriptoria ensured that Brian in many respects drafted his own script. Finely wrought and greatly expanded by generations of his descendants, it stands as a masterful monument to Brian as medieval myth. Entangled within it is a man of might whose historical reflex was the most powerful of rulers in his day, comparable with other outstanding leaders of previous and later times. What sets him apart is his superior story, skilfully recreated in different guises and at various times down through a millennium, from the south-west of Ireland to Iceland's south-east. Elaborate and engaging, it is a tale that bears retelling, the craft of its manifold creators always to the fore. Its much manipulated message is that Brian is Ireland's greatest king.

Notes

CHAPTER ONE: ACCESSING BRIAN

1 Gwynn, *Book of Armagh*, p.ciii and fol. 16v; AU 1014.
2 For a discussion of the nature of annalistic evidence and of the interrelationships between the extant chronicles, see Charles-Edwards, *Chronicle*, 1, pp.1–59.
3 Places and territories mentioned in the text are depicted on maps 18 and 19.
4 AU 1014.
5 See Gwynn, 'Brian in Armagh', pp.41–3, 44–8.
6 See Kelleher, 'Rise of the Dál Cais', p.234 and Ó Corráin, 'Irish origin legends', pp.70–1.
7 AU¹ 1224 and 1375.
8 See Ní Úrdail, 'Seachadadh'.
9 See Ní Úrdail, 'Seachadadh', pp.187–91.
10 See Campbell Ross, 'Representation'.

CHAPTER TWO: BEFORE BRIAN

1 AU; CS, pp.194–5 (placing his birth erroneously about 923).
2 See Meyer, 'Brian Borumha', pp.71–3. 'Bórama' means 'cattle tribute' and may have denoted the place where such tribute was taken; that its meaning was understood is indicated by a reference to the battle of Clontarf by a twelfth-century poet, Gilla na Náem ua Duind, as 'the battle of Brian of the cattle' (*cath Briain in buair*): Best, Bergin, O'Brien, *Book of Leinster*, 1, p.141, line 4361.
3 AU 841: *Longport oc Duiblinn* 'A naval camp at Dublin'; AU 942: *Geinnti for Duiblinn beos* 'Heathens still in Dublin'. Colmán Etchingham has suggsted to me that a

Viking fleet on the River Liffey in 837 (AU) could have overwintered and that there may have been other Vikings who settled earlier.

4 AU; Rathlin Island off the coast of Antrim had been identified with Rechru, since it was thought that the Isle of Skye was laid waste in the same attack. However, Clare Downham has questioned the raid on Skye: 'Imaginary Viking-raid'.

5 For an account of Viking activities in the ninth century, see Ó Corráin, *Ireland before the Normans*, pp.81–2, 89–96 and Ó Corráin, 'Vikings in Scotland and Ireland', pp.323–5. Raids on churches in the period are analysed by Etchingham, *Viking Raids*.

6 AU.

7 AU; this is discussed by Ó Corráin, *Ireland before the Normans*, p.93.

8 AU; the terms have been discussed by Dumville, 'Old Dubliners'.

9 Ó Cuív, 'Personal names', pp.87–8, n.19.

10 For discussion of the poem, see Ní Mhaonaigh, 'Friend and foe', pp.399–400.

11 AU: 'The heathens were driven from Ireland, i.e. from the fortress of Dublin, by Máel Finnia son of Flannacán with the men of Brega and by Cerball son of Muiricán with the Leinstermen; and they abandoned a good number of their ships and escaped half dead after they had been wounded and broken' (*Indarba ngennti a hEre .i. longport Atha Cliath o Mael Findia m. Flandacain co feraibh Bregh ocus o Cerball m. Muiricain co Laignibh co farcabsat drecht mar dia longaibh co n-erlasat lethmarba iarna nguin ocus a mbrisiuth*). See also CS, pp.178–9.

12 AU.

13 Graham-Campbell, 'Archaeological reflections' and Higham, 'Northumbria', both of which references I owe to Fiona Edmonds.

14 New fleets arrived in Waterford, for example, in 914 and again the following year: AU.

15 AU.

16 AU 919.

17 Smyth, *Scandinavian York and Dublin* and Downham, *Viking Kings*.

18 For these and other tenth-century activities, see Ó Corráin, *Ireland before the Normans*, pp.101–4 and Downham, 'Vikings in Southern Uí Néill', pp.235–43.

19 AFM *s.a.* 935 (= 937).

20 Arnold, *Symeonis Monachi Opera*, 2, p.93 (§84); Woolf, 'Amlaíb Cuarán', p.36.

21 AU 945: 'Blacair gave up Áth Cliath and Amlaíb succeeded him' (*Blacáir do thelcudh Atha Cliath ocus Amlaibh tara eisi*); for an account of his career, see Woolf, 'Amlaíb Cuarán'; see also Etchingham, 'North Wales', pp.165–71.

22 AU.

23 AU.

24 AU 945.

25 AU 947.

26 AU; a later hand claims that the perpetrators were Dublin Vikings.

27 AU; Dobbs, 'Ban-Shenchus', *Revue Celtique* 47, pp.313, 337; 48, pp.188, 227; Woolf, 'Amlaíb Cuarán', p.41.

28 Dobbs, 'Ban-Shenchus', *Revue Celtique* 48, pp.188, 227.

29 Dobbs, 'Ban-Shenchus', *Revue Celtique* 47, pp.314, 338; 48, pp.189, 227.

30 AU; the battle is discussed by Etchingham, 'North Wales', pp.173—5.

31 CS, pp.226—7; see also ATig., 2, pp.233—4.

32 ASC 943.

33 See Bhreathnach, 'Documentary evidence' and 'Columban churches'; I owe the
   latter reference to Fiona Edmonds.

34 CS, pp.226—7; see also ATig., 2, p.234.

35 'Amlaíb Cuarán', p.43.

36 See Downham, 'Vikings in Southern Uí Néill', pp.239—41.

37 See Holm, 'Viking Dublin', Valante, 'Dublin's economic relations' and Wallace, 'The
   Economy'.

38 AU 1013.

39 ATig., 2, p.235. See also AU 983; CS, pp.228—9.

40 'Vikings in Southern Uí Néill', p.242.

41 CS, pp.234—5; ATig., 2, p.242; Downham, 'Vikings in Southern Uí Néill', p.242.

42 AU.

43 The corresponding entry in AU designates him *rex Caisil* 'king of Cashel': 742.

44 For a discussion of the term, and the related one 'king of Tara', see Ó Corráin,
   'Nationality and kingship' and Charles-Edwards, *Early Christian Ireland*, pp.469—
   521.

45 AU 776; see Charles-Edwards, *Early Christian Ireland*, pp.595—6.

46 AU.

47 The Annals of Ulster, on the other hand, simply record it as *rigdhal mor* 'a great
   royal meeting': 838.

48 AU. His career and that of his son, Flann Sinna, is discussed by Jaski, 'Vikings',
   pp.315—25.

49 Note, for example, the series of entries AU 854, 856, 858.

50 AU 859: 'Máel Guala, king of Munster, warranted the alienation' (*ad-rogaidh Mael
   Gualai, ri Muman, a dilsi*).

51 AU 860.

52 CS, pp.168—9: 'Flann son of Máel Sechnaill plundered Munster and [took] away its
   hostages' (*Inradh Mumhan la Flann mac Maoileclainn et a braigde [do thabhairt] leis*).

53 CS, pp.180—1 mentions only the hostages of Connacht in this regard.

54 AU.

55 AI.

56 CS, pp.208—11.

57 AU.

58 AU 971.

59 AI; CS, pp.228—9; ATig., 2, p.235.

60 AU, AI.

61 Breatnach, 'Ecclesiastical Element', p.43.

62 Ní Dhonnchadha, 'Guarantor List', p.200.

63 AU.

64 AI; he is listed as one of eight sons of Cernach in the Dál Cais genealogies:
   O'Brien, *Corpus genealogiarum Hiberniae*, p.241 (153a46).

65 AI 747 where the place is given as Cúil Gese; AU 747 speaks of the battle of

Carn Ailche. For Corpre's Éoganacht lineage, see O'Brien, *Corpus genealogiarum Hiberniae*, p.220 (1512a6).

66 AU.

67 Radner, *Fragmentary Annals*, pp.150–63 (§423); Uí Thairdelbaig are mentioned pp.156–7, 160–1 where they are said to hail from their territory's heartland, Aineslis from Bórama (whence Brian acquired his name) and Conadar from Mag Adair.

68 The names of the two Uí Thairdelbaig do not occur in the contemporary accounts of the battle: AU, AI 908; CS, pp.180–3.

69 AI. His Uí Oengusso lineage is noted in a later source: Ó Donnchadha, *An Leabhar Muimhneach*, pp.316–7.

70 Ryan, 'Brian Boruma', p.357; Ó Corráin, 'Dál Cais', p.55.

71 For his genealogy, see O'Brien, *Corpus genealogiarum Hiberniae*, pp.237, 250 (152b27, 154a46).

72 AU 951 accord him the less inflated title, 'king of Thomond' (*rí Tuathmuman*); CS, pp.210–1 style him 'king of Dál Cais' (*rí Dáil cCais*).

73 Later sources claim that he was the first Dál Cais king to attack outside his own territory stating that he spent a month in Athlone besieging the Connacht men: Ó Donnchadha, *An Leabhar Muimhneach*, p.126.

74 CS, pp.206–7.

75 Dobbs, 'Ban-Shenchus', *Revue Celtique* 48, p.187.

76 CS, pp.204–5: 'Órlaith, daughter of Cennétig mac Lorcáin, was put to death by Donnchad mac Flainn, king of Ireland, after she was accused of sexual intercourse with Óengus, his son' (*Orlaith ingen Cinnéididh mic Lorcain do bas[ugud] la Donnchadh mac Flainn, rí Eirenn, iar na liudh for Aongus, for a mac*). The incident is discussed in Kelleher, 'Rise of the Dál Cais', pp.236–7.

77 CS, pp.208–11; the sons in question are called Echtigern and Donnacan (for Donn Cuan), both of whom are listed in the genealogies: O'Brien, *Corpus genealogiarum Hiberniae*, p.237 (152b32); see above p.20.

78 AI; O'Brien, *Corpus genealogiarum Hiberniae*, p.237 (152b34).

79 Ó Donnchadha, *An Leabhar Muimhneach*, p.127.

80 O'Brien, *Corpus genealogiarum Hiberniae*, p.360 (LL 320ab34).

81 For a brief account of Mathgamain's career, see Ó Corráin, *Ireland before the Normans*, pp.116–7.

82 AFM *s.a.* 957 (= 959).

83 AI; AFM *s.a.* 961.(= 963) By contrast, a resounding victory over Fergal ua Ruairc is recorded in a later source: Ó Donnchadha, *An Leabhar Muimhneach*, pp.127–8.

84 For the economic importance of Limerick and its relationship with its hinterland see, for example, Bradley, 'Interpretation', pp.62–5, Holm, 'Viking Dublin', pp.257–8, and Sheehan, 'Viking-age hoards', for which reference I am grateful to Fiona Edmonds.

85 AI, AU 967; Todd, *Cogadh*, pp.74–83.

86 AI.

87 AFM *s.a.* 970 (= 972).

88 AI 972.

89 AI 973.

90 Gwynn, 'Were the "Annals of Inisfallen" written at Killaloe?', p.25.

91 'Rise of the Dál Cais'.

92 *Ibid.*, p.236.

93 I owe this suggestion to my colleague, Fiona Edmonds. For an account of Munster kingship reflecting eighth-century politics, see O'Keeffe, 'Dál Caladbuig' and the discussion of this tract and a related one in Charles-Edwards, *Early Christian Ireland*, pp.534–48.

94 CS, pp.206–7 (*s.a.* 943).

95 Ó Corráin, *Ireland before the Normans*, p.115.

96 Kelleher, 'Rise of the Dál Cais', p.234; Ó Corráin, 'Irish origin legends', pp.70–1.

97 O'Brien, *Corpus genealogiarum Hiberniae*, p.207 (149b47–8); this is repeated Todd, *Cogadh*, pp.54–5.

98 Mulchrone, *Bethu Phátraic*, p.123.

99 See Jackson, 'Date'.

100 Mac Eoin, 'Dating', pp.127–34; Dumville 'Dating'; Byrne and Francis, 'Two Lives', p.7.

101 AI; see above p.22.

102 Hughes, *Early Christian Ireland*, p.114.

103 AU, AI 934; AFM *s.a.* 932.

104 Gwynn, 'Were the "Annals of Inisfallen" written at Killaloe?', p.26.

105 Later sources claim that he assumed the kingship of Cashel on the death of Donnchad mac Cellacháin in 963: Todd, *Cogadh*, pp.70–1; Ó Donnchadha, *An Leabhar Muimhneach*, p.127.

106 AI 976: 'The capture of Mathgamain son of Cennétig, king of Cashel. He was treacherously seized by Donnubán and handed over to the son of Bran in violation of the guarantee and despite the interdiction of the elders of Munster and he was put to death by the latter [Bran's son]' (*Aurgabail Mathgamna meic Cennetich, rig Cassil; a aurgabail la Dondubán tre fell ocus a thabairt do mc. Brain tar sarugud ocus tar mallachtain sruthi Muman ocus a marbad la suide*).

107 Todd, *Cogadh*, pp.86–95; in a poem preserved only in a seventeenth-century version of the text, Mathgamain is said to have been under the protection not of Bairre but of St Ailbe of Emly and St Nessán (pp.96–7).

108 See Ní Mhaonaigh, '*Cogadh Gáedhel re Gallaibh* and Cork', pp.77–8 and references therein.

109 Todd, *Cogadh*, pp.88–9.

110 *Ibid.*, pp.92–3.

111 *Ibid.*, pp.56–7.

112 *Ibid.*, pp.64–71.

113 *Ibid.*, pp.76–85.

114 AI.

115 See Ní Mhaonaigh, '*Cogadh Gáedhel re Gallaibh* and Cork', pp.79–80.

116 Todd, *Cogadh*, pp.100–1.

Chapter Three: 'Emperor of the Irish'

1 Brian's birth is noted in certain chronicles (AU 941; CS, pp.194–5) though these entries may be retrospective; see p.15 above.

2 AU 1014; see above pp.7–8.

3 O'Brien, *Corpus genealogiarum Hiberniae*, p.124: 'No king has taken [the kingship of] Ireland after the death of Patrick apart from the lineage of Níall, except for two, i.e. Báetán and Brian' (*Sciendum est autem quod nullus rex de alio nisi de semine Néill nisi exceptis duobus id est Báetán et Brian regnauerunt Hiberniam post Patricii aduentu tenuit*).

4 Stokes, 'Death of Crimthann', pp.200–1: '… and kingship and overlordship will be with you and your children, except in the case of two of Fiachra's seed, namely Daithí and Ailill Molt, and one Munster king, namely Brian Boru; all those will be kings without opposition' (*… bid lat ocus lat chlaind co brath in rigi ocus in forlamus cenmotha dias do shil Fhiachrach .i. Dathi ocus Ailill Molt, ocus oenrigh a Mumain .i. Brian Boruma, cen fhresabra na riga sin uili*).

5 Murphy, *Early Irish Lyrics*, pp.90–1 (stanza 11).

6 AU; CS, pp.242–3.

7 Gwynn, *Book of Armagh*, p.ciii and fol.16v; Gwynn translates the passage in question as follows (substituting 'Irish' for his 'Scotic' and 'Scots'), 'Saint Patrick, when going to heaven, decreed that the entire fruit of his labour, as well of baptism and of causes as of alms, should be rendered to the apostolic city which in the Irish tongue is called Arddmacha [Armagh]. This I have found in the records of the Irish. [This] I have written, namely Caluus Perennis [= Máel Suthain], in the presence of Brian, Emperor of the Irish; and what I have written he has determined on behalf of all the kings of Maceria [Cashel]'. See also above p.12.

8 'Brian in Armagh', pp.44–6; see also Flanagan, *Irish Society*, p.179 who sees it as 'equally redolent of the high-flown contemporary titles used of the West Saxon royal house'.

9 O'Brien, *Corpus genealogiarum Hiberniae*, p.250; their association with Cas is set out on pp.206–8; see Kelleher, 'Rise of the Dál Cais', p.234 and Ó Corráin, 'Irish origin legends', pp.70–1; see also above p.25.

10 O'Brien, *Corpus genealogiarum Hiberniae*, p.237: 'Cennétig had twelve sons and five of them had descendants i.e. Brian from whom Síl Briain [Brian's seed] is descended, Mathgamain from whom Uí Mathgamna [the descendants of Mathgamain] are descended, Donn Cuan from whom Muinter Duind Chuain [Donn Cuan's people] are descended, Echthigern from whom are descended Uí Echthigirn [the descendants of Echthigern], Anluan from whom are descended Uí Chuirc [the descendants of Corc son of Anluan]' (*Dá mac déc oc Ceinnéitich ocus a cóic díb coa tá síl .i. Brian a quo Síl mBriain, Mathgamain a quo Húi Mathgamna, Donn-cuan a quo Muinter Duind-chuan, Echthigern a quo Húi Echthigirnn, Anluan ó tát Húi Chuircc meic Anluain*).

11 Dobbs, 'Ban-Shenchus', *Revue Celtique* 47, pp.314, 338; *Revue Celtique* 48, pp.188, 227.

12 O'Brien, *Corpus genealogiarum Hiberniae*, p.238.

13 Dobbs, 'Ban-Shenchus', *Revue Celtique* 48, p.228.

14 AI.

15 AI 1031.

16 AI, AU. See further below pp.101–7

17 Dobbs, 'Ban-Shenchus', *Revue Celtique* 47, pp.314, 338; *Revue Celtique* 48, pp.189, 227; the Norse narrative, *Brennu-Njáls saga*, on the other hand, wrongly states that Gormlaith was not the mother of any of Brian's children: Einar Ól. Sveinsson, *Brennu-*

Njáls saga, p.441.

18 Todd, *Cogadh* and Einar Ól. Sveinsson, *Brennu-Njáls saga*.

19 'Gormlaith, daughter of Murchad, wife of Brian. She it was who took the three leaps of which are said: 'Three leaps did Gormlaith perform which no other woman shall do till Doomsday: a leap into Dublin, a leap into Tara, a leap into Cashel, the plain with the mound which surpasses all'. Amlaíb Cuarán was her first husband, and Máel Sechnaill mac Domnaill after that, and Brian (*Gormlaith ingen Murchada ben Briain. Is sí sede ra ling na trí lémmend da n-ebrad: Trí lémend ra ling Gormlaith/ ní lingfea ben co bráth/ léim i nÁth Cliath, léim i Temraig/ léim i Cassel, Carnmaig ós chách. Amlaíb Cuarán a cétmuntar ocus Máel-Sechlainn mac Domnaill iar tain ocus Brian*): O'Brien, *Corpus genealogiarum Hiberniae*, p.13; translated by Ó Cuív, 'Personal names', p.86 n.3.

20 For these events see, for example, AI and Ní Mhaonaigh, 'Tales of three Gormlaiths', pp.18–19.

21 Amlaíb died in 981 (ATig., 2, p.234; CS, pp.226–7) and may have been considerably older than Gormlaith; their son, Sitric assumed the kingship of Dublin in the 990s.

22 Dobbs, 'Ban-Shenchus', *Revue Celtique* 48, pp.189, 228.

23 'Brian Boruma', p.366.

24 'Battle of Glenn Máma', pp.58–9.

25 CS, pp.232–3; ATig., 2, pp.239–40; AI 993, 997; AU 990.

26 AI. See further below pp.107–10.

27 AI. See further below pp.111–6.

28 AU, AI.

29 AU, AI.

30 AI.

31 AI and Kelleher, 'Rise of the Dál Cais', p.240.

32 AI.

33 Her name is preserved only in the medieval Welsh narrative, the Life of Gruffudd ap Cynan (*Historia Grufud vab Kenan*), and in the Latin text on which it is based: Evans, *Mediaeval Prince*, pp.26, 57; Russell, *Vita Griffini*, pp.56–7 (§6); see also Duffy, 'Ostmen', pp.392–3.

34 AU, AI 1000; CS, pp.238–9; ATig., 2, pp.244, 245.

35 Todd, *Cogadh*, pp.190–3.

36 Mathgamain was murdered in 976 (AI); see above pp.26–7

37 An account of Brian's career can be found in Ó Corráin, *Ireland before the Normans*, pp.120–31 and Duffy, 'Brian Bóruma'. It has been mapped by Seán Duffy in his *Atlas of Irish History*, p.27; I am grateful to him for allowing me to reprint the map below (map 20).

38 AI; CS, pp.224–5; ATig., 2, p.231.

39 AI 977.

40 AU, AI 978; CS, pp.224–5; ATig., 2, p.232.

41 AI.

42 AI; CS, pp.228–9; ATig., 2, p.235.

43 AI 983.

44 AI 983.

45 AI 984: 'and they exchanged hostages there … as a guarantee of both together providing a hosting to attack Dublin' (*coro chloemclaiset giallu and … im imthairec sluagid do dul ar Áth Cliath*).

46 AU 983.

47 See Etchingham, 'North Wales', p.175.

48 AI.

49 CS, pp.230–1; ATig., 2 pp.237–8.

50 AI.

51 AI 987.

52 AI.

53 AI 990.

54 AI; see Ó Corráin, 'Dál Cais', pp.52–3.

55 AU; CS, pp.232–3; ATig., 2, p.239.

56 AI 991; see also AU 991.

57 A Tig., 2, pp.239–40; CS, pp.232–3.

58 AI.

59 CS, pp.234–5; ATig., 2, p.241.

60 AI.

61 AI 996.

62 AI 997.

63 AI 998.

64 CS, pp.236–7.

65 AU 998.

66 AU, AI; the battle is discussed in Mac Shamhráin, 'Battle of Glenn Máma'.

67 CS, pp.236–7; ATig., 2, pp.243–4.

68 AU, AI 1000; CS, pp.238–9; ATig., 2, pp.244, 245. Sitric was Brian's son-in-law; see above p.33.

69 AU 1000; CS, pp.238–9; ATig., 2, p.245.

70 AU 1001; ATig., 2, p.246.

71 AU, AI 1001; CS, pp.238–9; A Tig., 2, p. 246.

72 CS, pp.238–9; ATig., 2, p.246.

73 AU, AI; CS, pp.238–41; ATig., 2, p. 247.

74 AU, AI 1002; CS, pp.240–1; ATig., 2, pp.246–7.

75 AI 1003.

76 AU 1004.

77 On this battle, see Byrne, *Irish Kings*, p.127, for which reference I am grateful to Fiona Edmonds.

78 AU 1005; AI 1005; CS, pp.242–3.

79 AU; CS, pp.242–3.

80 AU, AI; CS, pp.242–5.

81 AU, AI 1007.

82 AU 1007.

83 AI; see Ó Corráin, 'Dál Cais', p.86.

84 AU, AI; CS, pp.246–7.

85 AI; AU. Flaithbertach ua Néill's participation is recorded in AFM *s.a.* 1010 but Dál Cais involvement is mentioned only in an interlinear interpolation in AU; I owe this observation to Denis Casey.

86 AU 1012.

87 AU 1013; AI 1012.

88 AU.

89 AU, AI 1013.

90 AU 1013; CS, pp.248–9.

91 AU 1013.

92 AU, AI 1014; CS, pp.250–3.

93 Gwynn, 'Were the "Annals of Inisfallen" written at Killaloe?', Hughes, *Early Christian Ireland*, pp.110, 297–8; Grabowski and Dumville, *Chronicles and Annals.*

94 AU.

95 CS, pp.224–5; ATig., 2 p.231.

96 ATig., 2, pp.243–4: 'A hosting by Máel Sechnaill and Brian mac Cennétig to Glenn Máma … and Máel Sechnaill and Brian, with the men of Munster and Mide, went to Connacht and carried off its hostages and the best of its treasures' (*Sluaighedh la Mael Sechnaill ocus la Brian mac Cendétigh co Gleand Mama … ocus co ndechaid Mael Sechnaill ocus Brian co feraib Muman ocus Midhi a Condachtaib, co tucsad a ngíallu ocus a n-as deach a ssét*).

97 ATig. 2, pp.239–40, 245.

98 AU 1000: 'Brian then retreated without giving battle or making incursion – by the Lord's insistence' (*Do-luidh Brian tra fora chulu cen chath cen indriudh, cogente Domino*).

99 AI.

100 This runs counter to the opinion of Aubrey Gwynn that 'little credit is given to Brian in the Annals of Ulster for the events which led up to the battle of Clontarf', and to his claim that 'Maelsechlainn, not Brian, is here the central figure': 'Were the "Annals of Inisfallen" written at Killaloe?', p.26.

101 See above p.35. Gwynn, 'Brian in Armagh', p.39 has suggested that the bias in favour of Máel Sechnaill is most pronounced in the Annals of Tigernach, claiming that the history of these years has in fact been rewritten therein to reflect this. It should be noted, however, that owing to a lost folio the entries between 1001 and 1016 are missing in that chronicle. See also Downham, 'Vikings in Southern Uí Néill', p.243.

102 Gwynn, 'Were the "Annals of Inisfallen" written at Killaloe?'; Grabowski and Dumville, *Chronicles and Annals.*

103 AI: 'For these were the five kings of the Munstermen who ruled Ireland after the [introduction of the] Faith, i.e. Óengus son of Nad Fraích, and his son, i.e. Eochaid who ruled Ireland for seventeen years, and Cathal, son of Finguine, and Feidlimid, son of Crimthann, and Brian, son of Cennétig' (*Ar it hé .u. ríg ro gabsat Herind iar cretim do Mumnechaib, .i. Oengus macc Nad Fruich ocus a mc., .i. Eochaid, qui Hiberniam rexit .xuii. annis, ocus Cathal mc. Finguine ocus Feidlimmid macc Crimthain ocus Brian mc. Cennetich*).

104 Ní Mhaonaigh, '*Cogad Gáedel re Gallaib* and the annals', and references therein.

105 Todd, *Cogadh*, pp.56–9.

106 *Ibid.*, pp.58–69.

107 *Ibid.*, pp.74–81.

108 AI 967.

109 Todd, *Cogadh*, pp.100–3.

110 *Ibid.*, pp.102–3 and pp.44–5; see AI 977.

111 AU, AI 978; Todd, *Cogadh*, pp.106–7.

112 Todd, *Cogadh*, pp.106–7.

113 AI 985.

114 Todd, *Cogadh*, pp.106–7.

115 *Ibid.*, pp.106–9; AI 983.

116 Todd, *Cogadh*, pp.108–9.

117 AI 988, 993; Todd, *Cogadh*, pp.108–9.

118 AI 988.

119 Todd, *Cogadh*, pp.108–9.

120 *Ibid.*, pp.108–9; AI 997.

121 Todd, *Cogadh*, pp.108–19; AU, AI 999.

122 AI.

123 Todd, *Cogadh*, pp.118–33.

124 AU, AI.

125 Todd, *Cogadh*, pp.132–5.

126 AU 1005.

127 AU, AI 1006.

128 Todd, *Cogadh*, pp.134–5.

129 *Ibid.*, pp.136–7.

130 *Ibid.*, pp.136–9.

131 *Ibid.*, pp.138–9.

132 *Ibid.*, pp.138–41.

133 AI 995, 1012.

134 Todd, *Cogadh*, pp.142–65.

135 *Ibid.*, pp.146–7.

136 AU 1009 where Flaithbertach is said to make a foray into Brega.

137 Todd, *Cogadh*, pp.150–1; AU 1013.

138 Todd, *Cogadh*, pp.150–1.

139 AU, AI 1013.

140 AI.

141 Todd, *Cogadh*, pp.150–1.

142 *Ibid.*, pp.150–213.

143 The *Cogadh* gives his age at the time as eighty-eight (*ibid.*, pp.204–5); if his birth date of 941 in the chronicles is to be believed, he was in fact seventy-three.

144 *Ibid.*, pp.154–5, 196–205.

145 For discussion and examples, see, McCone, *Pagan Past*, pp.107–37.

146 Todd, *Cogadh*, pp.204–7.

147 *Ibid.*, pp.52–9.

148 *Ibid.*, pp.60–71; the specific quote is on pp.68–9.

149 *Ibid.*, pp.60–1.

150 For such tropes, see, for example, Clancy, 'Court' and O'Leary, 'Foreseeing driver'.

151 Todd, *Cogadh*, pp.100–1.

152 *Ibid.*, pp.136–7; Knott, *Togail*.

153 Todd, *Cogadh*, pp.138–9; see above p.41.

154 AI: 'A defeat of the foreigners of Limerick by Mathgamain son of Cennétig at Sulchóit and Limerick was burned by him before noon on the following day' (*Maidm for Gullu Luimnich re Mathgamain m. Cennetich oc Sulchuait, ocus loscud Lumnich dó ría medón laí arna bárach*).

155 AI 999, 1000; AU 999. CS, pp.236–7 records it as a joint-expedition by Brian and Máel Sechnaill, as noted above p.35; for discussion, see Mac Shamhráin, 'Battle of Glenn Máma'.

156 Todd, *Cogadh*, pp.76–7; see also pp.110–1, *cath fulech, fichda, forderc, feochair, fearda, feramail, agarb, aniartha, escardemail*.

157 *Ibid.*, pp.110–1; AU 999 where his father's name is given as Etigén.

158 Todd, *Cogadh*, pp.112–5. The versified dialogues between Mathgamain and Brian which follow the account of Sulchóit are only preserved in the seventeenth-century version of the *Cogadh*: pp.76–9, 80–1.

159 *Ibid.*, pp.78–9

160 *Ibid.*, pp.114–5.

161 *Ibid.*, pp.78–9: Their girls … young women … and youths were taken (*Tuccait a n-ingena … a hócmna … ocus a maccaimi*); see also pp.114–5.

162 *Ibid.*, pp.82–3: 'a big line of Viking women in a circle on the hills of Sangal, bent with their hands on the ground, and the youths of the hosts marshalling them (?) from behind' (*lini mór do gailsechaib na nGall i cncocanaib Sangail imacuart, ocus siat croma, ocus a lama ar lar, ocus gilli na sluag ga mairescud ina ndegaid*).

163 *Ibid.*, pp.116–7.

164 *Ibid.*, pp.82–3.

165 *Ibid.*, pp.118–9.

166 See Ní Mhaonaigh, '*Cogad Gáedel re Gallaib* and the annals'.

167 For details, see Ní Mhaonaigh, '*Cogad Gáedel re Gallaib*: some dating considerations', pp.368–74.

168 Dillon, *Lebor na Cert*; see Candon, 'Barefaced effrontery'.

169 See Ní Mhaonaigh, '*Cogad Gáedel re Gallaib*: some dating considerations', pp.374–6.

170 *Irish Kings*, p.70.

171 Ó Corráin, 'Dál Cais'.

172 *Ibid.*, p.56.

173 Grabowski and Dumville, *Chronicles and Annals*.

174 Ní Mhaonaigh, '*Cogad Gáedel re Gallaib* and the annals', p.120.

175 AI.

176 AU.

177 *Ireland before the Normans*, p.127.

178 Gwynn, 'Brian in Armagh'; see above p.30.

179 AI 1007, 1010.

180 Gwynn, 'Brian in Armagh', pp.48–50. The annalistic entries read as follows: AU 1052: 'Muiredach Ua Sencháin, steward of Munster, died in peace' (*Muiredach H. Sinachan maer Muman, in pace dormierunt*) (in the Annals of the Four Masters he is termed *maor Patraic hi Mumain* 'Patrick's steward in Munster'); AU 1072: 'Gilla Críst ua Longáin, steward of Munster, died' (*Gilla Crist H. Longan maer Muman do éc*); AU 1073: '[and] Cormac ua Clothagáin, steward of Munster [they] died in penitence' (*Cormac H. Clothagáin moer Muman in penitentia mortui sunt*); AU 1113: 'Díarmait Ua Cellaig, successor of Ua Suanaig, Díarmait Ua Longáin, steward of Munster … died in repentance' (*Diarmait H. Ceallaigh comarba hU Suanaigh, Diarmait H. Longan maer Muman … in penitentia mortui sunt*) (CS describes the latter as *airccinnech Arda Patraic*; and AI reads *comarba Aird Phatraic*). There are references to a steward of Dál Cais (*moer Dáil Cais*) at AU 1053 and 1108, for which references I am grateful to Denis Casey.

181 AU 1103.

182 AU 1113: 'A hosting by Muircertach Ua Briain and Leth Moga, consisting of both laity and clergy, to Grenóc. However, Domnall, grandson of Lochlann, with the nobles of the north of Ireland, went to Cluain Caín of the Fir Rois and they confronted one another continuously for a month until Cellach, successor of Patrick, with the staff of Jesus, made a year's peace between them' (*Slogadh la Muircertach H. mBriain ocus la Leith Mogha eter loech ocus cleiriuch co Grenoic. Domnall imorro m. m. Lochlainn co maithibh tuaiscirt Erenn co Cluain Cain Fer Rois co mbadar fri re mis cind comar co ndernai Ceallach comarba Patraic ocus bachall Isu beus sith mbliadhna etarru*).

183 Dillon, *Lebor na Cert*; Candon, 'Barefaced effrontery'; see above p.46.

184 O'Brien, *Corpus genealogiarum Hibernaie*, p.124; see above p.29.

185 'Rise of the Dál Cais', p.234; see above pp.24–5.

186 Kelleher, 'Rise of the Dál Cais', p.234; Ó Corráin, 'Irish origin legends', pp.70–1; see above p.25.

187 Gwynn, *Metrical Dindshenchas*, 1, pp.14–27.

188 Gwynn, *Metrical Dindshenchas*, 4, pp.146–63.

189 Joynt, 'Echtra'.

190 Stokes, 'Death of Crimthann', pp.172–207.

191 Murray, *Baile in Scáil*, p.4.

192 See, for example, Ó Riain, 'Psalter of Cashel'.

193 *Ibid.*, p.109.

194 Gwynn, *Metrical Dindshenchas*, 4 , pp.136–43; Arbuthnot, *Cóir Anmann*, 1, pp.101–4, 139–41 (§104).

195 Todd, *Cogadh*, pp.54–7.

196 It should be noted that at least one other eleventh-century author linked Uí Néill and Munster; a poem on the loss of a pet goose addressed to Mór, wife of Máel Sechnaill, includes a stanza addressed to Brian: Murphy, *Early Irish Lyrics*, pp.90–1; see above p.30.

197 Byrne, *Irish Kings*, p.257.

198 Macalister, *Lebor Gabála*; for discussion of the text, see Carey, *National Origin Legend*.

Chapter Four: 'Brian's Battle'

1 Jón Jóhannesson, *Austfirðinga sögur*, p.302 (*Þorsteins saga Síðu-Hallssonar* 'Þorsteinn Síðu-Hallsson's saga'). The Norse material is discussed in Helgi Guðmundsson, *Um haf innan*, for which reference I am grateful to Jonathan Grove.

2 For a detailed description of the battle, see Ryan, 'Battle of Clontarf'; Ó Corráin, 'Brian Boru' and Downham, 'Battle of Clontarf' contain more general accounts.

3 Goedheer, *Irish and Norse Traditions*, pp.50, 55 (stanza 47).

4 Todd, *Cogadh*, pp.196–203.

5 AU¹ 1224.

6 Goedheer, *Irish and Norse Traditions*, pp.50, 55 (stanza 51): 'When will there come the like of Brian, south or north, east or west, who will protect the Irish against evil, as he alone protected?' (*Cuin thucfas shamhail Briain/ theas ná thuaigh, toir ná thiar/ neach fhóirfeas Gaoidhil air ghoimh/ mar do fhóir sion a n-aonar?*).

7 AI 1014.

8 CS, pp.250–1. Lochla(i)nn refers to the territory whence Vikings came; on the changing meaning of the term, see Ní Mhaonaigh, 'Literary Lochlann' and references therein and Etchingham, 'Location'. As in AI, CS records the slaying of Leinstermen in the battle and refers to it as 'a defeat against Vikings and Leinstermen' (*raoineadh for Galloibh ocus for Laignibh*), pp.252–3.

9 AU 1014.

10 AU 1014. The estimate in *Chronicum Scotorum* is greater, since there allegedly fell there '3,000 foreigners' (*tricha ced do Galloibh*): pp.252–3.

11 AU 1014; see also CS, pp.250–1.

12 Hudson speculates on a possible context, *Viking Pirates*, pp.75, 134. Colmán Etchingham has suggested to me, however, that Brian's links with the Islesmen may lend credibility to this Scottish connection: see his 'North Wales'.

13 AI 958. Alongside, Tuathal, heir-apparent, of the Leinstermen, CS also contains the supplementary name of an heir-apparent of Uí Fhailgi, son of Brocarbán mac Conchobair, whereas AU adds the name of Domnall mac Fergaile, king of the Fortúatha Laigen; see Table 1 below, pp. 189–91.

14 These are Oittir Dub; Suartgair; Donnchad ua Eruilb; Grisene; Luimne; Amlaim mac

Laghmainn: AU 1014; the same list is found in ALC pp.10–1.

15 Downham, 'England and the Irish Sea zone', p.61, and references therein.

16 'Clann Eruilb', p.164; see also Ó Corráin, 'Vikings', pp.307–8.

17 Glún Iairn was a half-brother of Máel Sechnaill mac Domnaill, with whom he allied on occasion. Dubgall's son, Mathgamain, was slain on a raid in Munster in 1013: AI.

18 AU; see above p.37.

19 On the nature of the settlement at Dublin from its foundation until 1014, see Clarke, 'Bloodied eagle' and 'Proto-towns', pp.344–64.

20 AU.

21 AI 1000.

22 See, for example, AU 1000; AI 1002, 1006, 1007.

23 AU.

24 AI 1013; see also AU 1013.

25 AI 1014.

26 According to a later compilation, the Annals of Loch Cé, Brian declared war on the Dublin Vikings and the Leinstermen 'to bring them under his rule as he has brought them before' (dia ttabhairt fó a réir amail dus fucc ríamh): ALC 1014, pp.2–3. On Dublin as economic hub in this period see, for example, Holm 'Viking Dublin', Valante, 'Dublin's economic relations' and Wallace, 'The Economy'.

27 AI 1003.

28 AU 1013; he took great spoils and countless captives on the same expedition, as noted above p.37.

29 Jones, Brut … Peniarth, p.11; Jones, Brut … Red Book, pp.20–1; Jones, Brenhinedd, pp.50–1.

30 Jones, Brut … Peniarth, p.xxxviii. According to Jones, down to the year 1282, the Peniarth 20 and Red Book versions of the Brutiau represent 'two independent translations of the same [Latin] original' now lost and Brenhinedd y Saesson is a 'condensed version' of that original chronicle: Brut … Peniarth, pp.xxxvi–vii; see also Lloyd, 'Welsh chronicles'.

31 ab Ithel, Annales Cambriæ s.a. 1013 (p.22): 'Brian, king of Ireland together with his son, was killed by (A)Scuthin, i.e. king of Dublin' (?) (Bianus rex Hiberniæ cum filio suo Ascuthin, scilicet rege Dulyn, occiditur). I am grateful to Fiona Edmonds for drawing my attention to this and to Torsten Meißner for discussion of its possible meaning.

32 Jones, Brenhinedd, pp.50–1; see also Jones, Brut … Peniarth, p.11. Jones, Brut … Red Book, pp.20–1: Brut … Red Book erroneously has Derotyr for Brodar.

33 Goedheer, Irish and Norse Traditions, pp.120–1.

34 Bourgain, Ademari, p.173 §55, lines 11–16.

35 Landes, Relics, p.134.

36 Bourgain, Ademari, p.lxviii.

37 Karl Ferdinand Werner terms him a 'Geschichtsschreiber' (fabricator of history): 'Ademar von Chabannes', p.306, while John Gillingham describes his work as a 'brilliant but wayward history': 'Ademar of Chabannes', p.9.

38 Bourgain, Ademari, p.173 §55, lines 6–10.

39 Todd, Cogadh, pp.192–3.

40 Goedheer, Irish and Norse Traditions, pp.120–1; Einar Ól. Sveinsson, Brennu-Njáls saga, p.452; Jón Jóhannesson, Austfirðinga sögur, p.302.

41 A brief biography can be found in Kenney, Sources, pp.614–6.

42 This material is discussed by Mac Carthy, Codex.

43 As noted above p.35, Brian's brother, Marcán, was abbot there: Ó Corráin, 'Dál Cais',
    p.52.
44 Mac Carthy, *Codex*, p.8.
45 See Mac Niocaill, *Medieval Irish Annals*, pp.29–31.
46 ALC 1014, pp.12–3; see Freeman, 'Annals', pp.327–9.
47 Freeman, 'Annals', p.329.
48 ALC 1014.
49 The interrelationships are briefly discussed in Mac Niocaill, *Medieval Irish Annals*,
    pp.29–31.
50 The lists of the dead in the chronicle accounts are presented in tabular form in Table 1
    below pp.189–91.
51 ALC 1014, pp.2–5.
52 ALC 1014, pp.4–5: 'Grisíne, a knight of the Flemings, and Gresiam of the
    Northmen'(*Grisíne corad Pléimionnaibh ocus Greisiam a Normannaibh*).
53 AU 1013. The Ua Ruairc king in question is Niall Ua Ruairc (AU 1013); the author of
    the *Cogadh* substitutes his great-grandfather, Fergal (died 966). For material concerning
    this family in the text, see Ní Mhaonaigh, 'Bréifne bias', particularly, p.143.
54 Todd, *Cogadh*, pp.146–7: 'Flaithbertach plundered Mide and devastated most of it. On
    that occasion, Osli son of Dubcenn mac Ímair, an officer of Brian – he was one of
    his stewards – was slain and many more' (*Do roni Flatbertach crech i Midi, acus ro inretar
    formor Midi leis. As diside ro marbad Osli mac Dubcind mic Imair, fer grada do Brian, ocus
    mormaer da maeraib e, ocus sochaide eile*). Colmán Etchingham has suggested to me that
    Osli may be historical, a son of Dubecenn mac Ímair killed by Brian in 977 (ATig.
    p.231.)
55 Todd, *Cogadh*, pp.148–9: 'and Máel Mórda mac Murchada, Sitric mac Amláib, as well
    as Vikings and Leinstermen overtook them [Máel Sechnaill and his men] and they
    killed one of their three plundering parties ... After that a great hosting was made by
    Vikings and Leinstermen. They attacked Mide as far as Fabar Féchín and took great
    spoils and countless cattle away from the sanctuary of Fabar' (*ocus ro arraid orto Mael
    Morda mac Murchada ocus Sitriuc mac Amlaib ocus Gaill ocus Lagin ocus ro marbsat in tres
    creach da crechaib uli ... Da ronad morsluaged iarsin la Gallaib ocus re Lagnib ocus ro hinredh
    Midhi leo co Fabur Fechin ocus rucsat brait mor ocus buar diairmiti leo a Termuind Fabair*).
    ALC 1014, pp.2–3: 'A hosting by Amláib's son and Máel Mórda, together with Vikings
    and Leinstermen to Mide and Brega and after that to Féichín's sanctuary. Countless
    cows and extensive spoils were taken by then' (*Slúaighedh la mac Amhlaoíbh ocus la
    Máolmórda ocus Galla ocus Laighne a Midhe ocus a mBreghaibh ocus iarsin go termann
    Féichín, go ruccsat bú díarmhidhe ocus broide adbal leó*).
56 Todd, *Cogadh*, pp.150–3; ALC 1014, pp.4–5.
57 ALC 1014, pp.4–5; Todd, *Cogadh*, pp.152–3.
58 These two visions have been examined by Meidhbhín Ní Úrdail, to whom I am
    grateful for providing me with a copy of her work. She notes that the scribe of the
    Clontarf entry, Pilib Ballach Ó Duibhgeannáin, was known to be particularly interested
    in the supernatural and that this may account for their inclusion here. This discussion
    will form part of the commentary to her edition of the Modern Irish account of the
    battle, *Cath Cluana Tarbh*, which will be published by the Irish Texts Society.
59 ALC 1014, pp.6–9; the quote cited is on pp.8–9.
60 ALC 1014, pp.8–11.
61 ALC 1014, pp.10–11. This animosity is underlined by the sentence with which this
    section of the annalistic entry ends: 'Thus, every evil omen was overwhelming them

until the following morning came with its daylight, i.e. Good Friday' (*Ro bhuí trá gach michelmain a cinn a cheli doibh amhlaid sin no go tanic maiden an laoi cona lan shoillsi .i. oeine chasg*).

62 Todd, *Cogadh*, pp.200–1. There is another account of this vision in a poem by the fourteenth-century poet, Gofraidh Fionn Ó Dálaigh: Mac Cionnaith, *Dioghluim Dána*, pp.321–5.

63 Todd, *Cogadh*, pp.154–5, 210–11.

64 *Ibid*., pp.186–7.

65 *Ibid*., pp.186–7, 188–9, 192–5, 198–9.

66 *Ibid*., pp.198–9, 200–1.

67 On this particular interpolation, see Ní Mhaonaigh, 'Bréifne bias', pp.140–1.

68 Todd, *Cogadh*, pp.170–3.

69 *Ibid*., pp.182–5.

70 *Ibid*., pp.172–3: 'I am destined to die on the day that you [Murchad] die' (*a beith i ndan dam bas dagbail in la da gebtasu bas*).

71 *Ibid*., pp.174–5.

72 Examples have been discussed by Sayers, '*Airdrech, sirite*'.

73 Todd, *Cogadh*, pp.212–15; ALC 1014, pp.12–15; AU 1014.4.

74 ALC 1014, pp.12–15; AU 1014.3, 1014.4, 1014.5, 1014.6, 1014.7, 1014.8, 1014.9.

75 ALC 1014, pp.14–15; AU 1014.10.

76 ALC 1014, pp.2–3.

77 O'Brien, *Corpus genealogiarum Hiberniae*, pp.360–1 (LL 320 ab 33–6).

78 Best and O'Brien, *Book of Leinster*, 3, p.514, lines 15966–9.

79 Stokes, 'On the deaths of some Irish heroes', pp.314–5.

80 Hudson, *Prophecy of Berchán*, pp.33, 79 (stanzas 69 and 70).

81 *Ibid*., pp.32–3, 79 (stanzas 67 and 70).

82 *Ibid*., pp.33, 79 (stanza 71): '… both Viking and Irish will be worse off on account of it/ their contests will be bloody'(… *Gaill is Gáedil i n-ulc de/ bidh forderg a comraicte*).

83 See Ní Mhaonaigh, '*Cogad Gáedel re Gallaib*: some dating considerations' and above p.13.

84 These furnish the information on royal succession provided in Todd, *Cogadh*, pp.2–5.

85 See, for example, the Dál Cais genealogy employed, *ibid*., pp.52–5, 66–7.

86 Todd, *Cogadh*, pp.10–11; Hudson, *Prophecy of Berchán*, stanzas 7–9 (pp.22–3, 72). The seventeenth-century copy of the *Cogadh* also contains two additional stanzas: Todd, *Cogadh*, pp.204–5; Hudson, *Prophecy of Berchán*, stanzas 71 and 73 (pp.33, 79).

87 Todd, *Cogadh*, pp.150–1.

88 *Ibid*., pp.150–3.

89 *Ibid*., pp.154–5.

90 *Ibid*., pp.206–7. Some of these names also occur as leaders of fleets arriving in Ireland as Viking incursions began: 'and Eoin Barún's fleet … and that of Suimín and Suainín, and finally the fleet of the Red Girl' (*ocus loinges Eoan Barun … ocus loinges Suimin, ocus loinges Suainin, ocus loinges na hInghine Ruaidhe fa dheoigh*): pp.40–1.

91 *Ibid*., pp.178–9: 'a fierce, bloody, intense, red, furious, vigorous, manly, virile, harsh, rough, implacable, unfriendly battle' (*cath fichda, fuleach, frithir, forderg, forruamanda, feochair, ferda, feramail, anmin, agarb, anniartha, escardemail*). See also p.44.

92 *Ibid*., pp.190–3.

93 *Ibid*., pp.206–9: 'Amlaíb's son himself, i.e. the king of Dublin, did not come to the battle on that day and that is the reason why he was not killed, since no Viking of any rank escaped alive, if he came there' (*Ní thainic mac Amlaib fein .i. ri Atha Cliath isin*

chath an la sin, ocus is é sin fo dera gan a mharbadh, uair ni dheachaidh Gall maínech as beó da ttainic ann). See also p.33.

94 *Ibid.*, pp.208–9: 'and Dublin would also have been attacked that day, were it not for Amlaíb's son and those who were with him' (*ocus ro ragthai ar Ath Cliath fós an la sin muna beith mac Amhlaibh ocus an lucht bai maille fris*).

95 *Ibid.*, pp.154–5.

96 *Ibid.*, pp.168–9; this is omitted in the seventeenth-century copy of the text.

97 This happened one month after the battle itself, according to one manuscript version: *Ibid.*, p.182, n. 1.

98 *Ibid.*, pp.182–3.

99 Later literary accounts of the battle assign to him an entirely culpable role, for which see Ní Úrdail, 'Seachadadh', pp.185–7.

100 AU 1014: 'A hosting by Brian mac Cennétig meic Lorcáin, king of Ireland, and by Máel Sechnaill, king of Tara, to Dublin' (*Sloghud la Brian m. Cenneitigh m. Lorcain, la righ nErenn, ocus la Mael Sechlainn m. Domnaill, la righ Temhrach co hAth Cliath*); see also CS, pp.250–1. For a discussion of his role, see Downham, 'Vikings in Southern Uí Néill', p.243.

101 Todd, *Cogadh*, pp.148–9.

102 *Ibid.*, pp.154–5.

103 For details, see Ní Mhaonaigh, '*Cogad Gáedel re Gallaib*: some dating considerations', pp.363–6.

104 Todd, *Cogadh*, pp.168–71.

105 Brian marched against Desmond in 987, for example: AI.

106 The men of Desmond marched with Brian's great-grandson, Muirchertach, to Armagh in 1103, for example: AI.

107 Todd, *Cogadh*, pp.212–5.

108 *Ibid.*, pp.86–9. Cian was married to Brian's daughter, Sadb: Kelleher, 'Rise of the Dál Cais', p.240.

109 For details, see Ní Mhaonaigh, '*Cogadh Gáedhel re Gallaibh* and Cork', pp.77–80.

110 At one point, Murchad's cousin, Conaing, is described as *rí Desmuman* 'king of Desmond': Todd, *Cogadh*, pp.184–5.

111 *Ibid.*, pp.166–7.

112 Brian himself was involved in planning the battle: *Ibid.*, pp.154–5. When the forces actually met in combat, however, 'his cushion was spread under him and he opened his psalm-book' (*ro scailed a pell fae ocus ro oslaic a shaltair*): pp.196–7.

113 *Ibid.*, pp.158–9.

114 *Ibid.*, pp.162–5.

115 *Ibid.*, pp.166–9; the reference to Máel Sechnaill's men is omitted in the Ó Cléirigh version of the narrative; see also pp.68, 69 above.

116 *Ibid.*, pp.168–9; this is also omitted in the Ó Cléirigh version of the text. A textual fragment preserved in the fourteenth-century manuscript, Rawlinson B486 (36ra1) appears also to pertain to the battle of Clontarf, enumerating three battalions and focussing in particular on Brian's Munster allies: for a brief description, see Ó Cuív, *Catalogue*, p.132.

117 Todd, *Cogadh*, pp.172–5.

118 *Ibid.*, pp.178–83, 188–93.

119 *Ibid.*, pp.154–5.

120 *Ibid.*, pp.174–7.

121 *Ibid.*, pp.184–5.

122 *Ibid.*, pp.192–3.

123 *Ibid.*, pp.186–9; the equation with Hector is also found in the Rawlinson B486 fragment, n.116 above.

124 *Ibid.*, pp.186–9.

125 *Ibid.*, pp.194–7.

126 *Ibid.*, pp.190–1.

127 *Ibid.*, pp.188–9, pp.194–5.

128 *Ibid.*, pp.178–9.

129 The preceding battle between the combined forces of Uí Briúin and the Conmaicne against Uí Chennselaig is an interpolation, on which see Ní Mhaonaigh, 'Bréifne bias'.

130 Todd, *Cogadh*, pp.184–7.

131 *Ibid.*, pp.172–3; the version written by Mícheál Ó Cléirigh in the seventeenth century adds the clarifying comment 'on account of their compactness' (*ar a ccomdlús*).

132 *Ibid.*, pp.190–1; see also the description of the advance of Murchad's Dál Cais followers pp.190–1.

133 *Ibid.*, pp.190–1; Todd read *lasanna* though the manuscript has the correct *lasamna*.

134 *Ibid.*, pp.182–3.

135 *Ibid.*, pp.182–3.

136 *Ibid.*, pp.210–1.

137 For a description of early medieval Irish warfare, see Charles-Edwards, 'Irish warfare' and Flanagan, 'Irish and Anglo-Norman warfare'.

138 Todd, *Cogadh*, pp.158–9. On the use of bows and arrows, see Bradbury, *The Medieval Archer*.

139 O'Brien, 'Location and context'. On Viking swords specifically, see Walsh, 'A summary classification'. Illustrations of Viking weapons and other material are reproduced in the centrefold of this volume.

140 Todd, *Cogadh*, pp.160–3.

141 *Ibid.*, pp.202–3; by contrast the nature of the *tuaga* 'axes' wielded at an earlier point in the battle is not specified: pp.180–1.

142 *Ibid.*, pp.180–1.

143 *Ibid.*, pp.196–7.

144 For a general description of Viking weaponry, see Foote and Wilson, *The Viking Achievement*, pp.263–85 and Griffith, *The Viking Art of War*.

145 This is a common theme throughout the narrative. Todd, *Cogadh*, pp.52–3, for example, reads 'because of the excellence of their shining, polished, thrice-riveted, heavy, gleaming mail-coats and of their hard, sturdy, strong swords, as well as their well-rivetted long spears and the other sharp, swift, glistening various arms besides' (*re febas a lurech lainderda luchtmara tredualach trom trebraid taitnemach ocus claidium cruaid comnert comchalma ocus a sleag semnech sithlebur ocus na narm naig nathlom etrocht ecsamail arcena*).

146 *Ibid.*, pp.202–3.

147 *Ibid.*, pp.180–1; see also pp.190–1.

148 *Ibid.*, pp.194–5; see also pp.188–9 where it is claimed that neither *sciath* 'shield' nor *lureach* 'mail-coat' could withstand Murchad's blows.

149 *Ibid.*, pp.194–5.

150 Charles-Edwards, 'Irish warfare', p.27.

151 This is in keeping with the evidence from Anglo-Saxon England where an entry in the Anglo-Saxon Chronicle for 1008 requiring a helmet and mail shirt from every eight hides suggests 'that a goodly number of warriors in the hosts of Aethelred must have been respectably armed', as Matthew Strickland has noted: 'Military technology', p. 367.

152 Dillon, *Lebor na Cert*, pp.4–5, 8–9, 10–11, 30–1, 32–3, 56–7, 58–9, 66–7, 68–9, 70–1, 78–9, 80–1, 82–3; see Flanagan, 'Irish and Anglo-Norman warfare', p.55.

153 We may compare the approach adopted by those who sculpted the Aberlemno Pictish symbol stone who for similar reasons may have deliberately portrayed their opponents, the Northumbrians, as being heavily armed: Strickland, 'Military technology', p.356.

154 Battle-standards are also referred to in eleventh- and twelfth-century annalistic entries; see Flanagan, 'Irish and Anglo-Norman warfare', p.59.

155 On this and other interpolations inserted at the same time, see Ní Mhaonaigh, 'Bréifne bias'.

156 Todd, *Cogadh*, pp.156–7. Reference to Fergal's standard also occurs pp.176–7.

157 *Ibid.*, pp.198–9.

158 *Ibid.*, pp.200–1.

159 *Ibid.*, pp.202–3.

160 *Ibid.*, pp.196–201.

161 *Ibid.*, pp.202–3.

162 *Ibid.*, pp.192–3.

163 *Ibid.*, pp.192–3.

164 *Ibid.*, pp.190–3. Dubgall's bridge is also referred to in the Annals of Tigernach under the year 1112 when Cenél nÉogain raid Fine Gall, as far as *drochat Dubgaill*. It was near where Fr Mathew Bridge now stands: Ó Murchadha, *Annals of Tigernach*, p.135. It is presumably equivalent to the *pons Ostmannorum* 'bridge of the men of the East' referred to in Latin sources, suggesting that the Norse were responsible for its construction: Clarke, 'Topographical development', p.45. *Caill Tomair* was burned by Brian and his men in a previous attack on Dublin in 1000 (AI).

165 Todd, *Cogadh*, pp.190–3. There are occasional references to certain groups holding their ground, pp.192–3 and 200–1.

166 *Ibid.*, pp.154–5. See also ALC 1014: 'Clontarf in old Mag nElta, to the north of Dublin' (*Clúain Tarbh i sen Muigh Ealta, ré hAth Clíath atthúaidh*).

167 Todd, *Cogadh*, pp.184–5.

168 *Ibid.*, pp.114–5.

169 *Ibid.*, pp.192–3. Clontarf is mentioned on two further occasions in the text (pp.176–7, 184–5), but in material inserted later, on which see Ní Mhaonaigh, 'Bréifne bias'.

170 Todd, *Cogadh*, pp.154–5.

171 *Ibid.*, pp.210–1.

172 *Ibid.*, pp.190–1; see also pp.180–1. The text specifies (pp.208–9) that Áth Cliath itself was not attacked; see above p.67.

173 AU, AI 1014; CS, pp.250–1.

174 For a map of Medieval Dublin, see Clarke, *Dublin*. An artist's impression of Dublin about the year 1000 is reproduced in the centrefold of this volume.

175 Dunbabin, *France*, pp.150–4; on the movement in general, see Cowdrey, 'Peace and truce of God' and Head and Landes, *Peace of God*.

176 Hallam and Everard, *Capetian France*, p.24.

177 Riley-Smith, *The Crusades*, pp.1–2.

178 Keen, *The Penguin History of Medieval Europe*, pp.121–2.

179 Stringer, 'Reformed monasticism'.

180 Todd, *Cogadh*, pp.138–41.

181 Strickland, 'Slaughter, slavery or ransom', p.53.

182 'Provoking or avoiding battle?', p.317.

183 See Allmand, 'The reporting of war', p.17.

184 Todd, *Cogadh*, pp.196–9; see also Strickland, 'Provoking or avoiding battle?', pp.317–8.

185 'Provoking or avoiding battle?', p.340.

186 Todd, *Cogadh*, pp.160–1.

187 *Ibid.*, pp.204–5.

188 *Ibid.*, pp.186–7; Murchad is also described as the best of Adam's sons, pp.166–7.

189 *Ibid.*, pp.152–3; see also pp.158–9.

190 *Fire and Iron*, p.160.

191 *Njáls Saga*, pp.123–30; see also Hagland, 'Njáls saga'.

192 Lehmann and Schnorr von Carolsfeld, *Die Njalssage*, pp.161–5; Finnur Jónsson, *Den oldnorske og oldislandske litteraturs historie*, 2:2, pp.525–40.

193 *Old-Norse Sources*, p.3.

194 *Njáls Saga*, pp.231–6.

195 See Sayers, 'Clontarf', p.181.

196 Lehmann and Schnorr von Carolsfeld, *Die Njalssage*, pp.161–5; Bugge, *Norsk sagaskrivning*, pp.59–66; Einar Ól. Sveinsson, *Brennu-Njáls saga*, p.xlvii.

197 Ó Corráin, 'Viking Ireland', pp.447–52 and Hudson, "Brjáns saga".

198 Jón Jóhannesson, *Austfirðinga sögur*, p.301. The key text reads as follows: 'They [Earl Sigurd and Þorsteinn] went to Ireland and fought against King Brian and there many remarkable things happened afterwards, as is said in his saga' (*Þeir fóru síðan til Írlands ok bǫrðusk við Brján konung, ok urðu þar mǫrg tiðendi senn, sem segir í sǫgu hans*). For its ambiguity, see *ibid.*, pp.ci–cviii and Lönnroth, *Njáls Saga*, pp.226–7.

199 "Brjáns saga", pp.249, 254 and 260.

200 For a direct comparison between *Njáls saga* and *Orkneyinga saga*, see Hudson, "Brjáns saga", pp.248–54.

201 Bugge, *Norsk sagaskrivning*, pp.59–66; Ó Corráin, 'Viking Ireland', p.449; Hudson, "Brjáns saga", pp.254 and 261.

202 "Brjáns saga", p.262.

203 Todd, *Cogadh*, pp.188–9, the bravery of Brian's son, Murchad, being testified by his enemies, *senchaidi Gall ocus Lagen* 'Viking and Leinster chroniclers', as noted above p.72. Vikings watching the battle from inside the battlements are also claimed to have attested 'that they saw flashes of lightning in the expanse of air on all sides' (*co faictis saigneana tentidi fon aer eradbul ar cach leth uathib*), pp.180–1.

204 Sayers, 'Clontarf', p.183; Ó Corráin, 'Viking Ireland', pp.448–9.

205 Hudson, "Brjáns saga", pp.260–1.

206 Einar Ól. Sveinsson, *Brennu-Njáls saga*, p.445.

207 *Ibid.*, pp.446, 448.

208 *Ibid.*, p.445.

209 *Ibid.*, p.449.

210 *Ibid.*, p.450.

211 *Ibid.*, pp.450–2.

212 *Ibid.*, pp.452–3. See Hill, 'Evisceration', for which reference I am grateful to Jonathan Grove.

213 See Ní Mhaonaigh, 'Tales of three Gormlaiths', pp.22–3.

214 Einar Ól. Sveinsson, *Brennu-Njáls saga*, pp.440–1.

215 *Ibid.*, p.442: 'King Brian forgave his enemies the same crime three times, but if they transgressed more often, he let them be judged in accordance with the law, and from such a thing it can be seen what kind of king he was' (*Brjánn konungr gaf upp útlǫgum sínum þrysvar ina sǫmu sǫk; en ef þeir misgerðu optar, þá lét hann dæma þá at lǫgum, ok má af þvílíku marka, hvílíkr konungr hann var*).

216 *Ibid.*, p.441, detailing how his foster-son, Kerþjálfaðr, was the son of Brian's erstwhile enemy, Kylfir.

217 *Ibid.*, p.446.

218 'Some observations', pp.70–1.

219 *Ibid.*

220 For reformist ideas in the *Cogadh*, see Ní Mhaonaigh, 'Pagans and holy men', pp.149–50; see also above pp.77–9.

221 Haki Antonsson, 'Some observations', pp.77–87 and references therein.

222 For a comparison between this poem and the *Cogadh*, see Goedheer, *Irish and Norse Traditions*, pp.56–9.

223 *Ibid.*, pp.50, 55 (stanza 50); this stanza is cited by Haki Antonsson, 'Some observations', p.71.

224 Goedheer, *Irish and Norse Traditions*, pp.49, 54 (stanza 37).

225 *Ibid.*, pp.50, 55 (stanza 47); the complete stanza is quoted above pp.53–4.

226 Goedheer, *Irish and Norse Traditions*, pp.50, 55 (stanza 50).

227 Todd, *Cogadh*, pp.200–3.

228 For a comparison between them, see Hudson, "Brjáns saga", pp.256–60.

229 Todd, *Cogadh*, pp.142–3; for a discussion of this passage, see Ní Mhaonaigh, 'Tales of three Gormlaiths', pp.20–1.

230 Todd, *Cogadh*, pp.144–7.

231 Einar Ól. Sveinsson, *Brennu-Njáls saga*, p.440: 'She had been married to a king called Brian but now they were divorced' (*Brjánn hét konungr sá, er hana hafði átta, ok váru þau þá skilið*); 'but she had become so angry at King Brian after their divorce that she wished him dead' (*en svá var hon orðin grimm Brjáni konungi eptir skilnað þeira, at hon vildi hann gjarna feigan*), pp.441–2.

232 *Ibid.*, p.445.

233 In any event, she is with Brodar who is specifically located there the day before the battle: *ibid.*, p.449.

234 See Ní Mhaonaigh, 'Tales of three Gormlaiths', pp.21–4.

235 See Dronke, *Role of Sexual Themes* and O'Donoghue, 'Women in *Njáls saga*'.

236 According to the seventeenth-century writer, Geoffrey Keating: 'However, Máel Mórda remembered the queen's words' (*Acht cheana fá cuimhin lé Maolmórda comhrádh na ríoghna*): Comyn and Dineen, *Foras Feasa ar Éirinn*, 3, pp.268–9. A later account of the battles states: 'That exchange greatly affected the Leinster king and he was sad on account of it' (*Do chuaidh an comhrádh sin go mór fá rígh Laighean ocus ba chumhthach é thríd*): Mac Neill, 'Cath Cluana Tairb', p.8. Gormlaith's role in later accounts has been discussed by Ní Úrdail, 'Seachadadh', pp.184–5.

237 See Hudson, "Brjáns saga", pp.257–9.

238 Todd, *Cogadh*, pp.150–1. He and his companion, Amlaíb, son of the king of Lochlainn, are termed earls of Cair (for Cáer Ebroc 'York') and of the northern Saxons; the seventeenth-century version terms Brodar 'son of the king of Lochlainn' and, mistakenly, 'earl of Cair Ascadal', listing him along with his brother, Ascadal, another earl; the Annals of Loch Cé designate him earl of York: ALC 1014, pp.4–5.

239 Todd, *Cogadh*, pp.152–3.

240 *Ibid.*: '2,000 swift, harsh, plundering hard-hearted, strange, wondrous Danes' (*fiche cet Danar dian, dolig, dibercach, durcraideach do Anmargachaib allmardaib ingantachaib*).

241 He is listed among the dead as son of Oisli, earl of Cáer Ebroc: *ibid.*, pp.207–8.

242 *Ibid.*, pp.202–3.

243 Einar Ól. Sveinsson, *Brennu-Njáls saga*, pp.452-3; see above p.81.

244 *Ibid.*, pp.446–7; the supernatural nature of these events is discussed by McTurk, 'Supernatural', p. 112.

245 Einar Ól. Sveinsson, *Brennu-Njáls saga*, pp.447–8.

246 *Ibid.*, p.445.

247 *Ibid.*, p.446.

248 Finnbogi Guðmundsson, *Orkneyinga saga*, p.26. See also *Ólafs saga Tryggvasonar* where Sigurd is offered the choice of baptism or death: Bjarni Aðalbjarnarson, *Heimskringla*, I, p.292.

249 Einar Ól. Sveinsson, *Brennu-Njáls saga*, pp.444, 451.

250 *Ibid.*, p.441.

251 See Ní Mhaonaigh, 'Pagans and holy men', pp.149–51 and above pp.77–9.

252 See Constable, *The Reformation of the Twelfth Century*, pp.257–95 and Ní Mhaonaigh, 'Pagans and holy men', especially p.153, and references therein.

253 A number of these are discussed in Ní Mhaonaigh, 'Pagans and holy men'.

254 Radner, *Fragmentary Annals*.

255 Radner, *Fragmentary Annals*, pp.94–5 (§235). For an analysis of the presentation of Vikings in this text, see Downham, 'The good, the bad and the ugly'.

256 Radner, *Fragmentary Annals*, pp.96–7 (§244).

257 AU 856, CS, pp.154–5; CS, pp.156–7; see Charles-Edwards, *Chronicle*, 1, pp.310–2; 2, pp.4–5.

258 Radner, *Fragmentary Annals*, pp.104–5 (§260).

259 *Ibid.*, pp.96–9 (§247). An account of the battle of Chester in the same text also refers to Irish foster-children among the Norse: 'for many were the Irish foster-children among the pagans' (*ar ba hiomdha dalta Gaoidhealach ag na paganaibh*), pp.170–3 (§429).

260 *Ibid.*, pp.98–9 (§250), as well as in two extended passages concerning the hero of the narrative, Cerball mac Dúnlainge, pp.100–1 (§254) and pp.108–9 (§277).

261 F.T. Wainwright suggested that the passages were inserted 'before 1200': 'Ingimund's invasion', p.158; he is followed by Radner, *Fragmentary Annals*, p.198.

262 Lukman, 'An Irish source'.

263 Einar Ól. Sveinsson, *Brennu-Njáls saga*, pp.450, 452.

264 Todd, *Cogadh*, pp.202–3.

265 *Ibid.*, pp.192–3, 196–9.

266 *Ibid.*, pp.202–3; Einar Ól. Sveinsson, *Brennu-Njáls saga*, p.453.

267 Einar Ól. Sveinsson, *Brennu-Njáls saga*, p.450.

268 *Ibid.*, p.452.

269 AU, AI; ATig. p.260; CS pp.266–7.

270 AI: 'Amlaíb's son, king of Dublin, died' (*Mac Amlaíb, rí Átha Cliath, do éc*).

271 Todd, *Cogadh*, pp.206–9.

272 *Ibid.*, pp.168–9; see above pp.68–9.

273 Einar Ól. Sveinsson, *Brennu-Njáls saga*, p. 449 and n.; see also Sayers, 'Clontarf', p.173.

274 Einar Ól. Sveinsson, *Brennu-Njáls saga*, p.451. On the raven banner in general, see Lukman, 'Raven banner' and Orchard, 'Literary background', for which references I am grateful to Jonathan Grove.

275 Einar Ól. Sveinsson, *Brennu-Njáls saga*, p.452.

276 Todd, *Cogadh*, pp.166–7, 208–9; Sayers, 'Clontarf', pp.173–4.

277 Ó Corráin, 'Viking Ireland', pp.448–9.

278 Einar Ól. Sveinsson, *Brennu-Njáls saga*, pp.454–8, at p.457 (stanza 8). The poem has been re-edited, translated and discussed in detail by Poole, *Viking Poems*, pp.116–56. John Hines addresses the poem, also providing text and translation in *Old-Norse*

Sources, pp.24–5; his translation is adopted here (p.24, stanza 8).

279 Einar Ól. Sveinsson, *Brennu-Njáls saga*, pp.457–8 (stanzas 7 and 10); Hines, *Old-Norse Sources*, pp.24–5 (translation).

280 Einar Ól. Sveinsson, *Brennu-Njáls saga*, p.457 (stanza 7).

281 *Ibid.*, p.454.

282 *Old-Norse Sources*, pp.3–7.

283 *Ibid.*, p.5.

284 Poole, *Viking Poems*, pp.122–5, though he carefully concludes that the 'conflicts in the evidence rule out a firm conclusion on the date of the battle commemorated in 'Darraðarljóð" (p.124).

285 It is commemorated in Irish annalistic compilations: AU, AI 919; CS, pp.190–1.

286 AU 919: 'The heathens won a battle against the Irish at Dublin, in which fell Niall son of Áed, king of Ireland' (*Bellum re ngentibh occ Duiblinn for Goidhelu du i torcair Niall m. Aedho ri Erenn*).

287 Todd, *Cogadh*, pp.212–5.

288 Benjamin Hudson notes in passing that Berchán's idea that there was no victor is 'more in keeping with contemporary Norse opinion expressed in the poem *Darraðarljóð'*: *Prophecy of Berchán*, p.18.

289 *Ibid.*, pp.33, 79 (stanzas 70, 71).

290 Einar Ól. Sveinsson, *Brennu-Njáls saga*, p.457 (stanza 7).

291 For a detailed analysis of the weaving motif, see Poole, *Viking Poems*, pp.131–42.

292 Einar Ól. Sveinsson, *Brennu-Njáls saga*, p.455 (stanza 2); Hines, *Old-Norse Sources*, p.24 (translation).

293 Einar Ól. Sveinsson, *Brennu-Njáls saga*, pp.456–7 (stanzas 4–6).

294 *Ibid.*, p.457 (stanza 8); Hines, *Old-Norse Sources*, p.24 (translation); the reference here appears to be to the death-tales of Irishmen.

295 Einar Ól. Sveinsson, *Brennu-Njáls saga*, p.459.

296 *Ibid.*, pp.459–60.

297 McTurk treats these supernatural events as an artistic unit in 'Supernatural', pp.116–7.

298 Einar Ól. Sveinsson, *Brennu-Njáls saga*, pp.454, 459.

299 "Vefr Darraðar".

300 'An unsolved problem'.

301 On the circumstances of its composition, see Finnbogi Guðmundsson, 'On the writing of *Orkneyinga saga'*.

302 Finnbogi Guðmundsson, *Orkneyinga saga*, p.27.

303 *Ibid.*, p.25.

304 Einar Ól. Sveinsson, *Brennu-Njáls saga*, p.451; this episode is discussed in Sayers, 'Clontarf', pp.166–7 and Hudson, "Brjáns saga", pp.249–50. See also Lukman, 'Raven' and Orchard, 'Literary background'. See also p.89 above.

305 "Brjáns saga", pp.248–52.

306 Jón Jóhannesson, *Austfirðinga sögur*, pp.301–2.

307 *Ibid.*, p.301.

308 *Ibid.*, p.300; for the relationship between the two, see Lönnroth, *Njals Saga*, pp.227–31.

309 Jón Jóhannesson, *Austfirðinga sögur*, p.301.

310 Sayers, 'Clontarf', pp.174–6; Hudson, "Brjáns saga", p.248.

311 Jón Jóhannesson, *Austfirðinga sögur*, p.301.

312 *Ibid.*, p.302.

313 *Ibid.*, pp.302–3.

314 *Ibid.*, p.301.

315 e.g. *ibid.*, p.302.

316 Bjarni Aðalbjarnarson, *Heimskringla*, 2, p.160.

317 He is included in the sixteenth-century list of recognised Irish saints put together by the Jesuit priest, Henry Fitzsimons: Grosjean, 'Édition', p.349, no.72 and Ó Riain, '*Catalogus*', p.408, no.28, for which reference I am grateful to Professor Ó Riain. Similarly, Reverend O'Hanlon devotes many pages to 'blessed Brian Boru, king and martyr' in his nineteenth-century publication, *Lives of the Irish Saints*, 4, p.276.

318 See Ní Úrdail, 'Seachadadh'.

Chapter Five: 'The Like of Brian'?

1 The phrase is that of the thirteenth-century poet, Muireadhach Albanach Ó Dálaigh: Goedheer, *Irish and Norse Traditions*, pp.50, 55 (stanza 51).

2 Todd, *Cogadh*, pp.154–5. This may reflect an actual expedition undertaken by his brother, Murchad, before the battle: AU 1013.

3 Todd, *Cogadh*, pp.200–1.

4 *Ibid.*, pp.210–1.

5 *Ibid.*, pp.214–5.

6 *Ibid.*, pp.216–7: 'And they said to Brian's son and to Dál Cais to go into the nearest wood to get stakes against which they could place their backs to be standing while the battle was being fought'(*Ocus do raidhedar re mac Briain, ocus re Dal cCais dol fon ccoill fa nesa dóibh, ocus indlaighe do thabhairt leo co mbeidis a ndromanna riu ina sesamh an fedh do beith an cath aga chur*).

7 AU; ATig. pp.254–5; CS pp.262–3.

8 ALC 1014, pp.8–11.

9 See Ryan, 'The O'Briens in Munster' (1941), pp.143–6 and Ó Corráin, *Ireland before the Normans*, pp.131–3.

10 AU 1014; CS, pp.252–3.

11 *Ibid.*

12 AU 1015.

13 CS, pp.254–5.

14 AU; AI; CS, pp.258–9; ATig., 2, p.249; Ryan, 'The O'Briens of Munster' (1941), p.141.

15 CS, pp.262–3, see also ATig., 2, pp.254–5; AU simply states that Tadc was killed by the Éile, AI noting that he was murdered *tre fhell* 'treacherously' (1023).

16 AI 1063: 'Tairdelbach ua Briain seized the kingship of Munster' (*Tairdelbach Hua Briain do gabail ríge Muman*); AI 1064: 'Donnchad mac Briain went to Rome' (*Donnchad mc. Briain do dul do Róim*).

17 AU 1022: 'Máel Sechnaill mac Domnaill, high-king of Ireland, pillar of the dignity and nobility of the western world, died' (*Mael Sechlainn m. Domnaill airdri Erenn, tuir ordain ocus oirechais iarthair domain, do ecaib*); see also CS, pp.260–3; ATig., 2, pp.252–3.

18 AI 1016; see also the briefer record of the event CS, pp.256–7.

19 CS, pp.256–7.

20 CS, pp.258–9.

21 AU; ATig., 2, p.257.

22 AI 1026: 'and he spent three days peacefully in Dublin, with his encampment close to the fort'(*ocus co rabe féin tri thrath i nÁth Chliath i síd, ocus a longphort hi farrad in dúine*).

23 AI 1026.

24 'Shrine', pp.287–8, 293–4; the inscription reads, 'A prayer for Donnchad son of Brian, king of Ireland'(*Oroit do Dondchad macc Briain do rig Herend*): Warner, *The Stowe Missal*, 2, p.xlvi.

25 AI; CS, pp.264–7; ATig., 2, p.259.

26 ATig., 2, p.266; see also AU 1033.

27 AI 1031; see also AU.

28 AU 1034; AI 1035; CS, pp.270–3

29 AU; AI; CS, pp.272–3; ATig., 2, p.271.

30 ATig., 2, p.274: 'and they seized small spoils and Carthach overtook them and Ua Donncáin, king of Ara, was slain there' (*cor' gabsat gabala becca, conus tarraidh Carrtach ocus cor' marbadh and O Dondacan rí Áradh*).

31 AU 1045: 'Carthach son of Sáerbrethach, king of Éoganacht of Cashel, was burned with many nobles in a house set on fire by the grandson of Longarcán son of Donn Cuan' (*Carrthach m. Soerbrethaig, ri Eoganachta Caisil, do loscad i tigh theined do Hu Longarcan m. Duinn Cuan cum multis nobilibus ustis*); ATig., 2, p.277.

32 CS pp.266–7; ATig., 2, p.280 where Domanll is presumably an error for Donnchad.

33 *Ibid.*

34 AI 1049; ATig., 2, p.282.

35 CS, pp.278–9; ATig., 2, p.284; AI 1052 simply records the death of Domnall Bán Ua Briain, AU adding *do Connachtaibh* 'by the Connachta' in the same year.

36 AI 1053: 'Tairdelbach ua Briain beleaguered upper Dál Cais' (*cora gaib Tairdelbach Hua Briain forbaisi for huachtar Dál Chais*).

37 ATig., 2 pp.285–6.

38 ATig., 2, pp.287–8; AI 1054, 1055.

39 AI, AU 1058; ATig., 2, pp.290–1.

40 ATig., 2, p.292.

41 AI 1059; ATig., 2, p.292.

42 ATig., 2, p.293.

43 AU 1061; ATig., 2, pp.293–4.

44 AI 1062.

45 AI 1063; ATig., 2, pp.295–6.

46 AU 1064; ATig., 2, p.296.

47 CS, pp.230–1; AI 1002.

48 AI: 'and they exchanged hostages there with Cennétig's son' (*coro chloemclaiset giallu and ocus mc. Cennetich*).

49 AI: 'and Harald's grandson died in Munster' (*ocus hua Arailt do éc hi Mumain*); Etchingham, 'North Wales', p.180.

50 AI; her name is given in her obituary as Cacht where she is described as 'queen of Ireland' (*rígan Erenn*): ATig., 2, p.287; CS, pp.282–3.

51 AU 1035.

52 Etchingham, 'North Wales', p.182; for possible links with Waterford, see Duffy, 'Irishmen and Islesmen', p.97.

53 ATig., 2, p.284.

54 Hudson, 'Cnut and the Scottish kings', pp.355–6; Etchingham, 'North Wales', pp.181–2; see also Oram, *Lordship*, pp.18–19.

55 Waitz, 'Mariani Scotti Chronicon', p.559: 'Donnchad son of Brian, a king from Ireland and Echmarcach, king of the Rhinns, men of no mean standing among their own, came to Rome and died' (*Donnchad filius Briani, rex de Hibernia atque Echmarcach rex Innarenn, viri inter suos non ignobiles, Romam venientes obierunt*); Etchingham, 'North Wales', p.182, n.108. Donnchad's death is previously noted in the same chronicle, p.557; I am grateful to Denis Casey for drawing my attnetion to this.

56 AI.

57 AI 1040: 'that none should dare to steal, or do feats of arms on Sunday, or go out on Sunday carrying any load; and furthermore, that none should dare to fetch cattle within doors' (*conna laimthe gait do dénam na henggnam Domnaig na himthecht nach aire ar muin i nDomnuch; ocus dano na laimthe míl innille do thabairt hi tech*). Donnchad promulgated another unspecified *cáin mór* (great law) a decade later: AI 1050.

58 In this regard, it is reminiscent of the later portrayal of Brian as the ruler of a peaceful land in which thieves no longer roam: Todd, *Cogadh*, pp.138–9.

59 Dobbs, 'Ban-shenchus', *Revue Celtique* 48, p.190; she was the mother of Donnchad's son, Murchad.

60 AU 1014; CS, pp.252–3, on which occasion Gormlaith's brother, Ruaidrí, was killed.

61 Dobbs, 'Ban-shenchus', *Revue Celtique* 48, p.190; see also p.229 where their son's name, Murchad, appears to have been omitted. Her death-notice is at AU 1080: 'Derbforgaill, daughter of Brian's son, wife of Diarmait mac Maíl na mBó died in Emly' (*Derbfhorgaill ingen m. Briain ben Diarmata m. Mail na mBo do écaib i nImligh*).

62 ATig., 2, pp.285–6.

63 See Etchingham, 'North Wales', p.183.

64 See, for example, AI 1053, 1055, 1058, 1062.

65 AI; he is titled *rígdamna Érenn* alone in ATig., 2, p.300.

66 AI 1068: 'Tairdelbach ua Briain went to Leinster and brought away many valuables, including Brian's sword, the standard of the king of the Saxons, and many other treasures from Diarmait, king of Leinster' (*Tairdelbach Hua Briain do dul i lLaignib co tuc seotu imda as, .i. claideb Briain ocus mergge ríg Saxan, ocus seotu imda archena ó Diarmait, o ríg Laigen*). Colmán Etchingham has suggested to me that this may be an example of the common practice of giving *tuarastal* 'a stipend' by a superioir king to an inferior one. However, Seán Duffy sees the return of the sword to Munster as marking 'a restoration of Munster dominance': 'The career of Muirchertach Ua Briain', p.58.

67 AI.

68 AI 1070.

69 AI 1071.

70 AI: 'Diarmait mac Maíl na mBó, king of Leinster, and of Osraige, was killed in battle in Mide, i.e. by ua Maíl Shechnaill and by ua Briain, and a great host of Leinstermen and foreigners fell together with him' (*Diarmait mc. Mail na mBó, rí Laigen ocus Osraige, do marbad hi Mide a cath, .i. do Hú Maíl Shechnaill ocus do Hú Briain, ocus sochaide mor do Laignib ocus do Gallaib do thoittim immalle fris*).

71 AU 1072; ATig., 2, p.302; CS, pp.290–1.

72 AI 1072.

73 AI 997.

74 AI 1073; see also AU 1073.

75 AI, AU 1075.

76 *Ireland before the Normans*, p.138.

77 AI 1075.

78 ATig., 2, pp.305–6; CS, pp.292–3 [1079].

79 AU.

80 AI 1076.

81 AU 1076.

82 AI 1079; ATig., 2, p.305.

83 ATig., 2, p.305; see Ó Corráin, *Ireland before the Normans*, p.139.

84 AI.

85 AI 1080: 'Donn Slébe Ua hEochada took the kingship of the Ulaid' (*Donn Slébe Hua*

Eochada do gabail ríge Ulad); AI 1081: 'The king of the Ulaid came into the house
of Tairdelbach Ua Briain, i.e. he received a stipend from him' (*Rí Ulad do thíchtain
i tech Tairdelbaig Hui Briain, .i. co ruc innarrad huad*). An earlier attempt at expansion
northwards by Tairdelbach on a hosting to Airgialla in 1075 was unsuccessful (AU).

86 AU 1083; ATig., 2, p.307.

87 ATig., 2, p.308; CS, pp.294–5; AI 1084 suggests that Tairdelbach seized the initiative
   marching 'into the northern part of Ireland against the son of In Cailech Ua Ruairc'
   (*i Leth Cuind do shaigid m. Cailich Hú Ruairg*).

88 AU 1084. On the northern Uí Briain, see Hogan, 'The Uí Briain kingship'.

89 ATig., 2, p.309: 'A great tribulation of disease struck Tairdelbach ua Briain, and such
   was its extent that his hair was struck off him' (*Treblaid mor galair for Thoirrdelbach Hua
   mBriain, cor' be a méd cor' benadh a folt de*).

90 AI, AU; ATig., 2, p.310 and CS, pp.294–5 term him 'king of the greater part of Ireland'
   (*rí urmóir Erenn*).

91 AU 1073; Duffy, 'Irishmen and Islesmen', p.102.

92 Clover and Gibson, *Letters of Lanfranc*; see Gwynn, 'Lanfranc', 'Pope Gregory', 'St.
   Anselm', and 'Gregory VII'.

93 Clover and Gibson, *Letters of Lanfranc*, pp.70–1 (no.10).

94 See Candon, 'Barefaced effrontery', p.4; Hudson, 'William the Conqueror', pp.149–51.

95 Hudson, 'William the Conqueror', p.151.

96 AI 1079; Hudson speculates that they were requesting permission for a settlement at
   Dublin, 'William the Conqueror', p.154.

97 On Muirchertach's career, see Ryan, 'The O'Briens in Munster' (1942), Candon,
   'Muirchertach Ua Briain' and Duffy, 'The career of Muirchertach Ua Briain'.

98 AI 1086.

99 'Barefaced effrontery', p.13.

100 AU 1086; Tadc and Muirchertach were full brothers, their mother being Derbforgaill,
    daughter of the king of Osraige (Dobbs, 'Ban-shenchus', *Revue Celtique* 48, p.190);
    Diarmait was their half-brother.

101 AFM *s.a.* 1087; however, Diarmait's involvement is not noted in other sources (AI
    1087; ATig., 2, p.311; CS, pp.296–7) and the Leinster king is recorded as having
    plundered in Waterford, where Diarmait was *dux*, the following year, in an internecine
    dispute between Donnchad's branch of the family and that of his cousin, Énna, son of
    Diarmait mac Maíl na mBó (AI 1088).

102 AI 1088.

103 AFM *s.a.* 1091; see Duffy, 'Irishmen and Islesmen', p.105 and n.58.

104 AI 1093: 'Diarmait, son of Tairdelbach ua Briain, submitted to Muirchertach, i.e. his
    brother, and they made peace and covenant in Cashel and Lismore, with the relics of
    Ireland, including the staff of Jesus, as pledges and in the presence of Ua hÉnna and
    the nobles of Munster' (*Diarmait m. Tairdelbaig Huí Briain do thíchtain i tech Muirchertaig,
    .i. a brathar, ocus co ndersat síth ocus chomluge i Cassiul ocus i lLis Mór fo minnaib Herenn im
    Bachaill Ísu i fiadnaisi Huí Énnai ocus mathi Muman*).

105 'Irishmen and Islesmen', pp.103–4.

106 AI.

107 AI 1089.

108 CS, pp.298–9.

109 AI 1089.

110 AI 1092.

111 His acquisition of Dublin is recorded in the Manx Chronicle: Broderick, *Cronica*, fol.

33r. The Annals of Inisfallen record Muirchertach's recovery of it as a major event: 'Great warfare in this year between Ua Briain and Leth Cuinn and Gofraid, king of Dublin. Muirchertach went on a hosting to Dublin, imprisoned Ua Conchobair Fháilgi, and banished Gofraid therefrom' (*Coccad mór isin bliadain eter Hua mBriain ocus Leth Cuind ocus Gofraid, ríg Átha Cliath, co ndeochaid Murchertach for sluagud co hÁth Cliath goro chumrig Hua Conchobair Fhailgig, ocus cor innerp Gofraid a hÁth Cliath*). For these events, see Duffy, 'Irishmen and Islesmen', pp.106–8.

112 AU; ATig., 2, pp.313–4; CS, pp.296–9.

113 ATig., 2, p.315; see also CS, pp.298–301.

114 AU 1090.

115 ATig., 2, pp.316–7; CS, pp.300–1.

116 ATig., 2, pp.318–9; CS, pp.300–1; according to the Annals of Inisfallen (1092) Muirchertach himself took the kingship of Connacht (*Murchertach Hua Briain do gabail ardrige Chonnacht*), bestowing it on Ua hEidin the following year (AI 1093).

117 ATig., 2, pp.319–20; CS, pp.300–3; AU, AI 1093.

118 See Ó Corráin, *Ireland before the Normans*, p.145.

119 According to some sources, the murder was perpetrated by the Luigne of Mide: ATig., 2, p.320.

120 AI 1094; ATig., 2, p.320.

121 AI 1094: 'The men of Mide were partitioned in two between Donnchad Ua Maíl Shechnaill and Conchobar, son of Máel Sechnaill, and hostages were given by both to Muirchertach' (*Fir Mide do rainn i ndé eter Donnchad Ua Maíl Sechnaill ocus Conchobar mc. Mail Sechnaill, ocus geill uadib a ndis do Muirchertach*).

122 AI 1105: 'A hosting by Muirchertach Ua Briain into Mide and he banished Donnchad Ua Maíl Shechnaill' (*Slúage la Muircertach Ua Briain i Midi coro innarb Doncad Ua Maíl Shechnaill*); see also AU 1105.

123 ATig., 2, p.330; elsewhere he is said to have been slain by kinsmen: AI, AU 1106.

124 AI 1003.

125 When Muirchertach's power was failing, for example, Ua Conchobair partitioned Munster in two to keep it weak: AU 1118.

126 AU 1097, 1099, 1102, 1107, 1109, 1113.

127 AU.

128 AI, AU; ATig., 2, p.325; CS, pp.306–7.

129 AU, AI 1103; ATig., 2, pp.327–8; CS, pp.306–9.

130 AU 1104.

131 CS, pp.306–7: 'Magnus came to invade Ireland' (*Magnus do tiactain do gabáil Erenn*); see Etchingham, 'North Wales', p.148 and also Power, 'Magnus Barelegs' and 'Meeting in Norway'; I am indebted to Fiona Edmonds for the latter reference.

132 Broderick, *Cronica*, fol. 33v; see Duffy, 'Irishmen and Islesmen', pp.108–13.

133 ATig., 2, p.327: AU 1102.

134 Bjarni Aðalbjarnarson, *Heimskringla* 3, pp.224–5; Monsen and Smith, *Heimskringla*, p.595; see also AI 1102; Jones, *Brut ... Red Book*, pp.44–5.; Jones, *Brut ... Peniarth*, p.24; Jones, *Brenhinedd*, p.99.

135 'Irishmen and Islesmen', p.113.

136 AI 1102: 'In this year Muirchertach Ua Briain made a marriage-alliance with the French and with the Norsemen' (*In quo anno doróne Muircheartach Hua Briain clemnas re Francaib ocus Lochlannchaib*), the latter being a reference to the union of Sigurd and Bladmynja. See also Jones, *Brut ... Red Book*, pp.42–3; Jones, *Brut ... Peniarth*, p.23; Jones, *Brenhinedd*, p.97; Curtis, 'Muirchertach O'Brien'.

137 Candon, 'Muirchertach Ua Briain', pp.411–3.

138 AI: 'In that year, a camel, an animal of remarkable size, was brought from the king of
Alba to Muirchertach Ua Briain' (*Isin bliadain sin tucad in camal, quod est animal mírae
magnitudinis, o ríg Alban do Muircertach U Briain*); on possible reasons for the gift, see
Candon, 'Muirchertach Ua Briain', p.414.

139 Jones, *Brut ... Red Book*, pp.36–9; Jones, *Brut ... Peniarth*, pp.20–1; Jones, *Brenhinedd*,
pp.90–1.

140 Jones, *Brut ... Red Book*, pp.60–1; Jones, *Brut ... Peniarth*, p.30; Jones, *Brenhinedd*,
pp.108–11.

141 See Flanagan, *Irish Society*, pp.66–7.

142 Elrington and Todd, *Whole Works*, 4, pp.487–572; Gwynn, 'St. Anselm'.

143 See Candon, 'Barefaced effrontery', pp.4–6.

144 Elrington and Todd, *Whole Works*, 4, pp.564–6.

145 AU 1106 associates Cellach's assumption of episcopal orders with a circuit of Munster
he undertook in the same year.

146 ATig., 2, p.326: 'A meeting of the men of Ireland, both laymen and clerics, around
Muirchertach Ua Briain at Cashel, and it was then that Muirchertach Ua Briain gave
Cashel of the kings as an offering to Patrick and to the Lord' (*Comdail fer nErenn im
Muirchertach Húa mBriain i Caisil .i. laechaib, cleirchib, ocus is annsin tuc Muircertach Húa
Briain Caisil na righ a n-ídhbairt do Padraic ocus don Chomdidh*); see also CS, pp.306–7.
Information concerning the synod is embedded in later material: O'Grady, *Caithréim
Thoirdhealbhaigh*, 1, pp.174–5; 2, pp.185–6 and Ó Donnchadha, *An Leabhar Muimhneach*,
p.341. For discussion, see Candon, 'Barefaced effrontery'.

147 MacErlean, 'Synod'.

148 See Ó Corráin, *Ireland before the Normans*, p.149 and Candon, 'Barefaced effrontery'.

149 Candon, 'Barefaced effrontery', p.23.

150 AI 1114: 'Diarmait Ua Briain seized the kingship of Munster and banished
Muirchertach from Limerick to Killaloe' (*Diarmait Hua Briain do gabail rigi Muman
ocus Muircertach do innarba dó a Luimnuch co Cill Da Lua*); AI 1115: 'Muirchertach
came to Limerick and Diarmait was imprisoned by him' (*Muirchertach do thichtain co
Lumnech ocus Diarmait do cumrech leis*); AI 1116: 'Diarmait Ua Briain turned against
Muirchertach Ua Briain in violation of a mutual oath on the relics of Ireland ...
Muirchertach Ua Briain went to Lismore and assumed the pilgrim's staff' (*Diarmait
Ua Briain d'impúd ar Murchertach Ua mBriain dar comluga mind Hérend ... Murcheretach
Ua Briain co Les Mór co rragaib bachaill*).

151 AU; ATig., 2, p.342; CS, pp.320–1.

152 AU 1119; see also AI 1119; ATig., 2, p.344; CS, pp.320–1; the phrase echoes exactly that
used of Máel Sechnaill mac Domnaill, Brian Boru's northern contemporary, on his
death in 1022: AU; ATig., 2, pp.252–3; CS, pp.260–3.

153 AI 1113.

154 AI 1114: 'The king of Ireland was struck down by disease this year in the middle
of the summer. Alas, indeed, we find it impossible to relate the multitude of these
evils: battles and fights, raids and murders, violations of churches and holy places
throughout Ireland, both of laity and clergy! Woe to him who brought upon us
this sickness of the king of Ireland!' (*Galar do gabáil rig Érend isin bliadain so i medon
shamraid. Uch tra imad na n-olc so nucu n-etam a n-inisin: catha ocus chongala, crecha ocus
marbad duine, saraighthe cell ocus neimed fo Éirind eter tuaid ocus eclais! Mairg fo-uair duin in
galar so ríg Éirend!*).

155 AU 1118: 'A hosting by Tairdelbach Ua Conchobair ... to Munster ... and he gave

south Munster [Desmumu] to Mac Carthaig and north Munster [Tuadmumu] to the sons of Diarmait and took the hostages of both' (*Slogadh la Tairrdelbach H. Concobhair … isin Muman … co tard Desmumain do Mac Carrthaigh ocus Tuathmumain do macaibh Diarmada ocus co tuc a ngiallu diblinaib*).

156 The two-fold division of Munster was re-imposed in 1121 and again in 1127 (ATig., 2, pp.346, 353).

157 AI: 'Conchobar Ua Briain and Tairdelbach, his brother, turned against Ruaidrí's son [= Tairdelbach Ua Conchobair], and they brought Cormac from Lismore and gave him the kingship of Munster' (*Impoth do Concobor U Briain ocus do Tairdelbac da bratair, for mc. Ruadri co tucsat Chormac a Liss Mór, acus co tucsat rige Muman do*). See also ATig., 2, p.354.

158 '*Caithréim Chellacháin Chaisil*'.

159 See Stalley, 'Design and function', where he describes the chapel as 'a celebration of Mac Carthaig success in recapturing the kingship of Munster', linking it specifically with the propaganda tract (p.166).

160 Misc.Ir.Ann. 1134: 'A church built by Cormac son of Muireadhach Mac Carrthaigh at Cashel was consecrated with great honour by the archbishop of Cashel and the bishops of Munster' (*Teampall dorinneadh la Cormac mac Muireadhaigh Mic Carrthaigh a Caisil do coisrigadh la hairdeaspog Caisil agus la heaspogaibh Muman gu n-anóir móir*).

161 Misc.Ir.Ann. 1137 on which occasion their ally was a great-grandson of Diarmait mac Maíl na mBó.

162 ATig., 2, p.371; according to Misc.Ir.Ann. 1138, the deed was carried out by a henchman 'at the instigation of Tairdelbach son of Diarmait Ua Briain in his own house' (*ar furalimh Toirrdealbhaigh mic Diarmada h. Briain ana tigh fein*).

163 Misc.Ir.Ann.; ATig., 2, p.374; CS, pp.338–9.

164 ATig., 2, pp.378–9.

165 ATig., 2, pp.379, 381.

166 AFM *s.a.* 1150.

167 Misc.Ir.Ann.

168 ATig., 2, pp.387–8; see also Misc.Ir.Ann. 1151.

169 Misc.Ir.Ann.; ATig., 2, pp.391–2: 'That hosting was undertaken to restore Tairdelbach Ua Briain to power in Munster after he had been banished by Tairdelbach Ua Conchobair' (*D'indlacadh Thairrdelbaig Hui Briain ansa Mumain as uime do tinscnadh an sluaighedh sin iarna indarba la Tairrdelbach Hua Concobair*).

170 ATig., 2, pp.395, 405.

171 ATig., 2, p.398.

172 Misc.Ir.Ann. 1164.

173 ATig., 2, p.421; according to the more partisan Munster source, Misc.Ir.Ann., he was in fact 'king of almost all of Ireland' (*ri hEreann acht beac*).

174 For an account of these events, see Charles-Edwards, 'Ireland'.

175 For the background to and circumstances of this event, see Flanagan, *Irish Society*, pp.56–111.

176 AI 1171: 'The son of the Empress [Henry II] came to Ireland and landed at Waterford. The son of Cormac [Diarmait Mac Carthaig] and the son of Tairdelbach [Domnall Mór Ua Briain] submitted to him there…' (*Mc. na Perisi do thidach i nHerind goro gab ac Purt Lárgi go nnechaid mc. Cormaic ocus mc. Tairdelbaig ina theg and sin*); according to Gerald of Wales, Ua Briain submitted to Henry on the bank of the River Suir: Scott and Martin, *Expugnatio*, pp.92–5.

177 Dobbs, 'Ban-shenchus', *Revue Celtique* 48, p.233 and Orpen, *Song*, pp.150–1, lines 2041–2, for which reference I am indebted to Fiona Edmonds.

178 *Irish Society*, pp.226–7.

179 ATig., 2, pp.439, 440.

180 Flanagan, *Irish Royal Charters*, pp.127–74; he is also termed *rei de Lymerich* 'king of Limerick' in Orpen, *Song*, pp.148–9, line 2035.

181 Misc.Ir.Ann. where the implication is that he was 'king of Thomond'; AU describes him as 'king of Munster' (*ri Muman*).

182 Goedheer, *Irish and Norse Traditions*, pp.50, 55 (stanza 49).

183 *Ibid.* (stanza 51); this complete stanza has already been quoted above, pp.54, 148 n.6.

184 Scott and Martin, *Expugnatio*, pp.161–7; for this account, see Flanagan, *Irish Society*, pp.250–3.

185 Misc.Ir.Ann.

186 Frame, *Ireland*, p.19 and Empey, 'The settlement', pp.8, 13.

187 Goedheer, *Irish and Norse Traditions*, pp.49, 54 (stanzas 38, 39): 'Brian defended Ireland against the young, strong foreigners' (*Do leasaicc Brian an Banba/ air na Gallaibh glaschalma*); 'The foreigners left Ireland because of the slender-fingered hero' (*Do fhágbadar Goill Éirinn/ air eagladh an mhíledh mhéirsheing*). The poem is discussed in Simms, 'Battle', p.59 and Nic Ghiollamhaith, 'Dynastic warfare', pp.79–80, who speculates that it may have been written for Donnchad Cairprech.

188 Ní Úrdail, 'Two poems', pp.44–5 (stanza 23); Donnchad is also praised in a third poem ascribed to Muireadhach Albanach written to Murchad, son of Brian Dall Ua Briain: Bergin, *Irish Bardic Poetry*, pp.109, 261 (stanza 8).

189 Nic Ghiollamhaith, 'The Uí Briain'; Frame, *Ireland*, pp.24–5, 50–2.

190 Nic Ghiollamhaith, 'The Uí Briain'.

191 Nic Ghiollamhaith, 'Dynastic warfare', p.75.

192 For these events, see Simms, 'Battle', Nic Ghiollamhaith, 'Dynastic warfare' and Nic Ghiollamhaith, 'Kings and vassals'.

193 O'Grady, *Caithréim*.

194 Nic Ghiollamhaith, 'Dynastic warfare', p.77.

195 Trinity College Dublin Manuscript 1319; the fragment is contained in Rawlinson B 486: Ó Cuív, *Catalogue*, p.132. It consists of the names of those in Brian's battalion, as well as in a Thomond and a Desmond one. A number of the names are also found in Keating's account of the battle: Comyn and Dinneen, *Foras Feasa*, 3, pp.272–3.

196 This fact was already noted by Robin Flower in his introduction to O'Grady's posthumous edition, *Caithréim*, p.xiv. See also McNamara, 'Traditional motifs' and Nic Ghiollamhaith, 'Dynastic warfare', pp.78–9.

197 Todd, *Cogadh*, pp.74–5; O'Grady, *Caithréim*, 1, pp.11, 19; 2, pp.12, 21.

198 Todd, *Cogadh*, pp.112–05; O'Grady, *Caithréim*, 1, p.62; 2, p.58.

199 Todd, *Cogadh*, pp.204–5; O'Grady, *Caithréim*, 1, p.98; 2, pp.88–9.

200 Todd, *Cogadh*, pp.158–61; O'Grady, *Caithréim*, 1, pp.108–11; 2, pp.95–8.

201 Todd, *Cogadh*, pp.182–5; O'Grady, *Caithréim*, 1, pp.22–3, 114; 2, pp.23–4, 101.

202 Todd, *Cogadh*, pp.182–3; O'Grady, *Caithréim*, 1, p.117; 2, p.104.

203 Todd, *Cogadh*, pp.214–7; O'Grady, *Caithréim*, 1, pp.129–32; 2, pp.113–6.

204 Todd, *Cogadh*, pp.84–5; O'Grady, *Caithréim*, 1, p.9; 2, p.10.

205 Todd, *Cogadh*, pp.76–81; O'Grady, *Caithréim*, 1, p.13; 2, p.14.

206 Todd, *Cogadh*, pp.100–1; O'Grady, *Caithréim*, 1 p.11; 2, p.12.

207 Todd, *Cogadh*, pp.140–1; O'Grady, *Caithréim*, 1, p.29–30; 2, pp.31–2.

208 O'Grady, *Caithréim*, 1, pp.8, 60; 2, pp.9, 56–7. The key passage reads: 'since the Uí Chellaig are linked by birthright with Brian Boru's successful kin to a greater degree than any other people of the Connachta, since it is on account of Brian's generous

benefactions that the prosperity of that great family is maintained' (*óir is dúthchas do chloinn Chellaig sech gach cined Connachtach clann buanáithesach Bhriain Bhoraime, óir is tré raithbennachtaib Briain buanaigter maith na mórchlainne sin*).

209 O'Grady, *Caithréim*, 1, pp.126–7; 2, pp.111–2.

210 O'Grady, *Caithréim*, 1, p.9; 2, p.10.

211 Simms, 'Battle', p.60.

212 Mac Kenna, 'Poem' pp.134, 137 (stanza 37): 'Diarmait Ó Briain and the Brian whence he is descended – equal their achievement' (*Diarmaid Ó Briain 's an Brian ó ttá/ ionann a ngníomh*).

213 *Ibid.* (stanza 38): 'Though formidable his guidance on battle-front; his mercy is like that of Brian, Brian Boru the greatest of Ireland's kings, of whose race he comes' (*Brian Bóroimhe rogha ríogh bhFáil/ ar a bhfuil sliocht/ gidh eagail a rinnghliaidh a reacht/ in Bhriain a iocht*).

214 'Seachadadh'.

215 'Seachadadh', pp.187–91; Comyn and Dineen, *Foras Feasa*, 3, pp.156–7: 'on the authority of the book which is called *Cogadh Gall re Gaedhealaibh*' (*do réir an leabhair da ngairthear Cogadh Gall re Gaedhealaibh*).

216 Ó Muraíle, *Leabhar Mór na nGenealach*, 3, pp.44–51.

217 Best, 'Leabhar Oiris'.

Chapter Six: Assessing Brian

1 Jaski, *Early Irish Kingship*, p.13.

2 Ó Cróinín, *Early Medieval Ireland*, p.266.

3 On his death in 1224, Cathal Ua Conchobair is described as the best Irishman since Brian Boru's time, as noted above p.54: AU[1] s.a. 1223.

4 Goedheer, *Irish and Norse Tradition*, pp.49, 54 (stanza 37).

5 Chadwick, 'Vikings', p.33.

6 'Brian Boruma', pp.373–4.

7 *Ireland before the Normans*, p.125.

8 *Early Christian Ireland*, p.570.

9 *Irish Kings and High-Kings*, p.267.

10 Compare, for example, the account of Brian's raid on Uí Fhidgeinti (AI 977) with that of the battle of Belach Lechta the following year (AI 978).

11 See AI 982 and 993.

12 AI 983.

13 AI 995 and 1012.

14 AI 977: 'Ímar, king of the Vikings, and his two sons were killed on Scattery Island by Brian son of Cennétig' (*Imar rí Gall, ocus a da mc. do marbad i nInis Cathaig la Brian mc. Cennetich*).

15 AI 984.

16 'North Wales', p.175.

17 AI.

18 'Dál Cais'.

19 AI 990.

20 AU 1007.

21 AU.

22 'North Wales', pp.180–1.

23 AI.

24 AI 982, 983, 984.

25 AU 999.

26 AU.

27 AU 1005.

28 AI 721: 'For these were the five kings of the Munstermen who ruled Ireland after the [introduction of the] Faith, i.e. Áengus son of Nad Fraích, and his son, i.e. Eochaid, who ruled Ireland for seventeen years, and Cathal son of Finguine, and Feidlimid son of Crimthann, and Brian son of Cennétig' (*Ar it hé .u. ríg ro gabsat Herind iar cretim do Mumnechaib, .i. Oengus macc Nad Fruich ocus a mc., .i. Eochaid, qui Hiberniam rexit .xuii. annis, ocus Cathal mc. Finguine ocus Feidlimmid macc Crimthain ocus Brian mc. Cennetich*).

29 His career is discussed in Ó Corráin, *Ireland before the Normans*, pp.97–9.

30 See AU 823 and 836.

31 AU 827 and 838.

32 *Ireland before the Normans*, pp.98–9.

33 AU 847.

34 See, for example, AU 848; CS, pp.148–9.

35 AU 856; CS, pp.154–5.

36 AU 845.

37 Ó Corráin calls him a concocted 'super Viking': *Ireland before the Normans*, p.92.

38 The two accounts differ considerably from one another: Todd, *Cogadh*, pp.12–15; O'Meara, 'Giraldus Cambrensis', p.174 and O'Meara, *Gerald of Wales*, pp.120–1. See Stewart, 'Death of Turgesius', and Downham, 'Vikings in Southern Uí Néill', p.236.

39 AU 851; AU 859: they were also present at a later meeting at which Máel Sechnaill exerted control over Osraige and Munster.

40 See AU 856, 858, 859.

41 AU.

42 See, for example, AU 862.

43 AU 862; CS, pp.156–8; se above p.19.

44 Both brothers were murdered, Edward, however, in obscure circumstances: ASC, pp.79–8; Keynes, *Diplomas*, pp.163–74.

45 See Keynes, 'Declining reputation' and 'Re-reading', for which reference I am indebted to Professor Keynes.

46 Keynes, 'Declining reputation', pp.163–4, 166; the account is preserved in the Anglo-Saxon Chronicle.

47 'Declining reputation', p.168.

48 *Ibid.*, pp.168–73; Mynors, Thomson and Winterbottom, *William of Malmesbury*.

49 *Irish and Norse Traditions*, pp.38–9. Of Alfred, his Life claims, 'with his small band of nobles and also with certain soldiers and thegns, [he] was leading a restless life in great distress amid the woody and marshy places of Somerset. He had nothing to live on except what he could forage by frequent raids, either secretly or even openly from the Vikings' (*cum paucis suis nobilibus et etiam cum quibusdam militibus et fasellis, per sylvestria et gronnosa Summurtunensis pagae loca in magna tribulatione inquietam vitam ducebat. Nihil enim habebat quo uteretur, nisi quod a paganis … frequentibus irruptionibus aut clam aut etiam palam subraheret*): Stevenson, *Asser's Life*, p.41; Keynes and Lapidge, *Alfred the Great*, p.83. Similarly, for Brian, 'Great indeed was the hardship, suffering, bad food and bedding which they [Vikings] inflicted upon him in the huts of the harsh wilderness upon the hard, knotty, wet roots of his own native country, after they had killed his people, trusty officers and comrades, sorrowful, dispirited, wretched, unpitied, weary. For historians say that the foreigners cut off his people so that in the end he had no more

than fifteen followers' (*Mor, am, do duad ocus do docair ocus do drocuit ocus do drochlebaid, tuc sosum dosom, i fianbothaib fásaig for cruaidfremanaib corracha fliuchta a tiri duthaigi fodein, ar marbad a muintiri ocus aessa grada, ocus a comalta, co dub, domenmnach, truag, nemelach, torsech. Daig atberait na senchaidi go ro dithaigset gaill a muintir cunach rabi fo deoid na lenmain acht .u. duini dec)*: Todd, *Cogadh*, pp.60–3.

50 *Irish and Norse Traditions*, p.39.

51 '*Caithréim Chellacháin Chaisil*', p.69.

52 Stevenson, *Asser's Life*, p.28; Keynes and Lapidge, *Alfred the Great*, p.78.

53 Keynes and Lapidge, *Alfred the Great*, p.56.

54 The work ends in 893, six years before Alfred's death; Whitelock, *Genuine Asser*, p.5. Kirby suggests that what we have is 'an imperfect conflation of several separate shorter treatises on the king, all written at originally different times': 'Asser', p.13.

55 Early Irish examples of this genre include *Audacht Morainn*: Kelly, *Audacht*.

56 Scharer, 'Writing of history', pp.192–203; Stevenson, *Asser's Life*, pp.60–1; Keynes and Lapidge, *Alfred the Great*, p.92.

57 Todd, *Cogadh*, pp.204–5

58 *Ibid.*, pp.76–7.

59 'Writing of history', p.201.

60 See Keynes and Lapidge, *Alfred the Great*, p.57 where they note that the Life's circulation was confined to England, suggesting that its limited nature 'may be because Asser never completed it [the work] and hence made no arrangements to have the work copied and distributed'. Simon Keynes has drawn attention to the possibility that Gerald of Wales may have used Asser directly: *Anglo-Saxon England*, p.123, for which reference I am grateful to Professor Keynes.

61 Dutton, *Charlemagne's Courtier*, pp.15–39.

62 Gwynn, 'Brian in Armagh', p.46; see above p.26.

63 Althoff, *Otto III*.

64 See Loyn, 'Imperial style'.

65 The phrase is Loyn's, *ibid.*, p.111.

66 *Irish Society*, p.179.

Tables

AI	AU	CS	ALC	AB	AClon	AFM
BRIAN'S ALLIES	BRIAN'S ALLIES	BRIAN'S ALLIES	BRIAN'S ALLIES	BRIAN'S ALLIES	BRIAN'S ALLIES	BRIAN'S ALLIES
Dál Cais	Dál Cais	Dál Cais	Dál Cais	Dál Cais	Dál Cais	Dál Cais
Brian Bórama	Brian Bórama	Brian Bórama	Brian Bórama	Brian[1]	Bryan Borowa	Brian
Murchad son of Brian	Murchad son of Brian	Murchad son of Brian	Murchad son of Brian	Murchad son of Brian	Murrough son of Brian	Murchad son of Brian
Tairdelbach son of Murchad	Tairdelbach son of Murchad	Tairdelbach son of Murchad	Tairdelbach son of Murchad	Tairdelbach son of Murchad	Terence, Brian's grandchild	Tairdelbach son of Murchad
Conaing, Brian's nephew	Conaing, Brian's nephew	Conaing, Brian's nephew	Conaing, Brian's nephew	Conaing, Brian's nephew[1]	His nephew, Conyng mcDon Cwan[2]	Conaing, Brian's nephew[3]
	Brian's attendants: Eocho mac Dúnadaig; Níall ua Cuind; Cennétig's son	Brian's attendants: Eocho mac Dúnadaig; Níall ua Cuind; Cú Duilig, son of Cennétig	Brian's attendants: Eocho mac Dúnadaig; Niall mac Cuinn; Cú Duilig son of Cennétig	Brian's attendants: Eochu mac Dúnadaig; Níall ua Cuind; Cú Dulich son of Cennétig	3 noblemen of the king's bedchamber: Eachy mcDawny; Neale O'Coyne; Cowdaylye mcKennedy	Brian's attendants: Eochu mac Dúnadaig lord of Clann Scannláin; Níall ua Cuind; Cú Dulich son of Cennétig
Munstermen	Munstermen	Munstermen	Munstermen	Munstermen	Munstermen	Munstermen
Domnall mac Diarmata, king of Corcu Bascinn	Domnall mac Diarmata, king of Corcu Bascinn[4]	Domnall mac Diarmata, king of Corcu Bascinn[4]	Domnall mac Diarmata, king of Corcu Baiscinn[4]	Domnall mac Diarmata, king of Corcu Bascinn[4]	Donnell McDermott prince of Corka Avaiskin[4]	Domnall mac Diarmata, lord of Corcu Bascinn[4]
Mac Bethad mac Muiredaig, king of Ciarraige Luachra	Mac Bethad mac Muiredaig, king of Ciarraige Luachra[5]	Mac Bethad mac Muiredaig, king of Ciarraige Luachra[5]	Mac Bethad mac Muiredaig, king of Ciarraige Luachra[5]	Mac Bethad mac Muredaig, king of Ciarraige Luachra[5]	McBeachy McMorreaye Kloen, prince of Kerry Lawchra[5]	Mac Bethad mac Muiredaig Chlóin, lord of Ciarraige Luachra[5]
	Scannlán mac Cathail, king of Eoganachta Locha Léin	Scannlán mac Cathail, king of Eoganachta Locha Léin	Scannlán mac Cathail, king of Eoganachta Locha Léin	Scannlán mac Cathail, king of Eoganachta Locha Léin	Scannlan McCahall, prince of Eonaght of Loghlyen	Scannlán mac Cathail, lord of Eoganachta Locha Léin
	Mothla mac Domnaill, king of the Déissi[6]	Mothla mac Domnaill, king of the Déissi[6]	Mothla mac Domnaill, king of the Déissi[6]	Mothla mac Domnaill, king of the Déissi[6]	Mothlae mcDonell mcFoylan, prince of the Dessies[6]	Mothla mac Domnaill meic Fáeláin, lord of the Déissi[6]
	Gebenach ua Dubagáin, king of Fernmag[7]	Gebenach ua Dubagáin, king of Fernmag[7]	Geibendach ua Dubagáin, king of Fernmag[7]	Gebennach mac Dubcon, king of Fer Maigi[7]	Geveannagh McDowagan, king of Fearnmoy[7]	Gebenach ua Dubagáin, lord of Fer Maigi[7]

1 List of the dead at the battle of Clontarf.

AI	AU	CS	ALC	AB	AClon	AFM
Others	Others	Others	Others	Others	Others	Others
Tadc ua Cellaig, king of Uí Maine	two kings of Uí Maine	Tadc ua Cellaig, king of Uí Maine	Tadc son of Murchad, king of Uí Maine	Tadc mac Murchada, king of Uí Maine	Teig O'Kelly, prince of Imanie	Tadc ua Cellaig, lord of Uí Maine
	Máel Rúanaid ua hEidin, king of Aidne	Máel Rúanaid ua hEidin, king of Aidne	Mael Ruanaid ua hEidin, king of Aidne	Mael Ruanaid ua hEdin, king of Aidne	Moyleronye O'Hoynn, prince of Ayny	Mael Ruanaid ua hEidin, lord of Aidne
	Domnall mac Eimín meic Cainnig, mórmáer Marr	Domnall mac Eimín meic Cainnig	Domnall mac Eimín mic Cainnig, mórmaer Mair	Domnall mac Emin meic Cainnich Móir .i. mórmáer i nAlbain ('in Scotland')	Donnell McEvin McCaynich, earle of Dombarr in Scotland	Domnall mac Eimíne mic Cainnich, mórmáer i nAlbain ('in Scotland')
and many others	and many other nobles	and others	and many other nobles	and many other nobles		and many other nobles
BRIAN'S OPPONENTS	BRIAN'S OPPONENTS[8]	BRIAN'S OPPONENTS[8]	BRIAN'S OPPONENTS[8]	BRIAN'S OPPONENTS[8]	BRIAN'S OPPONENTS[8]	BRIAN'S OPPONENTS
Irishmen	Irishmen	Irishmen	Irishmen	Irishmen	Irishmen	Irishmen
Máel Mórda mac Murchada, king of Leinster	Máel Mórda mac Murchada, king of Leinster	Máel Mórda mac Murchada, king of Leinster	Máel Mórda mac Murchada, king of Leinster	Máel Mórda mac Murchada, king of Leinster	Mulmorrey McMurrogh, king of Leinster	Máel Mórda mac Murchada, king of Leinster
	Domnall mac Fergaile, king of the Fortuatha of Leinster		Domnall mac Fergaile, king of the Fortuatha of Leinster			
		Tuathal ua Ugaire, heir-apparent of Leinster				Tuathal ua Ugaire, heir-apparent of Leinster[9]
		mac Brogarbáin mic Conchobair, heir-apparent of Uí Fháilgi	Brogarbán mac Conchobair, king of Uí Fhailgi	mac Brogarbáin meic Conchobair, king of Uí Fhailgi	McBrogaroann, prince of Affaile	mac Brogarbáin mic Conchobair, heir-apparent of Uí Fháilgi
and Leinster royalty		and many others		and many other nobles		and a countless slaughter of the Leinstermen
	Vikings	Vikings	Vikings	Vikings	Vikings	Vikings
	Dubgall mac Amlaíb	Dubgall mac Amlaíb	Dubgall mac Amlaib	Dubgall mac Amlaíb		Dubgall mac Amlaíb
	Gilla Ciaráin mac Glúin Iairnn	Gilla Ciaráin mac Glúin Iairnn	Gilla Ciaráin mac Glúin Iarainn	Gilla Ciaráin mac Glúin Iarainn		Gilla Ciaráin mac Glúin Iairnn
	Siuchraidh mac Loduir, Earl of Orkney[10]	Siuchraidh mac Loduir, Earl of Orkney	Sighrud mac Lotair, Earl of Orkney[10]	Siffraith mac Lodair, Earl of Orkney		Sichfrith mac Lodair, Earl of Orkney
	Oittir Dub Suartgair		Uithir Dub Suairtghair			
	Donnchad ua Eruilb		Donnchad ua hEruilb			
	Griséne		Grissíne			
	Luimne		Luimne			
	Amlaíb mac Lagmainn		Amlaib mac Lagmainn			
	Brodar, leader of the fleet of Lochlainn	Brodar leader of the Danes	Brodar, leader of the fleet of Lochlainn	Brodar leader of the Danes	Brwader, Earle of the Island of the Orcades[11]	Brodar leader of the Danes
and the foreigners of the western world	6,000 others	3,000 other Vikings	6,000 others	1,000 others and 3,000 Vikings		1,000 armed men and 3,000 Vikings

1 (cont.) List of the dead at the battle of Clontarf.

1 Brian and Conaing are mentioned at the end of the list of dead in AB.

2 Conaing appears before Murchad and Tairdelbach in AClon.

3 Conaing appears between Murchad and Tairdelbach in AFM.

4 Domnall mac Diarmata appears after Mac Bethad mac Muiredaig in AU, CS, ALC, AB, AClon. and AFM.

5 Mac Bethad mac Muiredaig appears after Tadc Ua Cellaig and Máel Ruanaid ua hEidin in AU, CS, ALC, AB, AClon. and AFM.

6 Mothla mac Domnaill appears before Brian's three attendants in AU, CS, ALC, AB, AClon. and AFM.

7 Gebennach ua Dubagáin appears after Tadc Ua Cellaig and Máel Ruanaid ua hEidin and before Mac Bethad mac Muiredaig in AU, CS, ALC, AB, AClon. and AFM.

8 Brian's opponents are listed before his allies in AU, ALC, AB and AClon.

9 Tuathal ua Ugaire is listed after mac Brogarbáin in AFM.

10 The Earl of Orkney is listed before Gilla Ciaráin in AU and ALC.

11 Brodar is before Máel Mórda mac Murchada and mac Brogarbáin in AClon.

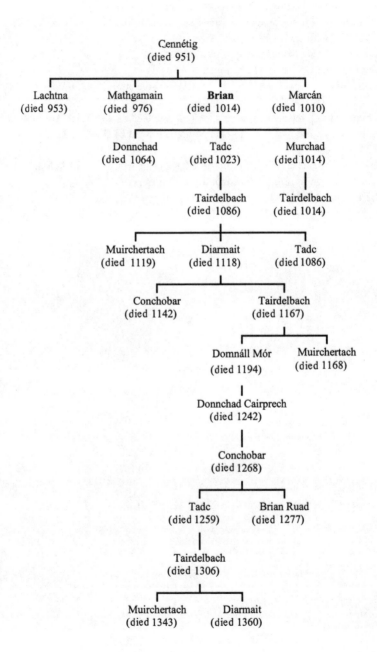

Cennétig
(died 951)

Lachtna
(died 953)

Mathgamain
(died 976)

Brian
(died 1014)

Marcán
(died 1010)

Donnchad
(died 1064)

Tadc
(died 1023)

Murchad
(died 1014)

Tairdelbach
(died 1086)

Tairdelbach
(died 1014)

Muirchertach
(died 1119)

Diarmait
(died 1118)

Tadc
(died 1086)

Conchobar
(died 1142)

Tairdelbach
(died 1167)

Domnáll Mór
(died 1194)

Muirchertach
(died 1168)

Donnchad Cairprech
(died 1242)

Conchobar
(died 1268)

Tadc
(died 1259)

Brian Ruad
(died 1277)

Tairdelbach
(died 1306)

Muirchertach
(died 1343)

Diarmait
(died 1360)

2 Brian and his descendants.

List of Illustrations and Maps

ILLUSTRATIONS

Maps

Chapter Page Illustrations

Guide to Further Reading

Full bibliographical references to the works cited are given in the Bibliography. The following is a list of key reading material on Brian Boru and his times.

Primary Sources

Annalistic Sources: Thomas Charles-Edwards (trans.), *The Chronicle of Ireland*, 2 vols, Translated Texts for Historians 44 (Liverpool, 2006).

Cogadh Gáedhel re Gallaibh: James Henthorn Todd (ed. and trans.), *Cogadh Gaedhel re Gallaibh: The War of the Gaedhil with the Gaill or the Invasions of Ireland by the Danes and Other Norsemen* (London, 1867).

Njáls saga: Einar Ól. Sveinsson (ed.), *Brennu-Njáls saga*, Íslenzk fornrit 12 (Reykjavík, 1954); Viðar Hreinsson (ed.), *The Complete Sagas of Icelanders including 49 Tales*, 5 vols (Reykjavík, 1997), vol.3, pp.1–200 ('Njal's saga').

Secondary Sources

Candon, Anthony, 'Muirchertach Ua Briain, politics, and naval activity in the Irish Sea, 1075–1119', in Gearóid Mac Niocaill and Patrick F. Wallace (eds), *Keimelia: Studies in Medieval Archaeology and History in*

Memory of Tom Delaney (Galway, 1988), pp.397–415.

Charles-Edwards, Thomas, 'Irish warfare before 1100', in Thomas Bartlett and Keith Jeffery (eds), *A Military History of Ireland* (Cambridge, 1996), pp.26–51.

Downham, Clare, 'England and the Irish Sea zone in the eleventh century', *Anglo-Norman Studies* 26 (2003), pp.55–73.

Downham, Clare, 'The Vikings in Southern Uí Néill to 1014', *Peritia* 17–18 (2003–4), pp.233–55.

Duffy, Seán, 'Irishmen and Islesmen in the kingdoms of Dublin and Man, 1052–1171', *Ériu* 43 (1992), pp.93–133.

Etchingham, Colmán, 'North Wales, Ireland and the Isles: the Insular Viking zone', *Peritia* 15 (2001), pp.145–87.

Goedheer, A.J., *Irish and Norse Traditions about the Battle of Clontarf* (Haarlem, 1938).

Hines, John, *Old-Norse Sources for Gaelic History*, Quiggin Pamphlets on the Sources of Mediaeval Gaelic History 5 (Cambridge, 2002).

Hudson, Benjamin, "Brjáns saga", *Medium Ævum* 71:2 (2002), pp.241–68.

Hudson, Benjamin, *Viking Pirates and Christian Princes: Dynasty, Religion, and Empire in the North Atlantic* (Oxford, 2005).

Lönnroth, Lars, *Njáls Saga: A Critical Introduction* (Berkeley, CA, 1976).

Ní Mhaonaigh, Máire, '*Cogad Gáedel re Gallaib*: some dating considerations', *Peritia* 9 (1995), pp.354–77.

Ní Mhaonaigh, Máire, 'Friend and foe: Vikings in ninth- and tenth-century Irish literature', in Howard B. Clarke, Máire Ní Mhaonaigh and Raghnall Ó Floinn (eds), *Ireland and Scandinavia in the Early Viking Age* (Dublin, 1998), pp.381–402.

Ó Corráin, Donncha, *Ireland before the Normans*, Gill History of Ireland 2 (Dublin, 1972).

Ó Corráin, Donnchadh, 'Viking Ireland – afterthoughts', in Howard B. Clarke, Máire Ní Mhaonaigh and Raghnall Ó Floinn (eds), *Ireland and Scandinavia in the Early Viking Age* (Dublin, 1998), pp.421–52.

Ó Corráin, Donnchadh, 'The Vikings in Scotland and Ireland in the ninth century', *Peritia* 12 (1998), pp.296–339.

Ryan, John, 'The O'Briens in Munster after Clontarf', *North Munster Antiquarian Journal* 2:4 (1941), pp.141–52 and 3:1 (1942), pp.1–52.

Ryan, John, 'Brian Boruma, king of Ireland', in Etienne Rynne (ed.), *North Munster Studies: Essays in Commemoration of Monsignor Michael Moloney* (Limerick, 1967), pp.355–74.

Bibliography of Works Cited in Notes

Icelandic names are cited alphabetically, in accordance with the first name.

Primary Sources

ab Ithel, J. Williams (ed.), *Annales Cambriæ*, Chronicles and Memorials of Great Britain and Ireland during the Middle Ages 20 (London, 1860).

Arbuthnot, Sharon (ed. and trans.), *Cóir Anmann: A Late Middle Irish Treatise on Personal Names*, 2 vols, Irish Texts Society 59–60 (London and Dublin, 2005–7).

Arnold, Thomas (ed.), *Symeonis Monachi Opera Omnia*, 2 vols, Rerum Britannicarum Medii Aevi Scriptores 75 (London, 1882–5).

Bergin, Osborn (ed. and trans.), *Irish Bardic Poetry: Texts and Translations* (Dublin, 1970).

Best, R.I. (ed.), 'The Leabhar Oiris', *Ériu* 1 (1904), pp.74–112.

Best, R.I., Osborn J. Bergin, M.A. O'Brien and Anne O'Sullivan (eds), *The Book of Leinster formerly Lebar na Núachongbála*, 6 vols (Dublin, 1954–83).

Bjarni Aðalbjarnarson (ed.), *Heimskringla*, 3 vols, Íslenzk fornrit 26–8 (Reykjavík, 1941–51).

Bourgain, Pascale (ed.), *Ademari Carbannensis Chronicon*, Corpus Christianorum, Continuatio mediaevalis 129 (Turnhout, 1999).

Broderick, George (ed. and trans.), *Cronica regum Mannie & Insularum: Chronicles of the Kings of Man and the Isles, BL Coton Julius Avii* (Belfast, 1979).

Charles-Edwards, Thomas (trans.), *The Chronicle of Ireland*, 2 vols, Translated Texts for Historians 44 (Liverpool, 2006).

Clover, Helen and Margaret Gibson (eds), *The Letters of Lanfranc, Archbishop of Canterbury* (Oxford, 1979).

Comyn, David and Patrick S. Dineen (eds and trans.), *Foras Feasa ar Éirinn le Seathrún Céitinn, D.D.*, 4 vols, Irish Texts Soceity 4, 8, 9, 15 (London and Dublin, 1902–14)

Dillon, Miles (ed. and trans.), *Lebor na Cert: The Book of Rights*, Irish Texts Society 46 (London and Dublin, 1962).

Dobbs, Margaret C. (ed. and trans.), 'The Ban-Shenchus', *Revue Celtique* 47 (1930), pp.283–339; 48 (1931), pp.163–234; 49 (1932), pp.437–89.

Dutton, Paul Edward (trans.), *Charlemagne's Courtier: The Complete Einhard*, Readings in Medieval Civilisations and Cultures 3 (Peterborough, Ontario, 1998).

Einar Ól. Sveinsson (ed.), *Brennu-Njáls saga*, Íslenzk fornrit 12 (Reykjavík, 1954).

Elrington, C.R. and James Henthorn Todd (eds), *The Whole Works of the Most Reverend James Ussher D.D.*, 17 vols (Dublin, 1847–64).

Evans, D. Simon, *A Mediaeval Prince of Wales: The Life of Gruffudd ap Cynan* (Llanerch, 1990).

Finnbogi Guðmundsson (ed.), *Orkneyinga saga*, Íslenzk fornrit 34 (Reykjavík, 1965).

Freeman, A. Martin (ed. and trans.), 'The Annals in Cotton MS. Titus A. XXV', *Revue Celtique* 41 (1924), pp.301–30.

Grosjean, Paul, 'Édition du *Catalogus praecipuorum sanctorum Hiberniae* de Henri Fitzsimon', in John Ryan (ed.), *Féil-Sgríbhinn Eóin Mhic Néill: Essays and Studies presented to Professor Eoin MacNeill* (Dublin, 1940), pp.335–93.

Gwynn, Edward (ed. and trans.), *The Metrical Dindshenchas*, 5 vols, Todd Lecture Series 8–12 (Dublin, 1903–35).

Gwynn, John (ed.), *Liber Ardmachanus: The Book of Armagh* (Dublin, 1913).

Hennessy, William M. (ed. and trans.), *Chronicum Scotorum: A Chronicle of Irish Affairs, from the Earliest Times to A.D. 1135; with a Supplement containing the Events from 1141 to 1150* (London, 1866).

Hennessy, William M. (ed. and trans.), *The Annals of Loch Cé: A Chronicle of Irish Affairs from A.D. 1014 to A.D. 1590*, 2 vols (London, 1871).

Hennessy, William M. and B. Mac Carthy (eds and trans.), *Annala Uladh: Annals of Ulster otherwise, Annala Senait, Annals of Senat; a Chronicle of Irish Affairs from A.D. 431–1131: 1155–1541*, 4 vols (Dublin, 1887–1901).

Hudson, Benjamin T. (ed. and trans.), *Prophecy of Berchán: Irish and Scottish High-Kings of the Middle Ages* (Westport, CT, 1996).

Jón Jóhannesson (ed.), *Austfirðinga sögur*, Íslenzk fornrit 11 (Reykjavík, 1950).

Jones, Thomas (trans.), *Brut y Tywysogyon or The Chronicle of the Princes Peniarth MS. 20 Version*, Board of Celtic Studies, University of Wales History and Law Series 11 (Cardiff, 1952).

Jones, Thomas (ed. and trans.), *Brut y Tywysogyon or The Chronicle of the Princes Red Book of Hergest Version*, Board of Celtic Studies, University of Wales History and Law Series 16 (Cardiff, 1955).

Jones, Thomas (ed. and trans.), *Brenhinedd y Saesson or The Kings of the Saxons, BM Cotton MS. Cleopatra B v and The Black Book of Basingwerk NLW MS. 7006*, Board of Celtic Studies, University of Wales History and Law Series 25 (Cardiff, 1971).

Joynt, Maud (ed. and trans.), 'Echtra mac Echdach Mugmedóin', *Ériu* 4 (1910), pp.91–111

Kelly, Fergus (ed. and trans.), *Audacht Morainn*, (Dublin, 1976).

Keynes, Simon and Michael Lapidge (trans.), *Alfred the Great: Asser's Life of King Alfred and Other Contemporary Sources* (Harmondsworth, 1983).

Knott, Eleanor (ed.), *Togail Bruidne Da Derga*, Mediaeval and Modern Irish Series 8 (Dublin, 1936).

Mac Airt, Seán (ed. and trans.), *The Annals of Innisfallen (MS. Rawlinson B. 503)* (Dublin, 1951).

Mac Airt, Seán and Gearóid Mac Niocaill (eds and trans.), *The Annals of Ulster (to A.D. 1131), Part I, Text and Translation* (Dublin, 1983).

Macalister, R.A.S. (ed. and trans.), *Lebor Gabála Érenn: The Book of the Taking of Ireland*, 5 vols, Irish Texts Society 34, 35, 39, 41, 44 (London and Dublin, 1938–56).

Mac Cionnaith, Láimhbheartach (ed.), *Dioghluim Dána* (Dublin, 1938).

Mac Kenna, Lambert (ed. and trans.) 'A poem by Gofraidh Fionn Ó Dálaigh', *Ériu* 16 (1952), pp.132–9.

Mac Neill, John (ed.), 'Cath Cluana Tairb', *Gaelic Journal* 7 (1896), pp.8–11, 41–4, 55–7.

Mac Carthy, B. (ed. and trans.), *The Codex Palatino-Vaticanus No. 830, Texts,*

Translations and Indices, Todd Lecture Series 3 (Dublin, 1892).

Monsen, Erling and A.H. Smith (trans.), *Heimskringla or the Lives of the Norse Kings by Snorre Sturlason* (Cambridge, 1932).

Mulchrone, Kathleen (ed.), *Bethu Phátraic, the Tripartite Life of Patrick: I, Text and Sources* (Dublin, 1939).

Murphy, Denis (ed.), *The Annals of Clonmacnoise being Annals of Ireland from the Earliest Period to A.D. 1408, translated into English A.D. 1627 by Conell Mageoghagan* (Dublin, 1896).

Murphy, Gerard (ed. and trans.), *Early Irish Lyrics: Eighth to Twelfth Century* (Oxford, 1956).

Murray, Kevin (ed. and trans.), *Baile in Scáil: 'The Phantom's Frenzy'*, Irish Texts Society 58 (London and Dublin, 2004).

Mynors, R.A.B., R.M. Thomson and M. Winterbottom (eds and trans.), *William of Malmesbury: Gesta Regum Anglorum/ The History of the English Kings*, 2 vols (Oxford, 1998–9).

Ní Úrdail, Meidhbhín (ed. and trans.), 'Two poems attributed to Muireadhach Albanach Ó Dálaigh', *Ériu* 53 (2003), pp. 19–52.

O'Brien, M.A. (ed.), *Corpus genealogiarum Hiberniae* (Dublin, 1962).

O'Donovan, John (ed. and trans.), *Annala Rioghachta Eireann: Annals of the Kingdom of Ireland by the Four Masters, from the Earliest Period to the Year 1616*, 2nd edn, 7 vols (Dublin, 1856).

Ó Donnchadha, Tadhg (ed.), *An Leabhar Muimhneach maraon le suim aguisíní* (Dublin, 1941).

O'Grady, Standish Hayes (ed. and trans.), *Caithréim Thoirdhealbhaigh*, 2 vols, Irish Texts Society 26–7 (London and Dublin, 1929).

Ó hInnse, Séamus (ed. and trans.), *Miscellaneous Irish Annals (A.D. 1114–1437)* (Dublin, 1947).

O'Keeffe, J.G. (ed.), 'Dál Caladbuig and reciprocal services between the kings of Cashel and various Munster states', in J. Fraser, Paul Grosjean and J.G. O'Keeffe (eds), *Irish Texts*, 1 (London, 1931), pp. 19–21.

O'Meara, John J. (ed.), 'Giraldus Cambrensis in Topographia Hibernie: text of the first recension', *Proceedings of the Royal Irish Academy* C 52 (1948–50), pp. 113–78.

O'Meara, John J. (trans.), *Gerald of Wales: The History and Topography of Ireland* (Harmondsworth, 1982).

Ó Muraíle, Nollaig (ed. and trans.), *Leabhar Mór na nGenealach: The Great Book of Irish Genealogies*, 5 vols (Dublin, 2003).

Ó Riain, Pádraig (ed.), 'The *Catalogus praecipuorom sanctorum Hiberniae*, sixty years on', in Alfred P. Smyth (ed.), *Seanchas: Studies in Early and*

Medieval Irish Archaeology, History and Literature in Honour of Francis J. Byrne (Dublin, 2000), pp.396–430.

Orpen, Goddard Henry (ed. and trans.), *The Song of Dermot and the Earl: An Old French Poem from the Carew Manuscript No. 596 in the Archiepiscopal Library at Lambeth Palace* (Oxford, 1892).

Radner, Joan N. (ed. and trans.), *Fragmentary Annals of Ireland* (Dublin, 1978).

Russell, Paul (ed. and trans.), *Vita Griffini filii Conani: The Medieval Latin Life of Gruffudd ap Cynan* (Cardiff, 2005).

Scott, A.B. and F.X. Martin (eds and trans.), *Expugnatio Hibernica: The Conquest of Ireland by Giraldus Cambrensis*, A New History of Ireland, Ancillary Publications 3 (Dublin, 1978).

Stevenson, William Henry (ed.), *Asser's Life of King Alfred, Together with the Annals of St Neots Erroneously Ascribed to Asser* (Oxford, 1904).

Stokes, Whitley (ed. and trans.), 'The Annals of Tigernach: fourth fragment A.D. 973–1088', *Revue celtique* 17 (1896), pp.337–420; 'The Annals of Tigernach: the continuation A.D. 1088-1178', *Revue celtique* 18 (1897), pp.9–59, 150–97, 268–303; reprinted as *The Annals of Tigernach*, vol. 2 (Felinfach, 1993).

Stokes, Whitley (ed. and trans.), 'On the deaths of some Irish heroes', *Revue celtique* 23 (1902), pp.303–48.

Stokes, Whitley (ed. and trans.), 'The death of Crimthann son of Fidach, and the adventures of the sons of Eochaid Muigmedóin', *Revue Celtique* 24 (1903), pp.172–207.

Todd, James Henthorn (ed. and trans.), *Cogadh Gaedhel re Gallaibh: The War of the Gaedhil with the Gaill or the Invasions of Ireland by the Danes and Other Norsemen* (London, 1867).

Waitz, G. (ed.), 'Mariani Scotti Chronicon', in G.H. Pertz (ed.), *Monumenta Germaniae Historica IV:5, Annales et Chronica aevi Salici* (Hannover, 1844), pp.481–562.

Warner, George F. (ed.), *The Stowe Missal: MS. D. II. 3 in the Library of the Royal Irish Academy, Dublin*, 2 vols, Henry Bradshaw Society 31–2 (London, 1906–15).

Whitelock, Dorothy (trans.), *The Anglo-Saxon Chronicle: A Revised Translation*, 2nd edn (London, 1965).

Secondary Sources

Allen, Richard F., *Fire and Iron: Critical Approaches to Njáls Saga* (Pittsburgh, PA, 1971).

Allmand, Christopher, 'The reporting of war in the Middle Ages', in Diana Dunn (ed.), *War and Society in Medieval and Early Modern Britain* (Liverpool, 2000), pp.17–33.

Althoff, Gerd, *Otto III*, trans. Phyllis G. Jestice (Pennsylvania, 2003).

Bhreathnach, Edel, 'The documentary evidence for pre-Norman Skreen, County Meath', *Ríocht na Midhe* 9:2 (1996), pp.37–45.

Bhreathnach, Edel, 'Columban churches in Brega and Leinster: relations with the Norse and the Anglo-Normans', *Journal of the Royal Society of Antiquaries of Ireland* 129 (1999), pp.5–18.

Bradbury, Jim, *The Medieval Archer* (Woodbridge, 1985).

Bradley, John, 'The interpretation of Scandinavian settlement in Ireland', in John Bradley (ed.), *Settlement and Society in Medieval Ireland: Studies Presented to F.X. Martin, o.s.a.* (Kilkenny, 1988), pp.49–78.

Breatnach, Liam, 'The Ecclesiastical element in the Old-Irish legal tract *Cáin Fhuithirbe*', *Peritia* 5 (1986), pp.36–52.

Bugge, Sophus, *Norsk sagaskrivning og sagafortælling i Irland* (Kristiania [Oslo] 1908).

Byrne, Francis J., *Irish Kings and High-Kings* (London, 1973).

Byrne, Francis J. and Pádraig Francis, 'Two Lives of Saint Patrick: *Vita Secunda* and *Vita Quarta*', *Journal of the Royal Society of Antiquaries of Ireland* 124 (1994), pp.5–117.

Campbell Ross, Ian, '"One of the principal nations in Europe": the representation of Ireland in Sarah Butler's *Irish Tales*', *Eighteenth-Century Fiction* 7:1 (October 1994), pp.1–16.

Candon, Anthony, 'Muirchertach Ua Briain, politics, and naval activity in the Irish Sea, 1075–1119', in Gearóid Mac Niocaill and Patrick F. Wallace (eds), *Keimelia: Studies in Medieval Archaeology and History in Memory of Tom Delaney* (Galway, 1988), pp.397–415.

Candon, Anthony, 'Barefaced effrontery: secular and ecclesiastical politics in early twelfth-century Ireland', *Seanchas Ard Mhacha* 14:2 (1991), pp.1–25.

Carey, John, *The Irish National Origin Legend: Synthetic Pseudohistory*, Quiggin Pamphlets on the Sources of Mediaeval Gaelic History 1 (Cambridge, 1994).

Chadwick, Nora K., 'The Vikings and the western world', in Brian Ó

Cuív (ed.), *The Impact of the Scandinavian Invasions on the Celtic-speaking Peoples c.800–1100 AD* (Dublin, 1962), pp.13–42.

Charles-Edwards, Thomas, 'Irish warfare before 1100' in Thomas Bartlett and Keith Jeffery (eds), *A Military History of Ireland* (Cambridge, 1996), pp.26–51.

Charles-Edwards, Thomas, *Early Christian Ireland* (Cambridge, 2000).

Charles-Edwards, Thomas, 'Ireland and its invaders, 1166–1186', *Quaestio insularis: Selected Proceedings of the Cambridge Colloquium in Anglo-Saxon, Norse and Celtic* 4 (2003), pp.1–34.

Chesnutt, Michael, 'An unsolved problem in Old Norse-Icelandic literary history', *Mediaeval Scandinavia* 1 (1968), pp.122–34.

Clancy, Thomas, 'Court, king and justice in the Ulster Cycle', in Helen Fulton (ed.), *Medieval Celtic Literature and Society* (Dublin, 2005), pp.163–82.

Clarke, Howard B., 'The topographical development of Early Medieval Dublin', *Journal of the Royal Society of Antiquaries of Ireland* 107 (1977), pp.29–51.

Clarke, Howard B., 'The bloodied eagle: the Vikings and the development of Dublin, 841–1014', *The Irish Sword* 18:71 (1991), pp.91–119.

Clarke, Howard B., 'Proto-towns and towns in Ireland and Britain in the ninth and tenth centuries' in Howard B. Clarke, Máire Ní Mhaonaigh and Raghnall Ó Floinn (eds), *Ireland and Scandinavia in the Early Viking Age* (Dublin, 1998), pp.331–80.

Clarke, Howard B., *Dublin, Part I to 1610*, Irish Historic Towns Atlas, No. 11 (Dublin, 2002).

Constable, Giles, *The Reformation of the Twelfth Century* (Cambridge, 1996).

Cowdrey, H.E.J., 'The peace and truce of God in the eleventh century', *Past and Present* 46 (1970), pp.42–67.

Curtis, Edmund, 'Murchertach O'Brien, high king of Ireland, and his Norman son-in-law, Arnulf de Montgomery, *circa* 1100', *Journal of the Royal Society of the Antiquaries of Ireland* 11 (1921), pp.116–24.

Downham, Clare, 'An imaginary Viking-raid on Skye in 795?', *Scottish Gaelic Studies* 20 (2000), pp.192–6.

Downham, Clare, 'England and the Irish Sea zone in the eleventh century', *Anglo-Norman Studies* 26 (2003), pp.55–73.

Downham, Clare, 'The Vikings in Southern Uí Néill to 1014', *Peritia* 17–18 (2003–4), pp.233–55.

Downham, Clare, 'The good, the bad and the ugly: portrayals of Vikings in "The Fragmentary Annals of Ireland"', in Erik Kooper (ed.), *The

Medieval Chronicle 3: Proceedings of the 3rd International Conference on the Medieval Chronicle Doorn/Utrecht 12–17 July 2002 (Amsterdam and New York, 2004), pp.27–39.

Downham, Clare, 'The battle of Clontarf in Irish history and legend', *History Ireland* 13:5 (September/October 2005), pp.19–23.

Downham, Clare, *Viking Kings of Britain and Ireland: The Dyasty of Ívarr to A.D. 1014* (Edinburgh, forthcoming).

Dronke, Ursula, *The Role of Sexual Themes in* Njáls saga, The Dorothea Coke Memorial Lecture in Northern Studies (London, 1981).

Duffy, Seán, 'Irishmen and Islesmen in the kingdoms of Dublin and Man, 1052–1171', *Ériu* 43 (1992), pp.93–133.

Duffy, Seán, 'Ostmen, Irish and Welsh in the eleventh century', *Peritia* 9 (1995), pp.378–96.

Duffy, Seán (ed.), *Atlas of Irish History*, 2nd edn (Dublin, 2000).

Duffy, Seán, "The western world's tower of honour and dignity': the career of Muirchertach Ua Briain in context', in Damian Bracken and Dagmar Ó Riain-Raedel (eds), *Ireland and Europe in the Twelfth Century: Reform and Renewal* (Dublin, 2006), pp.56–73.

Duffy, Seán, 'Brian Bóruma' at www.oxforddnb.com/view/article/3377.

Dumville, David N., 'The dating of the Tripartite Life of St Patrick' in David N. Dumville (ed.), *Saint Patrick A.D. 493–1993*, Sudies in Celtic History 13 (Woodbridge, 1993), pp.255–8.

Dumville, David N., 'Old Dubliners and New Dubliners in Ireland and Britain: a Viking-age Story', in Seán Duffy (ed.), *Medieval Dublin VI: Proceedings of the Friends of Medieval Dublin Symposium 2004* (Dublin, 2005), pp.78–93.

Dunbabin, Jean, *France in the Making 843–1180* (Oxford, 1985).

Empey, C.A., 'The settlement of the kingdom of Limerick', in James Lydon (ed.), *England and Ireland in the Later Middle Ages: Essays in Honour of Jocelyn Otway-Ruthven* (Dublin, 1981), pp.1–25.

Etchingham, Colmán, *Viking Raids on Irish Church Settlements in the Ninth Century: A Reconsideration of the Annals*, Maynooth Monographs Series Minor 1 (Maynooth, 1996).

Etchingham, Colmán, 'North Wales, Ireland and the Isles: the Insular Viking zone', *Peritia* 15 (2001), pp.145–87.

Etchingham, Colmán, 'The location of historical *Laithlinn/Lochla(i)nn*: Scotland or Scandinavia?' in Mícheál Ó Flaithearta (ed.), *Proceedings of the Seventh Symposium of Societas Celtologica Nordica* (Uppsala, 2007), pp.11–32.

Finnbogi Guðmundsson, 'On the writing of *Orkneyinga saga*' in Colleen E. Batey, Judith Jesch and Christopher D. Morris (eds), *The Viking Age in Caithness, Orkney and the North Atlantic* (Edinburgh, 1993), pp.204–11.

Finnur Jónsson, *Den oldnorske og oldislandske litteraturs historie*, 3 vols, 2nd edn (Copenhagen, 1920–4).

Flanagan, Marie Therese, *Irish Society, Anglo-Norman Settlers, Angevin Kingship: Interactions in Ireland in the Late 12th Century* (Oxford, 1989).

Flanagan, Marie Therese, 'Irish and Anglo-Norman warfare in twelfth-century Ireland', in Thomas Bartlett and Keith Jeffery (eds), *A Military History of Ireland* (Cambridge, 1996), pp.52–75.

Flanagan, Marie Therese, *Irish Royal Charters: Texts and Contexts* (Oxford, 2005).

Foote, Peter and David M. Wilson, *The Viking Achievement: The Society and Culture of Early Medieval Scandinavia* (London, 1970).

Frame, Robin, *Ireland and Britain, 1170–1450* (London, 1998).

Gillingham, John, 'Ademar of Chabannes and the history of Aquitaine in the reign of Charles the Bald', in Margaret Gibson and Janet Nelson (eds), *Charles the Bald: Court and Kingdom*, BAR International Series 101 (Oxford, 1981), pp.3–14.

Goedheer, A.J., *Irish and Norse Traditions about the Battle of Clontarf* (Haarlem, 1938).

Grabowski, Kathryn and David Dumville, *Chronicles and Annals of Mediaeval Ireland and Wales; the Clonmacnoise-group Texts*, Studies in Celtic History 4 (Woodbridge, 1984).

Graham-Campbell, James, 'Some archaeological reflections on the Cuerdale hoard', in D.M. Metcalf (ed.), *Coinage in Ninth-Century Northumbria: The Tenth Oxford Symposium on Coinage and Monetary History*, BAR British Series 180 (Oxford, 1987), pp.329–44.

Griffith, Paddy, *The Viking Art of War* (London and Mechanicsburg PA, 1995).

Gwynn, Aubrey, 'Lanfranc and the Irish church', *Irish Ecclesiastical Record* 57 (1941), pp.481–500 and 58 (1941), pp.1–15.

Gwynn, Aubrey, 'Pope Gregory VII and the Irish church', *Irish Ecclesiastical Record* 58 (1941), pp.97–109.

Gwynn, Aubrey, 'St. Anselm and the Irish church', *Irish Ecclesiastical Record* 59 (1942), pp.1–14.

Gwynn, Aubrey, 'Gregory VII and the Irish church', *Studi Gregoriani* 3 (1948), pp.105–28.

Gwynn, Aubrey, 'Were the "Annals of Inisfallen" written at Killaloe?', *North Munster Antiquarian Journal* 8 (1958), pp.20–33.

Gwynn, Aubrey, 'Brian in Armagh (1005)', *Seanchas Ard Mhacha* 9:1 (1978), pp.35–50.

Hagland, Jan Ragnar, 'Njáls saga i 1970- og 1980-åra: eit oversyn over nyare forskning', *Scripta islandica* 38 (1987), pp.36–50.

Haki Antonsson, 'Some observations on martyrdom in post-conversion Scandinavia', *Saga-Book* 28 (2004), pp.70–94.

Hallam, Elizabeth M. and Judith Everard, *Capetian France 987–1328*, 2nd edn (Harlow, 2001).

Head, Thomas F. and Richard Landes (eds), *The Peace of God: Social Violence and Religious Response in France around the Year 1000* (Ithaca, NY, 1992).

Helgi Guðmundsson, *Um haf innan: Vestrænir menn og íslenzk menning á miðöldum* (Reykjavík, 1997).

Higham, Nick, 'Northumbria, Mercia and the Irish Sea Norse, 893–926' in James Graham-Campbell (ed.), *Viking Treasure from the North West: The Cuerdale Hoard in its Context* (Liverpool, 1992), pp.21–30.

Hill, Thomas D., 'The evisceration of Bróðir in *Brennu-Njáls saga*', *Traditio: Studies in Ancient and Medieval History, Thought, and Religion* 37 (1981), pp.437–44.

Hines, John, *Old-Norse Sources for Gaelic History*, Quiggin Pamphlets on the Sources of Mediaeval Gaelic History 5 (Cambridge, 2002).

Hogan, James, 'The Uí Briain kingship in Telach Óc', in John Ryan (ed.), *Féil-sgríbhinn Eoin Mhic Néill: Essays and Studies Presented to Professor Eoin MacNeill* (Dublin, 1940), pp.406–44.

Holm, Poul, 'Viking Dublin and the city-state concept: parameters and significance of the Hiberno-Norse settlement' in Mogens Herman Hansen (ed.), *A Comparative Study of Thirty City-State Cultures: An Investigation Conducted by the Copenhagen Polis Centre*, Det Kongelige Danske Videnskabernes Selskab Historisk-filosofiske Skrifter 21 (Copenhagen, 2000), pp.251–62.

Holtsmark, Anne, "Vefr Darraðar", *Mall og Minne* (1939), pp.74–96.

Hudson, Benjamin, 'Cnut and the Scottish kings', *English Historical Review* 107 (1992), pp.350–60.

Hudson, Benjamin, 'William the Conqueror and Ireland', *Irish Historical Studies* 29 (1994–5), pp.145–58.

Hudson, Benjamin, "Brjáns saga", *Medium Ævum* 71:2 (2002), pp.241–68.

Hudson, Benjamin, *Viking Pirates and Christian Princes: Dynasty, Religion, and Empire in the North Atlantic* (Oxford, 2005).

Hughes, Kathleen, *Early Christian Ireland: Introduction to the Sources* (London, 1972).

Jackson, Kenneth, 'The date of the Tripartite Life of St. Patrick', *Zeitschrift für celtische Philologie* 41 (1986), pp.5–45.

Jaski, Bart, 'The Vikings and the kingship of Tara', *Peritia* 9 (1995), pp.310–51.

Jaski, Bart, *Early Irish Kingship and Succession* (Dublin, 2000).

Keen, Maurice, *The Penguin History of Medieval Europe* (London, 1991).

Kelleher, John V., 'The rise of the Dál Cais', in Etienne Rynne (ed.), *North Munster Studies: Essays in Commemoration of Monsignor Michael Moloney* (Limerick, 1967), pp.230–41.

Kenney, James F., *The Sources for the Early History of Ireland: An Introduction and Guide, Vol. 1, Ecclesiastical* (New York, 1929).

Keynes, Simon, 'The declining reputation of Æthelred the Unready' in David Hill (ed.), *Ethelred the Unready: Papers from the Millenary Conference*, BAR British Series, 59 (Oxford, 1978), pp.227–53, reprinted in David A.E. Pelteret (ed.), *Anglo-Saxon History: Basic Readings* (New York and London, 2000), pp.157–90.

Keynes, Simon, *The Diplomas of King Æthelred 'the Unready' 978–1016: A Study in their Use as Historical Evidence*, Cambridge Studies in Medieval Life and Thought, 3rd Series, 13 (Cambridge, 1980).

Keynes, Simon, 'Re-reading King Æthelred the Unready', in David Bates, Julia Crick and Sarah Hamilton (eds), *Writing Medieval Biography 750–1250: Essays in Honour of Professor Frank Barlow* (Woodbridge, 2006), pp.77–97.

Keynes, Simon, *Anglo-Saxon England: A Bibliographical Handbook for Students of Anglo-Saxon History*, revised edn (Cambridge, 2006).

Kirby, D.P., 'Asser and his Life of King Alfred', *Studia Celtica* 6 (1971), pp.12–35.

Landes, Richard, *Relics, Apocalypse and the Deceits of History: Ademar of Chabannes, 989–1034*, Harvard Historical Studies 117 (Cambridge, MA and London, 1995).

Lehmann, Karl and Hans Schnorr von Carolsfeld, *Die Njálssage inbesondere in ihrem juristischen Bestandtheilen: ein kritischer Beitrag zur altnordischen Rechts- und Literaturgeschichte* (Berlin, 1883).

Lloyd, John Edward, 'The Welsh chronicles', *Proceedings of the British Academy* (1928), pp.369–91.

Lönnroth, Lars, *Njáls Saga: A Critical Introduction* (Berkeley, CA, 1976).

Loyn, H.R., 'The imperial style of the tenth-century Anglo-Saxon kings', *History* 40 (1955), pp.111–5.

Lukman, Niels, 'The raven banner and the changing ravens: a Viking miracle from Carolingian court poetry to saga and Arthurian romance', *Classica et mediaevalia* 19 (1958), pp.133–51.

Lukman, Niels, 'An Irish source and some Icelandic *fornaldarsögur*', *Mediaeval Scandinavia* 10 (1977), pp.41–57.

Mac Eoin, Gearóid, 'The dating of Middle Irish texts', *Proceedings of the British Academy* 68 (1982), pp.109–37.

MacErlean, John, 'Synod of Ráith Breasail: boundaries of the dioceses of Ireland [AD 1110 or 1118]', *Archivium Hibernicum* 3 (1914), pp.1–33.

Mac Niocaill, Gearóid, *The Medieval Irish Annals*, Medieval Irish History Series 3 (Dublin, 1975).

Mac Shamhráin, Ailbhe, 'The battle of Glenn Máma, Dublin and the high-kinghip of Ireland: a millennial commemoration', in Seán Duffy (ed.) *Medieval Dublin II: Proceedings of the Friends of Medieval Dublin Symposium 2000* (Dublin, 2001), pp.53–64.

McCone, Kim, *Pagan Past and Christian Present in Early Irish Literature*, Maynooth Monographs 3 (Maynooth, 1990).

McNamara, Leo, 'Traditional motifs in the Caithréim Thoirdhealbhaigh', *Kentucky Foreign Language Quarterly* 8:2 (1961), pp.85–92.

McTurk, Rory, 'The supernatural in *Njáls saga*: a narratological approach', in John Hines and Desmond Slay (eds), *Introductory Essays on* Egils saga *and* Njals saga (London, 1992), pp.102–24.

Meyer, Kuno, 'Brian Borumha', *Ériu* 4 (1910), pp.68–73.

Ní Dhonnchadha, Máirín, 'The guarantor list of *Cáin Adomnáin*', *Peritia* 1 (1982), pp.178–215.

Ní Mhaonaigh, Máire, 'Bréifne bias in *Cogad Gáedel re Gallaib*, *Ériu* 43 (1992), pp.135–58.

Ní Mhaonaigh, Máire, '*Cogad Gáedel re Gallaib*: some dating considerations', *Peritia* 9 (1995), pp.354–77.

Ní Mhaonaigh, Máire, '*Cogad Gáedel re Gallaib* and the annals: a comparison', *Ériu* 47 (1996), pp.101–26.

Ní Mhaonaigh, Máire, 'Friend and foe: Vikings in ninth- and tenth-century Irish literature', in Howard B. Clarke, Máire Ní Mhaonaigh and Raghnall Ó Floinn (eds), *Ireland and Scandinavia in the Early Viking Age* (Dublin, 1998), pp.381–402.

Ní Mhaonaigh, Máire, 'Tales of three Gormlaiths in medieval Irish literature', *Ériu* 52 (2002), pp.1–24.

Ní Mhaonaigh, Máire, '*Cogadh Gáedhel re Gallaibh* and Cork', *Journal of the Cork Historical and Archaeological Society* 110 (2005), pp.73–83.

Ní Mhaonaigh, Máire, 'Literary Lochlann', in Wilson McLeod, James
E. Fraser and Anja Gunderloch (eds), *Cànan & Cultar/Language &
Culture: Rannsachadh na Gàidhlig 3* (Edinburgh, 2006), pp.25–37.

Ní Mhaonaigh, Máire, 'Pagans and holy men: literary manifestations of
twelfth-century reform', in Damian Bracken and Dagmar Ó Riain-
Raedel (eds), *Ireland and Europe in the Twelfth Century: Reform and
Renewal* (Dublin, 2006), pp.143–61.

Ní Úrdail, Meidhbhín, 'Seachadadh *Cath Cluana Tarbh* sna
lámhscríbhinní', in Ruairí Ó hUiginn (ed.), *Oidhreacht na
Lámhscríbhinní*, Léachtaí Cholm Cille 34 (2004), pp.179–215.

Nic Ghiollamhaith, Aoife, 'Dynastic warfare and historical writing in
North Munster, 1276–1350', *Cambridge Medieval Celtic Studies* 2 (1981),
pp.73–89.

Nic Ghiollamhaith, Aoife, 'The Uí Briain and the king of England,
1248–1276', *Dál gCais* 7 (1984), pp.94–9.

Nic Ghiollamhaith, Aoife, 'Kings and vassals in later medieval Ireland: the
Uí Bhriain and the Mic Conmara in the fourteenth century', in
T. B. Barry, Robin Frame and Katharine Simms (eds), *Colony and
Frontier in Medieval Ireland: Essays Presented to J.F. Lydon* (London, 1995),
pp.201–16.

O'Brien, Elizabeth, 'The location and context of Viking burials at
Kilmainham and Islandbridge, Dublin', in Howard B. Clarke, Máire Ní
Mhaonaigh and Raghnall Ó Floinn (eds), *Ireland and Scandinavia in the
Early Viking Age* (Dublin, 1998), pp.203–21.

Ó Corráin, Donncha, *Ireland before the Normans*, Gill History of Ireland 2
(Dublin, 1972).

Ó Corráin, Donnchadh, 'Dál Cais – church and dynasty', *Ériu* 24 (1973),
pp.52–63.

Ó Corráin, Donnchadh, '*Caithréim Chellacháin Chaisil*: history or
propaganda?', *Ériu* 25 (1974), pp.1–69.

Ó Corráin, Donnchadh, 'Nationality and kingship in pre-Norman
Ireland' in T.W. Moody (ed.), *Nationality and the Pursuit of National
Independence*, Historical Studies 12 (Belfast, 1978), pp.1–35.

Ó Corráin, Donnchadh, 'Irish origin legends and genealogy: recurrent
aetiologies', in Tore Nyberg and others (eds), *History and Heroic Tale: A
Symposium* (Odense, 1985), pp.51–96.

Ó Corráin, Donnchadh, 'Brian Boru and the battle of Clontarf', in Liam
de Paor (ed.), *Milestones in Irish History* (Cork and Dublin, 1986),
pp.31–40.

Ó Corráin, Donnchadh, 'Viking Ireland – afterthoughts', in Howard B. Clarke, Máire Ní Mhaonaigh and Raghnall Ó Floinn (eds), *Ireland and Scandinavia in the Early Viking Age* (Dublin, 1998), pp.421–52.

Ó Corráin, Donnchadh, 'The Vikings in Scotland and Ireland in the ninth century', *Peritia* 12 (1998), pp.296–339.

Ó Cróinín, Dáibhí, *Early Medieval Ireland 400–1200*, Longman History of Ireland 1 (London and New York, 1995).

Ó Cuív, Brian, 'Personal names as an indicator of relations between native Irish and settlers in the Viking period', in John Bradley (ed.), *Settlement and Society in Medieval Ireland: Studies Presented to F.X. Martin, o.s.a.* (Kilkenny, 1988), pp.79–88.

Ó Cuív, Brian, *Catalogue of Irish Language Manuscripts in the Bodleian Library at Oxford and Oxford College Libraries, Part I Descriptions* (Dublin, 2001).

O'Donoghue, Heather, 'Women in *Njáls saga*', in John Hines and Desmond Slay (eds), *Introductory Essays on* Egils saga *and* Njáls saga (London, 1992), pp.83–92.

O'Hanlon, John, *Lives of the Irish Saints*, 10 vols, 4 (Dublin and New York, [1894]).

O'Leary, Philip, 'A foreseeing driver of an old chariot: regal moderation in early Irish literature', *Cambridge Medieval Celtic Studies* 11 (1986), pp.1–16.

Ó Murchadha, Diarmuid, *The Annals of Tigernach: Index of Names*, Irish Texts Society Subsidiary Series 6 (London and Dublin, 1997).

Oram, Richard, *The Lordship of Galloway* (Edinburgh, 2000).

Orchard, Andy, 'The literary background to the *Encomium Emmae Reginae*', *Journal of Medieval Latin* 11 (2001), pp.156–83.

Ó Riain, Pádraig, 'The Psalter of Cashel: a provisional list of contents', *Éigse* 23 (1989), pp.107–30.

Ó Riain, Pádraig, 'The shrine of the Stowe Missal, redated', *Proceedings of the Royal Irish Academy* 91 C (1991), pp.285–95.

Poole, Russell G., *Viking Poems on War and Peace: A Study in Skaldic Narrative* (Toronto, 1991).

Power, Rosemary, 'Magnus Barelegs' expeditions to the west', *Scottish Historical Review* 65:2 (1986), pp.107–32.

Power, Rosemary, 'Meeting in Norway; Norse-Gaelic relations in the Kingdom of Man and the Isles, 1090–1270', *Saga-Book* 29 (2005), pp.5–66.

Riley-Smith, Jonathan, *The Crusades: A Short History* (London, 1990).

Ryan, John, 'The battle of Clontarf', *Journal of the Royal Society of Antiquaries of Ireland* 68 (1938), pp.1–50.

Ryan, John, 'The O'Briens in Munster after Clontarf', *North Munster Antiquarian Journal* 2:4 (1941), pp.141–52 and 3:1 (1942), pp.1–52.

Ryan, John, 'Brian Boruma, king of Ireland' in Etienne Rynne (ed.), *North Munster Studies: Essays in Commemoration of Monsignor Michael Moloney* (Limerick, 1967), pp.355–74.

Sayers, William, '*Airdrech, sirite* and other early Irish battlefield spirits', *Éigse* 25 (1991), pp.45–55.

Sayers, William, 'Clontarf, and the Irish destinies of Sigurðr Digri, Earl of Orkney, and Þorsteinn Síðu-Hallsson', *Scandinavian Studies* 63:2 (1991), pp.164–86.

Scharer, Anton, 'The writing of history at King Alfred's court', *Early Medieval Europe* 5:2 (1996), pp.177–206.

Sheehan, John, 'Viking age hoards from Munster: a regional tradition?', in Michael A. Monk and John Sheehan (eds), *Early Medieval Munster: Archaeology, History and Society* (Cork, 1988), pp.147–63.

Simms, Katharine, 'The battle of Dysert O'Dea and the Gaelic resurgence in Thomond', *Dál gCais* 5 (1979), pp.59–66.

Smyth, Alfred P., *Scandinavian York and Dublin: The History and Archaeology of Two Related Viking Kingdoms*, 2 vols (Dublin, 1975–79).

Stalley, Roger, 'Design and function: the construction and decoration of Cormac's Chapel at Cashel', in Damian Bracken and Dagmar Ó Riain-Raedel (eds), *Ireland and Europe in the Twelfth Century: Reform and Renewal* (Dublin, 2006), pp.162–75.

Stewart, James, 'The death of Turgesius', *Saga-Book* 18 (1970–3), pp.47–58.

Strickland, Matthew, 'Slaughter, slavery or ransom: the impact of the Conquest on conduct of warfare', in Carola Hicks (ed.), *England in the Eleventh Century: Proceedings of the 1990 Harlaxton Symposium*, Harlaxton Medieval Studies II (Stamford, 1992), pp.41–59.

Strickland, Matthew, 'Military technology and conquest: the anomaly of Anglo-Saxon England', *Anglo-Norman Studies* 19 (1997), pp.353–82.

Strickland, Matthew, 'Provoking or avoiding battle? Challenge, duel and single combat in warfare of the High Middle Ages' in Matthew Strickland (ed.), *Armies, Chivalry and Warfare in Medieval Britain and France: Proceedings of the 1995 Harlaxton Symposium*, Harlaxton Medieval Studies 7 (Stamford, 1998), pp.317–43.

Stringer, Keith, 'Reformed monasticism and Celtic Scotland: Galloway *c.1140–c. 1240* in Edward J. Cowan and R. Andrew McDonald (eds),

Alba: Celtic Scotland in the Medieval Era (East Linton, 2000), pp.127–65.

Thornton, David, 'Clann Eruilb: Irish or Scandinavian?', *Irish Historical Studies* 30 (1996), pp.161–6.

Valante, Mary, 'Dublin's economic relations with hinterland and periphery in the later Viking age', in Seán Duffy (ed.), *Medieval Dublin I: Proceedings of the Friends of Medieval Dublin Symposium 1999* (Dublin, 2000), pp.69–83.

Wainwright, F.T., 'Ingimund's invasion', *English Historical Review* 63:247 (1948), pp.145–69.

Wallace, Patrick F., 'The economy and commerce of Viking Age Dublin', in Klaus Düwel, Herbert Jankuhn, Harald Siems and Dieter Timpe (eds), *Untersuchungen zu Handel und Verkehr der vor- und frühgeschichtlichen Zeit in Mittel- und Nordeuropa, Teil IV: Der Handel der Karolinger- und Wikingerzeit*, Abhandlungen der Akademie der Wissenschaften in Göttingen, Philologisch-historische Klasse, dritte Folge, no.156 (Göttingen, 1987), pp.200–45.

Walsh, Aidan, 'A summary classification of Viking age swords in Ireland', in Howard B. Clarke, Máire Ní Mhaonaigh and Raghnall Ó Floinn (eds), *Ireland and Scandinavia in the Early Viking Age* (Dublin, 1998), pp.222–35.

Werner, Karl Ferdinand, 'Ademar von Chabannes und die *Historia pontificum et comitum Engolismensium*', *Deutsches Archiv für Erforschung des Mittelalters* 19 (1963), pp.297–326.

Whitelock, Dorothy, *The Genuine Asser*, The Stenton Lecture 1967 (Reading, 1968).

Woolf, Alex, 'Amlaíb Cuarán and the Gael, 941–81', in Seán Duffy (ed.), *Medieval Dublin III: Proceedings of the Friends of Medieval Dublin Symposium 2001* (Dublin, 2002), pp.34–43.

Index

TEMPUS – REVEALING HISTORY

William II Rufus, the Red King
EMMA MASON

'A thoroughly new reappraisal of a much maligned king. The dramatic story of his life is told with great pace and insight'
John Gillingham

£25

0 7524 3528 0

William Wallace The True Story of Braveheart
CHRIS BROWN

'A formidable new biography... sieves through masses of medieval records to distinguish the man from the myth' **Magnus Magnusson**

£17.99

0 7524 3432 2

Elizabeth Wydeville: The Slandered Queen
ARLENE OKERLUND

'A penetrating, thorough and wholly convincing vindication of this unlucky queen'
Sarah Gristwood

'A gripping tale of lust, loss and tragedy'
Alison Weir

A **BBC History Magazine** Book of the Year 2005

£9.99   978 07524 3807 8

The battle of Hastings 1066
M.K. LAWSON

'Blows away many fundamental assumptions about the battle of Hastings... an exciting and indispensable read' **David Bates**

A **BBC History Magazine** Book of the Year 2003

£12.99   978 07524 4177 1

The Welsh Wars of Independence
DAVID MOORE

'Beautifully written, subtle and remarkably perceptive' **John Davies**

£12.99

978 07524 4128 3

Medieval England
From Hastings to Bosworth
EDMUND KING

'The best illustrated history of medieval England' **John Gillingham**

£12.99

0 7524 2827 5

A Companion to Medieval England
NIGEL SAUL

'Wonderful... everything you could wish to know about life in medieval England'
Heritage Today

£19.99

0 7524 2969 8

The Prince In The Tower
MICHAEL HICKS

'The first time in ages that a publisher has sent me a book I actually want to read' **David Starkey**

£9.99

978 07524 4386 7

If you are interested in purchasing other books published by Tempus, or in case you have difficulty finding any Tempus books in your local bookshop, you can also place orders directly through our website

www.tempus-publishing.com

TEMPUS – REVEALING HISTORY

A History of the Black Death in Ireland
MARIA KELLY
'A fine example of how history can be made interesting to the layman' *The Irish Times*
£12.99
0 7524 3185 4

The Vikings
MAGNUS MAGNUSSON
'Serious, engaging history'
BBC History Magazine
£9.99
0 7524 2699 0

William the Conqueror
DAVID BATES
'As expertly woven as the Bayeux Tapestry'
BBC History Magazine
£12.99
0 7524 2960 4

Agincourt: A New History
ANNE CURRY
'A tour de force' *Alison Weir*
'*The* book on the battle' *Richard Holmes*
A BBC History Magazine BOOK OF THE YEAR 2005
£12.99
0 7524 2828 4

The Great Dying
The Black Death in Dublin
MARIA KELLY
'Pacy popular history… an infectious chronicle'
The Sunday Times (Irish edition)
£14.99
0 7524 2338 8

The English Resistance
The Underground War Against the Normans
PETER REX
'An invaluable rehabilitation of an ignored resistance movement' *The Sunday Times*
£12.99
0 7524 3733 X

Richard III
MICHAEL HICKS
'A most important book by the greatest living expert on Richard' *Desmond Seward*
£9.99
0 7524 2589 7

The Peasants' Revolt
England's Failed Revolution of 1381
ALASTAIR DUNN
'A stunningly good book… totally absorbing'
Melvyn Bragg
£9.99
0 7524 2965 5

If you are interested in purchasing other books published by Tempus, or in case you have difficulty finding any Tempus books in your local bookshop, you can also place orders directly through our website:
www.tempus-publishing.com